GRAHAME CLARK

GRAHAME CLARK

An Intellectual Life of an Archaeologist

BRIAN FAGAN

Westview
PRESS

A Member of the Perseus Books Group

Credits and permissions can be found on page 291, which constitutes a continuation of this copyright page.

Westview Press books are available at special discounts for bulk purchases in the United States by corporations, institutions, and other organizations. For more information, please contact the Special Markets Department at The Perseus Books Group, 11 Cambridge Center, Cambridge MA 02142, or call (617) 252-5298.

Published in 2001 in the United States of America by Westview Press, 5500 Central Avenue, Boulder, Colorado 80301-2877, and in the United Kingdom by Westview Press, 12 Hid's Copse Road, Cumnor Hill, Oxford OX2 9JJ

Find us on the World Wide Web at www.westviewpress.com

A CIP catalog record is available from the Library of Congress
ISBN 0-8133-3602-3

Designed by Jeffrey P. Williams
Set in 11.5-point Perpetua by Perseus Publishing Services

The paper used in this publication meets the requirements of the American National Standard for Permanence of Paper for Printed Library Materials Z39.48-1984.

10   9   8   7   6   5   4   3   2   1

for

MOLLIE CLARK

Honoris causa

Contents

Illustrations

Preface

If man has indeed made himself, he has only been able to do so by means of his economies.

Grahame Clark, *Economic Prehistory* [1]

I f, forty years ago, someone had predicted that I would write a biography of Grahame Clark, I would have laughed at such a ludicrous thought. Although I studied under him as an undergraduate and he supervised my graduate research, we never enjoyed much sustained conversation. In fact, I was terrified of him, confusing shyness for austerity. It was only when I started fieldwork on Iron Age villages in what was then Northern Rhodesia in 1960 that I realized the enormous influence he had exercised on my thinking. This intellectual mentorship continued during my doctoral research, much of it conducted far from Cambridge, and some of his ideas became part of my own thinking about the prehistoric past.

Many years have passed since I submitted the final draft of my dissertation into Grahame's formidable hands, and he was friendliness itself on the rare occasions that we met in later years. He had mellowed, and so had I, and it was deeply satisfying to encounter him in Cambridge when I delivered the first Geoffrey Bushnell Memorial Lecture in 1992 and had a chance to tell him in his old age just how much I had learned from him. Even then, the thought of my writing his biography would have strained the bounds of credibility.

Time and chance brought me to the role of biographer, the passage of time honing my writing skills and chance taking me to the Grahame Clark

Memorial Conference at the British Academy in London in November 1997. At the end of the meeting, I was cornered by Professor John Coles, one of Clark's literary executors, who invited me to become his biographer. After considerable soul searching, I accepted. This book, written at the formal invitation of Lady Clark and the literary executors, is the result.

I undertook the task with considerable trepidation but soon found myself engrossed in a complex, multifaceted life and in a journey that took me back to the nearly forgotten bucolic world of prehistoric archaeology in the 1930s, then to the Cambridge of the 1940s and 1950s and of my own undergraduate days. To chronicle Grahame Clark's intellectual life is to participate in the history of a discipline that he transformed, at first almost single-handedly, from something that was little more than artifact classification into a sophisticated study of the human past based on collaboration with scientists from many disciplines.

Grahame Clark was a very private man, with an austere, sometimes forbidding exterior. The public Grahame was a very different person from the private one. His archaeological friendships were relatively few, his acquaintances legion. He hid his emotions and preferred to talk about archaeology rather than exchange small talk. Stories of his awkwardness with students and others abound, but they are irrelevant to the biographer of a man whose intellectual influence on archaeology was enormous. Grahame Clark is one of the few archaeologists about whom the comment that Sir Christopher Wren's son made on his monument in Saint Paul's Cathedral is apposite: "Si monumentum requiris, circumspice" ("If you seek his monument, look around you"). His books and papers on archaeology, as well as the students he trained, many of them now gray-haired, surround one on every side. Clark's legacy to prehistory will endure for generations.

The history of archaeology has become a vigorous specialty within the discipline in recent years at three levels. The first is at a general level, that of anecdotal histories. Then there are intellectual assessments, such as the Canadian archaeologist Bruce Trigger's *History of Archaeological Thought*, which is on the reading list of every serious student.[2] Research at the third level is far more detailed and can be classified as formal historiography, in which the researcher goes back to the archive files of learned societies and academic departments, to the very often arcane trivia of academic politics of a half century ago or even earlier. This kind of research can be absorbing, and occasionally fascinating. It is also extremely time-consuming, especially for a researcher with many commitments, limited field time, and a base over 5,000 miles from the archives. In the case of Grahame Clark, I sensed that there was little to be gained from such research, for the main outlines, and indeed details, of his intellectual life are available in the public eye, and also in his own prolific writings. My concern with this book is to provide an assessment of his life's work for working scholars with a general interest in the development of archaeology, not for historians of archaeology. I think more detailed historiography, if appropriate, is best left for a future generation.

Quite apart from the issue of historiography, the writing of this biography presented unusual challenges. Clark's executors gave me unlimited access to his archives, which are deposited in the Cambridge University Library, including the manuscript of his last, incomplete book, *A Path to Prehistory*, which he ultimately intended to call *Man the Spiritual Primate*. In the event, the archives contained almost nothing of historical value, for Clark tended to destroy correspondence after dealing with it. The few letters that survive are not particularly illuminating. Much of his archive consists of notes on long outdated academic papers and research materials for his many books and papers, all of which are on public record. Fortunately for a biographer, Clark was a compulsive writer who published not only every piece of fieldwork and analysis he completed (which makes him almost unique among archaeologists) but also several almost hidden autobiographical sketches, the most important of which appears in his *Archaeology at Cambridge and Beyond* (1989).[3] His ideas and syntheses are fully published too, facilitating the task of an intellectual biographer. Accordingly, this biography is written in large part off Clark's own publications, a task that has involved reading virtually everything that he ever wrote, from his days as a Marlborough College schoolboy to his old age—I must be the only scholar ever to do so!

When I began the research, I anticipated that interviews with his former colleagues and students would prove to be a rich lode of informal material. The numerous interviews that I conducted, although enjoyable and informative (and sometimes reunions with archaeologists I had not seen in over forty years), proved disappointingly uninformative as far as Grahame Clark the person was concerned. To most of his colleagues, Clark was a strictly professional acquaintance who talked about little more than archaeology and occasionally reminisced. His former students were usually somewhat afraid of him, until they got to know him in later life. Consequently, this biography focuses almost entirely on Clark's academic contributions, while the man tends to stand in the background. Yet it matters little, for the Clark you encountered was the Clark you also met on paper. He was fundamentally a simple and direct thinker, with a brilliant gift for getting at the nub of a problem and a breadth of vision that could be astounding. Grahame Clark was conservative, sometimes magisterial, even rude, but his archaeology was sometimes tinged with genius—which is why he is worth a biography.

Few people would disagree with the assessment that Clark was one of the most important prehistorians of the twentieth century. He began his career in a world of artifact collectors, pioneered environmental archaeology and systems-ecological approaches, dug Star Carr, one of the most famous Stone Age hunter-gatherer sites in the world, and developed the first global synthesis of human prehistory. Several generations of students sat under him, with his proactive encouragement, and colonized the archaeological world. Yet he remains surprisingly invisible outside the narrow coterie of Mesolithic archaeologists and former Cambridge graduates. His personality was not one that invited celebrity; his lecturing style was dry rather than entertaining. He lacked the urbane sophistication of a Glyn Daniel or the self-aware flamboyance of a Mortimer Wheeler. Clark was a single-minded archaeologist who was most comfortable interacting with fellow specialists or writing in his study. He was not a gregarious man, which meant that his archaeological light was hidden under a bushel, especially in the United States, where his work was little known, except to a minority of practitioners, and was submerged in the 1960s by the loud rhetoric of processual archaeology.

The generations pass rapidly and I was surprised at how many archaeologists of the up-and-coming generation have never heard of Grahame Clark, and how little his work now figures in day-to-day research discussions. From the point of view of advancing research, one knows that Clark would be pleased, for his concern was with the progress of science. But the neglect is a pity, for there is much to be learned from his writings, even more than a generation later: his insistence that there are many forms of prehistory and history, his broad vision of the past, which overrode petty specialties, and his insistence on close teamwork with natural scientists— to mention only a few. Above all, his is a life illuminated by an intense passion for archaeology, for the achievements of humanity, a fire in the belly if you will, which often eludes us in these days of ardent specialization and papers on increasingly arcane topics of little interest except to those who write them. Grahame Clark was very much a renaissance archaeologist, rare in his day and even rarer in our own. There is much to learn from his long career of relevance to an archaeology that faces a difficult and uncertain future in the twenty-first century.

It is always difficult to write a biography of an acquaintance, no matter how slight. Inevitably, with the passage of years, scholars of high achievement like Grahame Clark tend to assume a more mythical stature than reality suggests. It is all too easy to fall into the trap of hagiography, which I have tried to avoid at all costs. Inevitably, there will be some readers who knew Grahame Clark better than I did. They are certain to disagree with some of the assessments in these pages. But I think that my appraisal of John Grahame Douglas Clark is an accurate one. He was one of the greatest archaeologists of a century that produced a remarkable number of gifted ones—and I wager that most people who knew him would agree with me.

Acknowledgments

This biography was written at the invitation of Lady Clark and Sir Grahame's literary executors. I am deeply grateful to Mollie Clark, both for many kindnesses and insights into the more personal aspects of Grahame's life and for reading the draft manuscript. Her advice and suggestions have been invaluable. She has, of course, made no attempt to change my intellectual assessments. The executors—Professor John Coles, Professor Paul Mellars, and Dr. Peter Rowley-Conwy—have encouraged me at every turn, commented on the manuscript, and corrected many errors of fact and perception. So have Professors Norman Hammond and Charles Higham. John Coles's memorial of Grahame Clark in the *Proceedings of the British Academy* for 1997 was an invaluable source, for he knew Clark far better than I.[4]

I owe a major debt to Pamela Jane Smith, whose research into Grahame Clark and the history of the Cambridge Department is the subject of her doctoral dissertation. I eagerly await the publication of the book, *Morning Coffee, Afternoon Tea*, resulting from her dissertation. She willingly gave me access to unpublished papers, helped me with sources, and read the manuscript. Without her assistance, this book would not have been written.

Dozens of colleagues and friends agreed to be interviewed, provided me with detailed materials, or supplied reminiscences in correspondence. It is impossible to name them all, but I owe special thanks to Leena Ahtola-Moorhouse of the Ateneum Art Museum, Helsinki, Paul Ashbee, Leslie Cram, Christopher Evans, John Evans, Peter Gathercole, Norman Hammond, Charles Higham, John Hurst, Ray Inskeep, Michael Jochim,

Vincent Megaw, R. J. Mercer, John Mulvaney, Julie Petrucci of Peterhouse, Colin Renfrew, Chris Scarre, Michael Thompson, and the late Claire Wilson.

The staff of the Davidson Library at the University of California–Santa Barbara were helpful far beyond the call of duty, as were the librarians providing me access to the Clark archive at the Cambridge University Library. I am also grateful to all those who provided permission to reproduce the illustrations in this book. The credits are listed in the captions. Photographs without credits either were taken by Grahame Clark or are in the possession of his family. Every reasonable effort was made to obtain permissions from copyright holders. Any questions in this matter should be directed to the author. The maps are the skillful work of Jack Scott.

Karl Yambert of Westview Press has been a supportive and perceptive editor, and I am grateful for his advice and insights.

Financial support for the lengthy research and travel involved in this project was generously provided by:

- The American Philosophical Society
- The Wenner Gren Foundation for Anthropological Research
- University of California—Santa Barbara Academic Senate and Interdisciplinary Humanities Center.

Brian Fagan
Santa Barbara, California

Author's Note

U nless otherwise stated, all radiocarbon dates cited in these pages are uncalibrated, since they are usually quoted in the context of the time they were released.

Site names and geographical locations are spelled, and used, as they were when Grahame Clark visited or referred to them.

Technical terms, such as Cambridge University nomenclature for degrees, are defined in the notes, which provide references for the text.

In the interests of more varied style, and with the concurrence of Lady Clark, I have used both "Grahame" and "Clark" to refer to Professor Sir Grahame in the text.

Given the comprehensive notes at the end of this book, it has been decided not to publish a complete listing of Grahame Clark's writings. An incomplete bibliography can be found in his edited *Economic Prehistory* (Cambridge: Cambridge University Press, 1989), with additions in Peter Rowley-Conwy, "Sir Grahame Clark," in Tim Murray, ed., *Encyclopedia of Archaeology,* vol. 2, *The Great Archaeologists* (Santa Barbara, Calif.: ABC-CLIO, 1999), pp. 507–529.

1

⬗

A Passionate
Connoisseur of Flints

*As an undergraduate I had already been a passionate connoisseur [of
flints] for more than a decade.*

*If anyone were to ask me why I have spent my life studying Prehistory, I
would only say that I have remained under the spell of a subject which
seeks to discover how we became human beings endowed with minds and
souls before we had learned to write.*[1]

"A Path to Prehistory"

A colleague once described him as "mattock faced," after one of the elk
antler implements he once discovered.[2] John Grahame Douglas Clark
was an imposing, remote man who hid his feelings behind a mask. Tall, thin,
and seemingly austere, he brought a high moral imperative and a complete
single-mindedness to archaeology. His devotion to, and absorption in, prehistory was so complete as to be intimidating, but scholars like him are the
foundation of many academic disciplines. Grahame Clark's long career from
the 1930s to the 1970s spanned an extraordinary transition in which
archaeology developed from a largely amateur pastime into a highly specialized scientific discipline. Working with minimal resources, he was one of
a handful of men and women who turned prehistoric archaeology from a

basically amateur pursuit into a multidisciplinary enterprise. He was a pioneer in ecological archaeology, was the first archaeologist to write a global prehistory of humankind, and encouraged an entire generation of young prehistorians to work abroad, far from the comfortable classrooms and laboratories of his beloved Cambridge.[3] Devout, hardworking, and not necessarily universally beloved, Grahame Clark was one of the greatest archaeologists of the twentieth century. He kept company with a small group of distinguished European contemporaries, among them the great synthesizer Vere Gordon Childe, Stone Age archaeologist Dorothy Garrod, and British specialist Stuart Piggott. He was in touch with American colleagues too, notably Gordon Willey of Harvard University and Richard MacNeish of Tehuacán Valley fame. His intellectual influence on archaeology will endure well into the twenty-first century.

John Grahame Douglas Clark was born on July 28, 1907, the elder son of Charles Douglas Clark and Maude Ethel Grahame Clark (née Shaw). His family was solidly upper middle class and moderately prosperous, his father a stockbroker and reserve army officer.[4] The family lived comfortably at Shortlands near Bromley in Kent, in southeastern England. By all accounts, Grahame's early childhood was a happy one. In 1914 his father sailed for service with the West Kent Regiment in France, Mesopotamia, and then India. The seven-year-old Grahame never saw his father again. Lieutenant Colonel Clark survived the Great War but succumbed to the virulent influenza pandemic that swept the world at the close of hostilities, dying just as his ship entered Plymouth Sound in 1919. He was buried with full military honors, which gave his son a lifelong distaste for funerals. Grahame Clark grew up without a father, a circumstance that had a lasting effect on his life. Brought up by his mother and a guardian uncle named Hugh Shaw, for whom he had deep affection, he became an intensely driven and emotionally self-sufficient boy, characteristics that endured throughout his life. His financial affairs were in the hands of trustees who paid for his public school and university education.

The family moved to Seaford on the edge of the Sussex Downs, where archaeological sites abounded. Grahame fell under the lure of flint collecting when a Mr. Bird, a retired Public Records Office official, showed him his collection of flint implements from Yorkshire. (The same gentleman taught him piquet, a card game Grahame played his entire life.) Some leaf-shaped arrowheads attracted Grahame's eye at once, kindling a lifetime interest in stone tools. He promptly started his own collection, riding far and wide on his pony over the chalk country of the Sussex Downs, where stone artifacts were plentiful. Then, as later, he became oblivious to everything when archaeology beckoned. On one occasion, his pony returned riderless. Grahame had spotted some flints and dismounted to collect them, promptly forgetting about his mount.

Schoolboy Archaeologist

In 1921, Grahame entered Marlborough College, a well-known public (private) school favored by middle-class families. The school lies in the Kennet Valley at the heart of Wessex, in the chalk country where Stonehenge and Avebury beckoned and the opportunities for archaeological exploration abounded (Figure 1.1).

Marlborough under headmaster Cyril Norwood prided itself, then as now, on its strict work ethic and moral code and on its tough academic standards, an atmosphere in which Clark flourished. He joined the Natural History Society and soon acquired the nickname "Stones and Bones." Members were excused from games at least once a week so they could participate in society activities. Grahame had ample time to indulge two enthusiasms: the pursuit of butterflies and moths and flint collecting in the countryside. Under the encouragement of the history master, Mr. Brentnall, members visited the Devizes Museum "by char-à-banc" to examine the collections of Bronze and Iron Age specimens. On another occasion, they were able to visit the Windmill Hill excavations near the famous Avebury stone circles, where the wealthy marmalade heir Alexander Keiller had started a long-term digging campaign in 1925. Windmill Hill was a Neolithic "causewayed camp," an enigmatic structure with irregular earthworks that was thought to be a Stone Age cattle enclosure. Keiller himself showed them "sections of three concentric works, and pointed out the peculiar causeways interrupting them every few yards."[5] Archaeology was not Grahame's major passion at the time. When the party climbed the nearby prehistoric earthwork known as Silbury Hill, he was more interested in the March Fritillary butterflies on the summit than in this remarkable monument.[6]

From 1923 to 1926, Grahame was a leading light of the Natural History Society. He led the way in recording the first appearances of butterflies and moths and collecting large numbers of specimens. In the end, stone tools

Figure 1.1   **Grahame Clark, age fifteen, a student at Marlborough College.**

won out over insects and engaged more and more of his time and enthusiasm. He advised other members and lectured on archaeology, while also learning how to draw in pen and ink, a skill that held him in good stead in later years. In his last year, he delivered a talk entitled "Progress in Prehistoric Times." The secretary reported: "He knew his subject very well."[7] Even in his teens, Clark had developed an intense curiosity about the ancient world that was to be the abiding passion of his life. At the same time, he absorbed ideas and values that remained with him for a lifetime.

The public school education of the day aimed at educating potential leaders of a global empire. Clark's Marlborough years inculcated within him an unspoken elitism typical of public schools of the day, a conviction that some were destined for prominence, wealth, and leadership, whereas most were not. With such attitudes came a commitment to empire, to the governance of less fortunate peoples, and to strong moral values based on service to God and country. An English public school education of the day, and right into the 1950s, was based on unspoken notions of class, on the principles of a society in which all people knew their place and human progress was closely tied to Britain's responsibilities as an imperial power.[8] A half century earlier, the pioneer anthropologist Edward Tylor had arranged human societies in a simple, progressive hierarchy of savagery (hunter-gatherer groups), barbarism (simple farmers), and civilization. Tylor's simplistic scheme was soon discredited in academic circles, but it lingered in public school classrooms. Few people believed that human progress was that simple, but the idea of advancement, of varying levels of society, formed a powerful undercurrent in much of Grahame Clark's later work and stemmed in part from his highly traditional and conservative public school education. Britain's public school–educated young men became clergymen, merchant princes, soldiers, and colonial administrators. They also became academics in an era when Oxford and Cambridge Universities were considered natural institutions for public school students to obtain their undergraduate degrees.

Grahame Clark came from a classic upper-middle-class background, in which notions of unspoken elitism and service were taken as gospel. Such attitudes were not necessarily wrong, nor were they overtly racist. They provided Grahame and thousands of other upper-middle-class young men and women with the leadership skills and moral underpinning they needed to make their way in the world. The general doctrines of human progress inculcated at Marlborough were a powerful and lifelong catalyst for a fledgling archaeologist's thinking, whose own mind moved far beyond elemental notions of linear evolution.

The first items on Grahame Clark's lengthy bibliography date to these formative Marlborough years. He published four papers while still a schoolboy, all of them in the Natural History Society's *Reports*. His first paper describes collections from his Downs wanderings, complete with percentages of artifacts. Only 3 percent of the collection comprised "weapons of war." The remaining 97 percent were scrapers, borers, knives, and other domestic artifacts. Thus the young author concluded that "the community must have been essentially a peaceful one."[9] A paper entitled "Sarsen Implements" quoted seventeenth-century antiquarian John Aubrey's *Natural History of Wiltshire*, which described such specimens as the stones that "framed the two stupendous antiquities of Avebury and Stonehenge." Clark classified sarsen hammerstones from Avebury, All Cannings Cross, and other locations, as well as some flaked specimens, which, he concluded, were used when flint was scarce. And "while fine sarsen was quite tractable it yet possessed a certain hardness and toughness not shared by flint."[10] The Sarsen paper shows a remarkable maturity of description for a young man not yet university trained. Plate II of the same paper is a well-executed drawing of a sarsen adze executed in the simple style that Clark was to develop to a high standard in his later articles and monographs, for he learned to draw while at Marlborough. Even as a schoolboy, Clark was determined to become a professional archaeologist. The single-minded teenage prehistorian was a mirror of the man.

A Changing Archaeological World

Grahame Clark began studying prehistory in a slowly changing archaeological world. Long-established ideas and antiquated research methods were giving way to new approaches and innovative methodologies that ranged far beyond the narrow universe of artifact classification.

The Flint Collectors

Grahame's earliest exposure to archaeology came in the narrow world of the flint collector. Already in 1867, a French prehistorian named Gabriel de Mortillet had proclaimed that the progress of humanity was inevitable. He measured such progress by using changing stone tool types from river valleys such as the Somme and from the stratified occupation levels in rockshelters and caves in southwest France's Dordogne. Cultural era gave way to cultural era in a smooth near geological sequence, as if human prehistory had passed through uniform periods throughout Europe and much of the world. De Mortillet called human progress "inevitable" and arranged the Stone Age accordingly.

The notion of orderly epochs of Stone Age prehistory seems absurd today, for we know just how diverse ancient human societies were. But de Mortillet's ideas died hard, for Stone Age archaeology was firmly based on French soil, in the rich caverns of southwestern France, and little was known of the prehistory of other parts of the world. We should not be surprised, since at the time no Stone Age sites elsewhere rivaled the richness and diversity of the Dordogne caves. Half a century of excavations in caves and rockshelters since de Mortillet's time yielded an increasingly elaborate cultural sequence for western Europe, summarized in 1912 by the French prehistorian Abbé Henri Breuil in a classic paper, *Les subdivisions du paleolithique superieur et leur signification*. This highly technical study served as a bible for all students of Stone Age societies and revealed considerably more cultural and technological diversity in the French caves than had been apparent in de Mortillet's day. But Breuil's analysis, while more elaborate than de Mortillet's, was completely artifact based. Prehistory was still a matter of stone artifacts and the occasional bone or antler tool, little more than a studied, and often minute, analysis of hundreds upon thousands of flint objects. Inevitably, in a world populated by few professional archaeologists, intellectual stagnation followed. It was not until the late 1920s, just as Grahame entered Cambridge, that convincing evidence of the diversity of Late Ice Age human culture came to light in the hands of archaeologists Gertrude Caton Thompson in Egypt's Nile Valley, Dorothy Garrod in Palestine, and Louis Leakey in Kenya. These researchers, as well as others, replaced the rigid evolution of prehistoric societies with much more flexible evolutionary schemes that took account of human diversity. Some years later, Grahame was to add an ecological dimension to these scenarios.

Prehistoric archaeology in the 1920s was, for the most part, in the hands of amateurs. Most professional archaeologists worked in museums poring over artifacts arranged in rows in glass cases. The amateurs were, for the most part, enthusiastic artifact typologists and collectors who haunted plowed fields, gravel quarries, and geological exposures in search of flint implements of every kind. Few of them ever conducted excavations, and those that they carried out were little more than searches for still more artifacts. Theirs was a narrow fellowship of local archaeologists—clergy, schoolteachers, solicitors, government officials, and small-town businessmen—who spent their summers collecting in the field, their winters engrossed in the minutiae of stone and pottery typologies. Many of them acquired artifacts just as they made money: by systematic, quiet application.[11] These were the amateur scholars whom young Clark met on the downs or through his excursions with the Marlborough College Natural History Society. They were collectors by inclination, academically more at home with geologists than historians. Their interests were ardently provincial and they rarely strayed more than a few kilometers from home. Platoons of these worthy, tweed-suited amateurs gathered at meetings of local archaeological societies to display their finds and debate artifacts as if they were stamp collections.

By the mid-1920s, these men and women had established the broad subdivisions of British prehistory—an ill-defined Upper Palaeolithic dating to the late Ice Age, which was a pale reflection of the sophisticated Aurignacian and Magdalenian cultures of France, some ill-defined later Stone Age hunter-gatherer societies, which hung on after the retreat of the glaciers, and later Neolithic, Bronze, and Iron Age farming cultures. Each period was marked by characteristic artifacts, stone tools, pottery styles, and metal objects, subdivided into endless local variations. Chronology was a matter of guesswork, little more than vague estimates developed from comparing artifact styles with better dated specimens across the Channel. The archaeology Clark first learned was that of the amateur collector, whose activities revolved around gathering artifacts in the field, doing occasional crude excavations, and endlessly cataloging arrowheads and scrapers. British Stone Age archaeology was provincial, self-satisfied, and little more than a sophisticated form of stamp collecting.

But Grahame's initial experience had its merits, limited as they were. Young Clark acquired the basics of archaeology by listening carefully to his fellow collectors and met many local archaeologists who knew their flint implements thoroughly, an essential qualification for any prehistorian to this day. His first papers are typical of an archaeological genre that filled the pages of local archaeological societies in the 1920s—page after page of descriptions of stone tools of all kinds. Clark absorbed himself in the genre, which, from the beginning, he seems to have found very limiting.

The leading figures in the field were men obsessed with stone tools, among them an Ipswich tailor named J. Reid Moir, one of the founders of the Prehistoric Society of East Anglia (1908), perhaps the most active of all local archaeological societies in Britain in the 1920s. He was convinced that he had found evidence for primordial Pliocene humans in eastern England in the form of crudely chipped stone tools, which he named "eoliths" or "dawn stones." Over the years, Reid Moir doggedly collected thousands of eoliths from Pleistocene and Pliocene gravels and glacial deposits in East Anglia, which he proclaimed to be of human manufacture. He was elected a fellow of the Royal Society for his pains. During the 1930s, geologists proved beyond all reasonable doubt that the eoliths were of natural origin and the controversy died. But Reid Moir and his allies went to their graves convinced that eoliths were indeed stone artifacts.[12] The eolith controversy was in full swing when Grahame came to archaeology, but he never succumbed to the eoliths' seductive temptations. However, the minutiae of stone tool classification and the thrill of finding prehistoric artifacts captivated him, just as it did hundreds of other amateurs from many walks of life. He retained an interest in stone tools throughout his career.

Landscape Archaeology

The archaeology of Grahame's youth was a pastime of the countryside—walking across plowed fields and collecting surface flints and potsherds. And therein lay a second pervasive skein of intellectual change. Some archaeologists spent a lifetime walking the land, looking at the past through a language of earthworks and burial mounds, field systems and stone circles—the imprint of ancient societies on the landscape. Their fieldwork had deep roots in a long tradition of antiquarian inquiry that went back to the days of William Camden and his immortal *Britannia*, the first systematic description of British antiquities. This was archaeology of the landscape, accomplished without expensive excavations, with notebook, pen, and camera, sometimes guided by an impressive novelty, aerial photographs. When Grahame was an undergraduate, Britain led the world in this kind of field archaeology, which grew naturally from amateur collecting, and also from the heavy imprint of the Romans on the British landscape. He soon learned of the researches of Cyril Fox, who boldly plotted distributions of archaeological sites in the Cambridge region against a background of soils and geology and made the distribution map an essential tool for all serious archaeologists.

Perhaps the most famous of these fieldworkers was O. G. S. Crawford, a genial soul who was known as everyone's uncle.[13] He founded the archaeological journal *Antiquity* in 1927, which aimed to bring well-written archaeology to a broader, well-read audience and is still being published. Its pages extolled field archaeology, in Britain and further afield. Clark was an early subscriber and received constant encouragement from this influential and friendly man.

Scientific Excavation

Although field observation was a strength of British archaeology in the 1920s, excavation was most emphatically not. A half century earlier, in the 1880s, General Augustus Lane Fox Pitt-Rivers had inherited the enormous Cranborne Chase estates in southern England. The general had long nurtured an interest in ethnography and now indulged a passion for archaeological excavation on his land. He dug Roman and prehistoric sites and earthworks with a meticulous attention to stratigraphy and minor finds that left his more casual contemporaries cold. Most of their excavations were crude, hasty searches for spectacular Roman finds that were little better than treasure hunts, with only minimal attention paid to stratigraphic observation. This was hardly surprising in an era when even professionals, such as Leonard Woolley, the world-famous excavator of the biblical city of Ur in Iraq, learned the craft in hasty apprenticeships under experienced diggers before being sent out on their own.

Pitt-Rivers described his sites in lavish, privately published volumes, which were neglected until the 1920s, when a handful of excavators applied his principles anew.[14] Among them was Mortimer Wheeler, who modeled his Romano-British excavations in the 1920s and 1930s along Pitt-Rivers's somewhat military lines. It was no coincidence that Wheeler had served with distinction as an artillery officer in World War I, an experience that made him a firm advocate of efficient organization in the field. His excavations soon attracted attention and student volunteers, who learned his methods and then applied them elsewhere. Clark never worked under Wheeler, but he visited his excavations on many occasions. In 1925, the wealthy Alexander Keillor, who owned much of the land around the Avebury stone circles in southern England, started long-term excavations at the nearby Windmill Hill Neolithic site, using scientific principles from the start. These excavations, and a few others, notably those of a German archaeologist named Gerhard Bersu, developed new standards for field archaeology. Keiller surrounded himself with young would-be archaeologists, among them the self-taught Stuart Piggott, who began to study

Neolithic pottery. Piggott became one of Clark's lifelong friends. Grahame himself never became known for his excavation skills, but he learned the new principles from the beginning.

Childe and The Dawn

Late in life, Clark wrote: "I was lucky enough to be born at a time when prehistory was at an early state of development and was still on the threshold of gaining academic recognition."[15] He came into archaeology at just the right moment, in time to be influenced by new and powerful intellectual strands in the world of archaeology, which was still small. By the time he left Marlborough, Clark was probably aware of an archaeological world beyond the narrow coterie of amateur flint collectors. He certainly knew of a new generation of textbooks and popular volumes that summarized what was known of the Stone Age. The French scholar Marcellin Boule, famous for his study of the La Chapelle-aux-Saints Neanderthal fossil, had published *Les hommes fossiles* in 1921. He portrayed Neanderthals as shambling, clumsy humans. The book became a classic, still in print as recently as the 1950s. R. A. S. Macalister's *A Text-Book of European Archaeology* was published in the same year, together with Cambridge archaeologist Miles Burkitt's widely read *Prehistory*. Clark undoubtedly read Burkitt's text before he went to university, for it was readily available and was a useful primer on what happened in prehistory for complete beginners, even if its tone was overly geological and much too provincial by modern scientific standards. These texts covered familiar intellectual territory. But Grahame soon became aware of a bold new synthesis of European prehistory—Vere Gordon Childe's *The Dawn of European Civilization*, published in 1925.

Australian-born Gordon Childe was an extraordinary archaeologist in an era of remarkable archaeological pioneers. He had arrived penniless in England from his Australian homeland three years earlier.[16] A committed socialist, he had begun his life in Australian politics but rapidly became disillusioned with the realities of political life. He studied some classical archaeology and philology at Oxford but was largely self-taught, except for some training in formal pottery analysis from the classical archaeologist John Beasley and "an impression" from the Minoan archaeologist Arthur Evans of the potential of potsherds as chronological markers. Unlike most of his contemporaries, Childe could speak numerous

European languages and acquire firsthand knowledge of even obscure sites in continental Europe. He immersed himself in artifact classifications and chronologies of all kinds. His very first lecture to the Society of Antiquaries of London in 1925 ended with a table boldly synchronizing the prehistoric successions in Britain, northern and central Europe, and the southern Danube between about 2500 and 1500 B.C. In the subsequent discussion, the austere and conservative Reginald Smith of the British Museum remarked on how he was "much refreshed" by the infusion of so much material from the Continent into discussion of a problem in British prehistory. Smith missed the point, but Childe had become convinced that it was possible to extract from archaeological data the kind of information to understand the "genesis of European civilization as a peculiar and individual manifestation of the human spirit."[17] His classic synthesis, *The Dawn of European Civilization,* set out to achieve that very task. This remarkable book changed archaeology forever.

Childe thought of European prehistory not just as artifacts but as a form of history distilled from archaeological data, with human cultures defined by artifacts set in time and space instead of people as the main players. He believed archaeology was a way of defining actual prehistoric communities of the past. The distribution maps of artifacts, cultures, and sites in *The Dawn* plotted cultural changes through the Neolithic and earlier Bronze Age.

The Dawn of European Civilization rippled through the provincial world of archaeology like a thunderclap and became the bible for Clark and others of his generation. Grahame himself remarked as late as 1975 that "we are working in a world, which was to a significant extent of his [Childe's] making."[18] While Clark was an undergraduate, Childe published a second influential masterpiece. *The Most Ancient East* was a masterly synthesis that traced the origins of food production and civilization in Egypt and Mesopotamia and set ancient European society in an even broader context, as a recipient of ideas such as food production from southwestern Asia. Again, in a startling move away from provincialism, Childe wrote archaeology as a form of history, with a broad brushed canvas. In large measure, Grahame's broad view of the past came from Childe's work and from a lifelong friendship that endured until Childe's death in 1957.

Grahame entered a newly restless archaeological world, where diverse intellectual strains were slowly creating a new, more sophisticated prehistoric archaeology, but one still bound by the deeply conservative traditions of a discipline founded in geology rather than anthropology and history. He went up to Cambridge with a thorough knowledge of artifact typology and stone tool technology from his schoolboy years and was already quite a knowledgeable archaeologist before he began to study professionally. He had developed cordial relationships with a wide range of amateur prehistorians long before he became an undergraduate, contacts that were to serve him well in later years. His childhood enthusiasm for archaeology had become a near obsession in his late teens. So he resolved to become that rarest of rarities, a professional archaeologist, and a prehistoric archaeologist at that.

Archaeology at Cambridge

Few universities took prehistoric archaeology seriously in the 1920s.[19] Archaeological training was still rudimentary, usually a matter of learning as you went along in the field. At both Cambridge and Oxford Universities, prehistoric archaeology first appeared as part of a broader curriculum in anthropology, as a postgraduate diploma aimed mainly at colonial administrators. The Institute of Archaeology was founded at Liverpool University in 1904 but became a shadow of its former self after World War I. The establishment of the Abercromby Chair of Prehistoric Archaeology at Edinburgh University in 1926 with Gordon Childe as the first incumbent placed the subject on a much firmer basis in the academic world. But Childe was more of a researcher and writer than a teacher, producing only one honors graduate during his stay in Scotland. Clark's only real option for undergraduate training was Cambridge University. There archaeology and anthropology were intertwined—to his lasting benefit.

Anthropology was first taught in the anatomy department at Cambridge under Professor Alexander Macalister as early as 1883 because that was where human evolution was taught. A board of anthropology was founded in 1904, under the leadership of, among others, anthropologist A. C. Haddon, celebrated for his expeditions to the Torres Straits, and William Ridgeway, a scholar with wide archaeological interests. Haddon worked hard to persuade the university that anthropology was of vital importance to future colonial administrators and missionaries about to work overseas. As a result, a diploma in anthropology was established in 1908, which turned out some notable anthropologists, among them A. R. Radcliffe-

Brown, famous for his groundbreaking research among the Andaman Islanders. Meanwhile, the gentle and charming Baron Anatole von Hügel raised the money for the University Museum of Archaeology and Ethnology, which opened in 1912. The new museum housed not only Haddon's remarkable collections but also a broad range of antiquities from the early prehistory to medieval times. A series of plaster casts of Maya stelae made at the city of Copán in Honduras and Quirigua in Guatemala by A. P. Maudslay, a Cambridge man, towered over the main gallery. Maudslay was famous for his eccentricities, such as using his ivory-backed hair brushes to clean glyphs in the field. Anthropology and archaeology blended in the displays of the university museum, which were intended as much for teaching as for research and for the general edification of the public. Any student of archaeology and anthropology was surrounded at once by technology ancient and modern.

Another strand in the development of archaeology at Cambridge was woven much earlier by John Disney, a Peterhouse graduate with a passion for classical archaeology. In 1851, Disney presented his collection of classical statuary to the university and endowed a chair in his own name. A series of classical scholars held the chair until 1892, when another classicist, William Ridgeway, was elected. Ridgeway was a very different breed of scholar with broad and catholic interests. He refused to "restrict it [archaeology] to the narrow sense of pots and pans with which it is too much bound up in many peoples' minds, but rather in the wider connotation of what are called in classical instruction antiquities and which is better expressed by the term anthropology, which embraces not only the material productions of man, but also all that pertains to his sociology and to his religion."[20] Between them, Haddon and Ridgeway founded a tradition of anthropology and archaeological anthropology that nourished and influenced Grahame Clark, his contemporaries, and future generations.

Ridgeway died in 1926, just as a faculty of archaeology and anthropology replaced the earlier board of anthropology with the ability to recruit a salaried staff to teach a one-part tripos for the first time.[21] The following year, just as Grahame Clark came to Cambridge, Ellis H. Minns, fellow of Pembroke College and university lecturer in palaeography, was elected to fill the vacant Disney Chair. Like Ridgeway, Minns was an eclectic scholar of unbounded curiosity. A classical scholar by training, he had far wider archaeological interests. He became an expert in Slavonic studies and

Russian archaeology, an authority on the "archaeology, ethnology, and history of the region between the Carpathians and the Caucasus."[22] Minns was a rigorous scholar who believed that artifacts were far more than functional objects and reflected the values of those who made them. Clark was influenced by Minns's ethical approach to scholarship, "the value of handling, scrutinizing and drawing specimens of ancient craftsmanship as a key to understanding them."[23] Minns's international perspective on the ancient world was a welcome counterbalance to the ardent provincialism of British and French archaeology.

Minns inherited a faculty that had previously lacked an adequate teaching staff. Archaeology was in the hands of Miles Burkitt, an unpaid university lecturer and graduate in geology with private means, who had come to prehistory by accident when he became involved in the identification of eoliths sent to the Sedgewick Museum of Geology by Reid Moir in the early years of the century. Burkitt soon came into contact with the Abbé Henri Breuil across the Channel and studied with him in France and Spain in 1913–1914. He learned artifact typology under Breuil and Hugo Obermaier, using the magnificent collections from sites such as the Castillo rockshelter in northern Spain and Laussel near Les Eyzies, Dordogne, while also acquiring a working knowledge of rock art and of excavation in the crude French style of that time.

Burkitt may have been conservative and old-fashioned, but he was a gifted teacher. His enthusiasm was infectious. He gave the first lectures on prehistory at Cambridge in 1914, published his textbook *Prehistory* in 1921, and was appointed lecturer in 1926, a post he held until 1958. For over thirty years, Burkitt made few changes in his lectures and even told the same stories he related in the 1920s. He showed lantern slides of his researches in France before World War I to Grahame Clark's generation and was still using them when the author was a Cambridge freshman in 1956. He rarely conducted original research and never ventured outside Europe, except for a memorable excursion to South Africa in 1927, which led to his third book, *South Africa's Past in Stone and Paint* (1928). For all his conservatism, Miles Burkitt exuded an old-fashioned excitement for prehistory, which was truly engaging. Several generations of archaeologists had their first exposure to the subject in Burkitt's classroom, to say nothing of hundreds of future colonial administrators. Burkitt assumed many of his undergraduates would pursue careers far from Britain and actively encouraged them to look for archaeological sites in later life. One of his favorite, and enduring, preambles, "when you are administering justice under a paw-paw tree," would be followed by an exhortation to follow some basic principle of sound archaeological practice. The preamble, and others of its ilk, endure in the reminiscences of his students to this day. Grahame Clark heard the same basic lectures in 1926 that we heard in 1956, which merely whetted his appetite for more.[24]

Undergraduate Years

Having failed to obtain a scholarship to St. John's College, Oxford, Grahame applied for one at Peterhouse in Cambridge, the college from which his history master at Marlborough had graduated. His interview with two fellows, Harold Temperley and Herbert Butterfield, seemed to go well, but he was not offered a scholarship. When he came up to Cambridge in 1926, it was as a pensioner of the college. As archaeology was a one-part, two-year tripos, Clark read history for his first two years and obtained a First.[25] These two years did nothing to shake his determination to become a prehistorian. While still an undergraduate, he published several papers, among them a study of "horned hollow scrapers," in *Sussex Archaeological Collections* (1927), in which he traced the evolution of the horned form from hollow scrapers. A second study on discoidal polished knives appeared in the *Proceedings of the Prehistoric Society of East Anglia* for 1928.[26] The paper plotted distributions of polished knives, which coincided well with Beaker distributions, so Grahame argued that the knives were spread by the Beaker folk. By this time, he had been studying stone tools for more than a decade. He was a lithic expert in his own right and was often consulted by fellow members of the Prehistoric Society of East Anglia.

The time in history was not wasted, for he attended lectures by such luminaries as the world historian G. M. Trevelyan. Grahame especially enjoyed Sir Alfred Clapham, professor of economic history, whose lectures left a lasting intellectual impression. Clapham was one of the first scholars to recognize the importance of the geographical distribution of archaeological sites on ancient landscapes as a way of understanding changing patterns of human settlement.[27] Clark's two undergraduate years in history were of seminal importance, for they left him open to the innovative researches of economic historian Michael Postan and other cutting-edge scholars of his generation, which played an important role in his thinking about economic archaeology in later years. In 1928, Grahame moved across to the faculty of archaeology and anthropology. His guardian, Hugh Shaw, had assumed he would enter his solicitor's office or become a stockbroker. Not unnaturally worried about future opportunities, Shaw called on Ellis Minns to inquire about career prospects in prehistoric archaeology. The Disney Professor was not optimistic, but Shaw wisely allowed his determined ward to proceed.

The curriculum for the archaeology and anthropology tripos covered the basic principles of anthropology, including physical anthropology, social anthropology, and the archaeology of the Stone and early Metal Ages of Europe and the Mediterranean, also material culture. Minns and Burkitt did most of the teaching, which was at an elementary level, but they approached the subject from the assumption that archaeology was an integral part of anthropology. From the outset, Grahame learned that archaeology was a source of information about human origins and the evolution of human culture. As such, it was a relevant way of approaching societies ancient and modern, all people on earth. Clark never forgot this fundamental point and soon "came to accept as an aim the promotion of World Prehistory," or so he wrote in remote retrospect.[28]

Clark elected to take an honors degree and spent two years studying archaeology and anthropology. He took to the work like a duck entering water, attending lectures in the Museum of Archaeology and Anthropology, surrounded on every side by ethnographic specimens from remote corners of the world, which reinforced the strong intellectual links between archaeology and anthropology in his mind. The curriculum ensured that he was exposed to both physical and social anthropology, which gave an anthropological dimension to the history that he had absorbed during his first two years.

Grahame began his tripos at the moment when the curriculum had two tracks, known as sections.[29] Section A covered anthropology and prehistoric archaeology. Section B, recently transferred from modern and medieval languages, was primarily concerned with the archaeology of the Celtic, Anglo-Saxon, and Norse-speaking peoples of Europe and was under the direction of Professor H. M. Chadwick, Elrington and Bosworth Professor of Anglo-Saxon. Undergraduates could qualify for an honors degree by taking both Sections A and B, which exposed them both to the Stone Age and to the Bronze Age antecedents of historic peoples. Chadwick himself had been trained as a classicist and then became interested in northern cultures, publishing a series of books on Celtic and Teutonic peoples that received wide acclaim. He was assisted by J. M. De Navarro, an American who spent most of his life in England and became an expert on the European Bronze Age and Iron Age. As an honors student, Grahame received an unusually broad grounding in prehistoric and later archaeology, while his historical studies added another perspective.

Clark was an undergraduate at a time when archaeological horizons were expanding rapidly in the hands of an exceptionally able group of field-workers far from Cambridge, many of whom became colleagues in later years. Their fieldwork and ideas permeated the tripos and were a powerful intellectual counterweight to the provincialism of so much East Anglian archaeology and to Miles Burkitt's somewhat narrow courses. He sat in on lectures by such luminaries as Leonard Woolley, who was in the midst of his spectacular Ur excavations. Gertrude Caton Thompson talked about her Fayum surveys and excavations west of the Nile River in Egypt, which were producing the earliest known evidence for agriculture in the world, dating to an estimated 4000 B.C. Gordon Childe lectured about Bronze Age Europe. The quiet and scholarly Dorothy Garrod, who had studied archaeology at Oxford University after World War I, had just completed her excavations at the Devil's Tower on Gibraltar, where she had unearthed an important fossil of a Neanderthal child. Garrod was also engaged in archaeological survey in Kurdistan. These experiences, and long residence abroad in her youth, gave Garrod much broader perspectives than most Cambridge archaeologists. Clark was in the audience in 1928 when she boldly informed the Prehistoric Society of East Anglia that the French Stone Age cultural sequence was not applicable outside the narrow confines of western Europe, an opinion that flew in the face of much conventional archaeological thinking at the time. As he completed the tripos, Garrod was holding a research fellowship at Newnham College, while she began her "very strenuous" excavations at the Mount Carmel caves in what was then Palestine in 1929. A decade later, Grahame reviewed her now classic monograph on Mount Carmel and describe it as "pure gold."

Young Louis Leakey, later to acquire international fame for his research into early human evolution, was the most colorful archaeologist associated with Cambridge at the time. He had gone down (graduated) a year before Clark arrived, but a research fellowship at St. John's gave him a base for his

East African archaeological expedition, which produced a remarkable, and exotic, Stone Age cultural sequence for East Africa, further undermining the Eurocentric perspective of the day. Grahame spent much time in Leakey's cluttered rooms at St. Johns, where boxes of stone artifacts were piled everywhere. Stories of Leakey's discoveries "served to underline for me the importance of excavation as the prime source of data for reconstructing the course of prehistory."[30]

One of Grahame's most vivid memories was of anatomist Sir Elliot Grafton Smith, famous for his diffusionist theories, lecturing in the well of the anatomy school, "rotating a fossil skull in his hands to demonstrate its crucial features."[31] His courses in social anthropology were taught by retired colonial civil servants. "I can still hear Col. Harding telling us that the essence of Anthropology was food and sex, keeping alive and perpetuating, not forgetting the social arrangements evolved by different communities to ensure these things," he wrote many years later.[32] Grahame and his fellow students had Radcliffe-Brown as compulsory reading, with notions of societies interacting with their natural environments. Forty years later, at the height of another theoretical furor, he remembered how "living systems and the interactions between their components were so to speak in the air. One grew up with a view of archaeology which some seem only to have rediscovered lately and by way of transatlantic proponents of the so-called New Archaeology."[33]

The tripos was not that demanding, but it offered a remarkable opportunity for an ambitious, serious-minded student to receive an unusually broad-based archaeological grounding. With the exception of Burkitt, the faculty had wide interests and an eclectic view of the ancient world, which knew few disciplinary or geographical boundaries. Students had free run of the museum and went to supervisions in colleges and private homes.[34] The Sedgewick Museum of Geology was also close at hand. By the time he graduated with first class honors in 1930, Grahame Clark had been exposed to a broad range of ideas and to archaeological researches in all corners of Europe and the Near East.

Perhaps Clark's strongest intellectual stimulus came from someone who was not at Cambridge at all. Cyril Fox had come up to Magdalene College immediately after World War I as a mature student to study archaeology. Fox had been working on local archaeology since 1914 and had attended Section B lectures that were still in the English tripos. Thanks to skilled lobbying by Professors Chadwick and Ridgeway, he was registered for a Ph.D. before he had even graduated with a B.A. The result was an extraordinary dissertation that used the collections of the university museum to plot the finds from successive periods from Neolithic to Anglo-Saxon on physical base maps that covered an area of some 113 square kilometers (44 square miles) around Cambridge. Fox used the distributions to argue for an expansion of human settlement from its beginnings on landscapes with relatively open vegetation to a "secondary zone" of heavier soils with dense forest and undergrowth. These soils were heavily exploited by the Romans and Anglo-Saxons, as opposed to earlier peoples, for they required a much heavier investment of labor without the prospect of immediate return.[35]

The Fox dissertation appeared as *The Archaeology of the Cambridge Region* in 1923 (reissued 1948) and became one of the classic monographs of twentieth-century British archaeology. Leading historians such as Alfred Clapham and G. M. Trevelyan were fascinated by the potential of archaeology for studying changing human settlement patterns, while the Fox research gave a new direction to the somewhat sterile process of artifact collection by emphasizing the importance of geology and geography in studying the past. Fox was hired as an assistant in the university museum for a short period but was soon lured away by Mortimer Wheeler to become keeper in antiquities at the National Museum of Wales. But his simple, soon outdated approach to settlement and environment exercised a strong influence on archaeologists of Clark's generation and can be seen in Grahame's research on Mesolithic Britain and in his later studies of much larger problems. It was they who replaced Fox's basic distribution maps with far more sophisticated formulations based, among other things, on paleo-environmental data.

First Excavations

The Cambridge archaeological curriculum gave undergraduates experience in describing and identifying artifacts, as it does today. But it suffered from one major weakness. The faculty did not engage in basic field research, so experience in excavation and survey had to be gained elsewhere. Clark found no one in Cambridge able to train him in the field, but he was fortunate enough to come in contact with Dr. Eliot Curwen, a former medical missionary in China, and his son physician Eliot Cecil Curwen. Both were enthusiastic and competent amateur archaeologists, Eliot junior being remarkable for his use of aerial photographs to find archaeological sites and ancient field systems that were nearly invisible on the ground. The Curwens were particularly interested in a chain of Iron Age hill forts along the Sussex Downs that had resisted Roman invaders.

Clark first met Curwen senior when he visited him at his home in Hove to inspect his extensive flint collection. He soon learned that the former missionary was an ardent creationist and believed in the absolute historical truth of the Scriptures. This meant that all of prehistory had to be confined within the mere 6,000 years of the Ussherian chronology, a somewhat limiting perspective for a student interested in the Stone Age. However, Curwen was a competent excavator in constant need of helpers, who used methods based on those of General Pitt Rivers, so Clark kept his mouth shut and had his first taste of excavation at Whitehawk Neolithic causewayed camp on the outskirts of Brighton.[36] Here Curwen and his son Cecil trenched through the earthworks and found potsherds like those from Windmill Hill near Avebury, recently excavated by Alexander Keillor, together with animal bones and flint artifacts.

In 1928, the Curwens excavated the entrances and fortifications of the Iron Age fort known as the Trundle, which overlooked Goodwood race course. In the course of this work, they found a much older "discontinuous ditch" below the Iron Age earthworks. Two years later, they returned to investigate these features, which turned out to be part of a Neolithic causewayed camp like Keillor's Windmill Hill. The excavators gathered in a small camp of bell tents in the shelter of the earthen ramparts during the blazing hot August of 1930. There Clark worked with two fledgling archaeologists who became lifelong friends: Stuart Piggott, who was already engaged in a study of Windmill Hill and other Neolithic pottery types, and Charles Phillips, a historian and enthusiastic archaeologist, later to become a fellow of Selwyn College and one of the principal excavators of the Sutton Hoo Anglo-Saxon ship in East Anglia just before World War II (Figure 1.2).

Grahame had become friends with Phillips the year before, when they happened to attend a meeting called by a small group of dissidents to set up a rival organization to the well-established Cambridge Antiquarian Society. Phillips recalled that he knew no one in the audience, so he sat down next to "the most respectable of them." The meeting was a disaster and Phillips's neighbor (Grahame) "was also fidgeting about with disapproval."[37] They

Figure 1.2   **Excavators at the Trundle, 1930. Grahame Clark is at left front, Stuart Piggott immediately behind him. Mrs. Curwen and daughter are at the center. (Photograph located by the late Ruth Daniel.)**

caught each other's eyes and slipped out, became friends over tea the next day, and frequently went on expeditions into the fens together. At the time, Phillips was surveying archaeological sites in the remote depths of Lincolnshire, among them areas like Risby Warren and Manton Warren, where there were wide expanses of sandy terrain in which Mesolithic flints of interest to Grahame abounded. The Trundle dig cemented a lifetime friendship, which rapidly became an important influence in Clark's archaeological career. Phillips was an expert at assessing landscapes and soon involved Clark in projects to identify hitherto unknown early Fenland and Lincolnshire communities, adding to his experience of the relationships between sites and their environments.

In the late 1920s, and thanks to O. G. S. Crawford, Phillips acquired a set of Royal Air Force aerial photographs of the fens, as well as cultivating the friendship of Major Gordon Fowler, the traffic manager of the huge Anglo-Dutch sugar processing factory at Ely. Fowler spent his days arranging the transport of sugar beet by barge and road, work that brought him in touch with many country people. He found large quantities of prehistoric pottery and learned of occasional ancient tree trunks found during plowing. His main interest was in the meandering silt banks that crisscrossed the fens, known as "roddens," which he was convinced were traces of a now vanished landscape. The aerial photographs showed a startled Phillips how a virtually invisible medieval and prehistoric landscape lay under the modern drainage system. Consequently, he started going into the fens armed with twenty-five-inch survey maps and the photographs, tracing Roman and earlier sites on the ground. Concurrently, botanists and geologists used the same tools to get a clear picture of the natural history of the fens since the Ice Age. All this research came together under the leadership of Grahame and others in the 1930s. Phillips's influence on Clark was seminal. In turn, Phillips readily acknowledged his own intellectual indebtedness.

Grahame seems to have enjoyed the Trundle excavations, where the company was congenial. Once again, trenches through the earthworks revealed Windmill Hill pottery and leaf-shaped arrowheads. Whitehawk and the Trundle represented the sum of Clark's formal training in excavation, although such limited training was nothing unusual before World War II. Most excavators worked alongside someone else for a short time and then learned on their own by trial and error. Grahame never learned the craft under Mortimer Wheeler, who trained a whole generation of excavators on Romano-British or Iron Age sites such as Verulamium or Maiden Castle. Although he never achieved fame as an excavator himself, his later, world-famous excavations at Star Carr show that he was a competent basic fieldworker, working closely with Phillips and others in his early days to acquire a broad field experience. He also resolved "to set an example by conducting excavations myself and encouraging students to join me as active helpers."[38] He followed this practice until the late 1950s.

Few people graduated with honors degrees in archaeology and anthropology before World War II. Only a handful of undergraduates studied prehistoric archaeology, even fewer Section B, which had only three or four students each year. During the 1930s, seven Cambridge graduates became professional archaeologists. Three of them—Grahame Clark, Glyn Daniel, and Charles McBurney—took doctorates at their alma mater and became members of the Cambridge faculty. In the early days, Cambridge generated its own staff, who then went on to train future generations of archaeologists, not only for British archaeology but for the wider world. Training archaeologists for a global role became a dominant theme of Grahame Clark's career.

2

✿

The Mesolithic Age in Britain

It is true that the cultures . . . were not as brilliant as those of Upper Palaeolithic date. . . . But at the same time though perhaps more miserable they are not at all despicable.

Miles Burkitt, foreword to *The Mesolithic Age in Britain*

Grahame Clark was proud that he made history by being the first candidate registered for a doctorate in archaeology after the founding of the Faculty Board of Archaeology and Anthropology in 1926. He was awarded a Hugo de Balsham Studentship at Peterhouse from 1930 to 1932 and encouraged by Miles Burkitt to tackle a broad topic: the British Mesolithic.

The Mesolithic: "A Sort of Dustbin"?

At the time, the Mesolithic was the poor relative of prehistoric archaeology. About 15,000 years ago, the ice sheets of the Würm glaciation, the last cold snap of the Ice Age, began to retreat. The thaw proceeded in fits and starts, with rapid deglaciation and then an abrupt, millennium-long cold snap about 12,000 years ago. Thereafter, the warming continued, ushering in modern climatic conditions in northern Europe.

The geography of northern and western Europe was radically different during the Late Ice Age. Huge ice sheets mantled Scandinavia and much of

Britain. Sea levels were ninety meters (300 feet) lower than they are today. The southern North Sea was dry land. Britain was part of the Continent and much of the English Channel, a land bridge. A vast expanse of rolling steppe-tundra extended from the Atlantic coast into Central Europe and beyond. Most Upper Palaeolithic hunter-gatherer groups lived in the more benign and sheltered river valleys of southwestern France, moving out on the plains in pursuit of reindeer and other prey during the summer months. The elaborate Magdalenian culture of the Dordogne and northern Spain with its magnificent art and finely crafted antler and bone tools was the apogee of Stone Age culture in Ice Age Europe and considered by archaeologists of the 1920s to be a climax of prehistoric achievement.

With the Postglacial warm-up, the geography and environment of ancient Europe changed dramatically. The Scandinavian ice sheets shrank rapidly, exposing what is now the Baltic Sea—first a lake, then various iterations of a brackish sea. At the same time, birches and conifers and then temperate oak forests spread rapidly over what had been a treeless landscape. Much of the once diverse Ice Age big-game fauna vanished, to be replaced by forest animals. The rich Upper Palaeolithic cultures of southwestern France gave way to what appeared to be impoverished forest cultures, with simple stone technologies, no antler artifacts, and apparently no artistic traditions. Most experts believed that the retreat of the ice sheets saw the Magdalenian hunter-gatherers of France retreating steadily northward with the glaciers. Sometime afterward, entirely new Neolithic (New Stone Age) farmers arrived in a deserted Europe from Asia and established an entirely new way of life. In other words, there was a complete hiatus between the Upper Palaeolithic and the Neolithic.

Not everyone agreed with this assessment. There were signs of human settlement, but they were very different from Upper Palaeolithic cultures and left a less conspicuous signature. As long ago as the 1840s, Danish archaeologists had excavated hunter-gatherer shell heaps that postdated the Ice Age but predated the Neolithic. These "kitchen middens" yielded the bones of migratory birds and freshwater fish but no signs of domesticated animals or grain. Soon, there were enough sites to justify a new terminological subdivision of the Stone Age. As early as 1872, the term "Mesolithic" (Middle Stone Age) was applied to these sites and to seemingly "degenerate" occupation layers in French caves above Upper Palaeolithic levels. One such culture was the Azilian of southern France and northern Spain (named after the Mas d'Azil cave in France's Ariège), a "crude" foraging culture remarkable only for simple painted stones. By the turn of the century, the Mesolithic was in wide terminological use and the notion of the *ancien hiatus* beloved by French prehistorians discredited. The Mesolithic was now seen as a brief transitional epoch between the Upper Palaeolithic and the Neolithic, the "new Stone Age" with its farming cultures. Whether the Neolithic originated in Mesolithic cultures or was attributable to immigrants was also unknown.

No one had a clear idea what the Mesolithic really was. It remained a kind of archaeological no-man's-land between the Upper Palaeolithic and the Neolithic, marked by seemingly dull and impoverished societies. "The cultures of this epoch are numerous and somewhat monotonous," Miles Burkitt wrote in his textbook, *The Old Stone Age*, still in print in 1964.[1] He thought of the Mesolithic as a period of cultural stagnation at the end of the Ice Age, which saw simplification of Upper Palaeolithic culture. The Mesolithic was a period of regression from the cultural achievements of the Late Ice Age, in which the extinction of big game led to a population crash and new, simpler hunting cultures based on forest animals and plant gathering. The people used less elaborate technology of smaller and lighter stone tools. Like his French colleagues, Burkitt grouped the Mesolithic cultures of Europe into the Maglemosian of the Baltic region and the "Azilio-Tardenoisian civilization," an all-embracing term that covered both the Azilian of northern Spain with its distinctive painted pebbles and the numerous microlithic sites of central and western Europe, named after a major site at Fère-en-Tardenois in central France. In Britain, he merely noted the presence of "many stations where microlithic flints occur."[2]

One can hardly blame Burkitt, for the British Mesolithic had received little attention from anyone but amateur collectors, who had assembled large collections of surface finds from open areas like the Pennines and Sussex Downs. It was considered a mere footnote to the flourishing cultures of the Late Ice Age. Until Grahame Clark came along, the British Mesolithic was "a sort of dust-bin into which any awkward industry which does not seem to belong to any period could be cast."[3] No one really understood the nature of Mesolithic cultural achievements, or whether the Mesolithic was a transition to farming or a genuine regression of European Stone Age culture. Was it "more advanced" than the Upper Palaeolithic, or simply something very different? As far as Britain was concerned, the problem was an intractable one, largely because the surviving archaeological record was little more than innumerable scatters of diminutive flint artifacts. Burkitt realized that young Grahame Clark with his passion for flints was the ideal person to define the British Mesolithic.

Travels

Dorothy Garrod had been the first scholar to study the British Upper Palaeolithic, which was culturally impoverished compared with the rich Cro-Magnon societies of southwestern France. She relegated the Mesolithic to a single chapter, "Epipalaeolithic Cultures," in her landmark *Upper Palaeolithic Cultures of Britain* (1926). Garrod followed French terminology and contented herself with a brief description of some major "Azilian stations" in Scotland, of Maglemose-like sites in East Anglia, also of the already famous Holderness Maglemose harpoons and "Tardenoisian industries" with their microliths that were "widely distributed" between Sussex and Scotland. She described the Tardenoisian of Britain as corresponding with "the earlier stages of the Tardenoisian of Belgium."[4]

Grahame knew little more about the Mesolithic than anyone else, but he had excellent contacts among amateur archaeologists in many parts of the country. He was as well qualified as anyone to sort out a confusing plethora of artifact scatters from Scotland to Sussex (Figure 2.1). Clark found himself very much on his own. His supervisor was Burkitt, who gave him free run of his remarkable offprint collection but otherwise left him to his own devices. However, he adopted his supervisor's Mesolithic terminology, for he agreed that Postglacial hunter-gatherer cultures were indeed transitional ones. He took Garrod's nine-page essay on the "Epipalaeolithic" as his starting point, with nothing but a few broad comparisons with similar microlithic cultures on the Continent as his cultural yardstick. Clark's task was to dissect Burkitt's metaphorical dustbin, starting almost from scratch, a formidable task even for a veteran prehistorian.

He realized at once that he needed to acquire an intimate knowledge of Mesolithic sites and cultures in mainland Europe. In 1929, he set off on the first of his pre–World War II journeys in search of the European Mesolithic, visiting Denmark and Sweden as the guest of archaeologist John af Klercker. His memories of this trip endured, among them a chance meeting with Sophus Müller, a legendary opponent of the European prehistori-

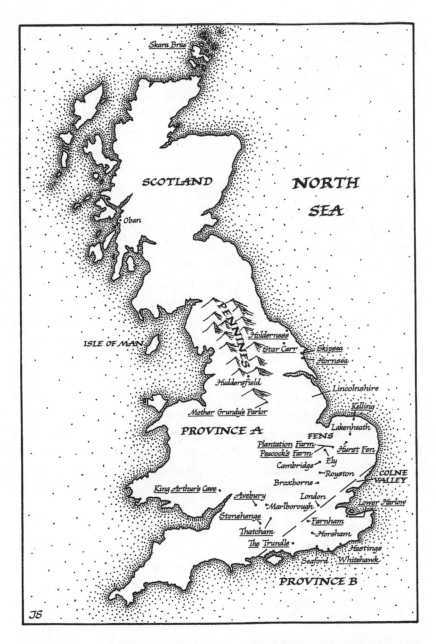

Figure 2.1 **Map of Mesolithic sites in Britain, showing Clark's "A" and "B" Provinces. Some other locations mentioned in later chapters are also included.**

an Oscar Montelius, in a Bronze Age gallery in the National Museum in Copenhagen, and a chance to handle the famous Ystad antler sleeve, adorned with finely etched deer. He was able to take a walk on the ancient beach of the Litorina Sea, a Postglacial shoreline of the Baltic Sea, an epiphanic experience. There he could appreciate for the first time the magnitude of the environmental changes that followed the Ice Age. He made lasting contacts with "Dr. Arne of Stockholm and Dr. Rydbeck of Lund," among the first of many Scandinavian scholars to exchange reprints with him.[5] The early years of Clark's archives in the Cambridge University Library are crammed with carefully annotated papers from northern colleagues, which provided the raw material for his continental analogies, and for his later work on the broader canvas of Mesolithic Europe.

Returning from his travels, Grahame embarked on a systematic examination of the numerous Mesolithic collections in British museums. He also used his connections with amateur archaeologists to assemble as complete a database as he could, focusing most of his attention on central and southern Britain (Figure 2.1). His researches took him far afield: to the British Museum, the Ashmolean in Oxford, the Manx Museum in Douglas, Isle of Man, Norwich Museum, Tunbridge Wells Museum, and the archaeology office of the Ordnance Survey—to mention only a few. He visited local amateurs all over the country, among them a Yorkshire solicitor named Francis Buckley, who had collected Stone Age artifacts in the walls of trenches on the western front before developing a serious interest in Mesolithic flints. Clark stayed with Buckley at Tunstead and accompanied him in the field (Figure 2.2). Buckley was an accomplished expert on old English glass and one of the first archaeologists to distinguish between the earlier and later Mesolithic on the basis of differences in stone tool forms. Many of Grahame's ideas on the subject came from his excursions with Buckley.[6] The acknowledgments in *The Mesolithic Age in Britain* read like a who's who of British archaeology at the time, including not only friends such as Piggott and Phillips and his Cambridge mentors but also well-known amateurs of the day, for example, A. L. Armstrong, J. P. T. Burchell, and J. E. Sainty. Three years later, in 1932, he presented his researches in a book that drew immediate attention from the narrow coterie of Stone Age archaeologists at home and abroad. *The Mesolithic Age in Britain* was published by Cambridge University Press, which published all of Grahame's writing. His published monograph also formed the core of his doctoral dissertation, which was submitted in January 1934.

Figure 2.2   **Francis Buckley photographed by Grahame Clark at the Wawcott Mesolithic site in the Pennines, northern England, probably in 1931.**

The Mesolithic Age

The Mesolithic Age in Britain is a remarkably mature work for someone starting out on an academic career. The style is spare and workmanlike and, characteristically, wastes no time in getting to the core of the matter, a distributional study of British Mesolithic assemblages. His aim was simple: "the recognition and definition of artefactual assemblages distinct from those ascribed either to the previously defined Palaeolithic or Neolithic Stone Ages."[7] The introduction notes how the British Neolithic had brought the beginnings of farming into closer focus, thanks to the Windmill Hill and Trundle excavations, and through the ceramic studies of Stuart Piggott. Furthermore, the Neolithic had been identified as an intrusive culture that was estimated to have entered Britain in the second half of the third millennium B.C. "The interest of this dating for us is that it gives room for a long Mesolithic," Clark wrote. "Between the close of the Pleistocene and the arrival of the Neolithic arts of life in this country, there is ample room for those Mesolithic cultures which form the subject of this book."[8]

The book begins with a general outline of the "Mesolithic Age" with a brief mention of the climatic changes that unfolded after the Ice Age. Here Clark drew on his knowledge of the new technique of pollen analysis (palynology) to reconstruct ancient vegetational changes, familiar to him from his Scandinavian reading and from a friendly association with his contemporaries, Cambridge botanists Harry Godwin and his wife, Margaret, who had learned palynological methods in Scandinavia with a view to studying climatic change from stratified deposits in the fens of East Anglia. Grahame's main concern was with human responses to climatic change. "Mankind seems to have reacted to these potent external stimuli in three different ways," he wrote, "by modification of his existing cultural equipment, by migration, or by new and revolutionary discoveries, which altered the character of his exploitation of natural resources from the food-gathering or parasitical to the productive." The purpose of his monograph was to pass in review over "these modifications and migrations of the old hunting cultures, which we may regard, in a certain sense, as the alternatives to the Neolithic cultures."[9] He assumed that Mesolithic and Neolithic cultures diverged from a common stock, Mesolithic cultures being "like the great apes, off the main line of human evolutionary progress." His real concern was how Stone Age cultures had changed under the "stress of climate change." Many scientists regarded Mesolithic cultures as "decadent." Clark did not engage himself in this fruitless debate but concerned himself purely with the "form and process" of the cultures, a scientific investigation that revealed the unique character of the Mesolithic.

Artifact Typologies

These forms and processes could only mean artifact typologies, for there was almost no other evidence for the British Mesolithic at the time, and most of that was from surface sites. Unlike many of his contemporaries, Clark examined the detailed characters of entire industries, not just carefully selected finished tools. Instead of using just type artifacts for classification, he looked at the presence or absence of tool types, percentages of different artifacts present, also the technology and raw material. He approached the various collections with several lines of evidence, hoping thereby to classify and date them more securely. His approach resembled that of Gordon Childe, whose books had exercised a strong influence on him. He assumed that artifact assemblages were cultures and that cultures represented people. In this way, he would use distinct assemblages such as those with axes, nongeometric microliths, or geometric forms, to identify distinct peoples, some of whom used distinct raw materials for toolmaking (Figure 2.3).[10] He also employed this multifaceted approach to make broad analogies with equivalent Mesolithic cultures on the Continent, where caves and rockshelters provided fine-grained stratigraphy virtually unknown in Britain. Distribution maps of different artifact forms and sites were a powerful weapon in his research armory too. At this point, he considered archaeology the study of past culture traits in time and space, and of the factors governing their distribution.

Mesolithic industries in Britain could be distinguished by three major elements: microliths, axes, and bone artifacts. If one artifact distinguishes Mesolithic cultures throughout Europe, it is the microlith. They are small, often geometrically shaped tools, made from tiny blades punch-struck from small conical lumps of fine-grained rock. They formed the sharp barbs of lethal hunting weapons—arrows, fish spears, harpoons, and lances, slotted into wooden or antler shafts—used against mammals and even birds on the wing. The wooden shafts are rarely found, but the microliths occur by the hundreds in even small sites, many of them made by the so-called microburin technique, which removed the thick end of the blade (Figure 2.4). Variations in the shape and percentages of microliths are still used to define different Mesolithic groups throughout Europe today and formed one of Clark's major research tools.

Clark recognized microlithic technology as a global phenomenon, even if the characteristic microburin technique associated with British specimens and many European Mesolithic assemblages was not universal. Here he differed immediately from all his predecessors except Garrod, for he assumed Britain was part of a much larger prehistoric world. He noted the presence of microliths as far afield as Scotland and Australia, from "Poland to the Cape [of Good Hope]." There were basic microlithic tool types that were modified in size and form under the influence of local climatic change.

Following the fashion of the day, Clark invoked population movements as the reason why microliths were manufactured in so many areas, the so-called Wilton culture with its microliths in South Africa, for example, having originated from a migration southward from East Africa. As for the

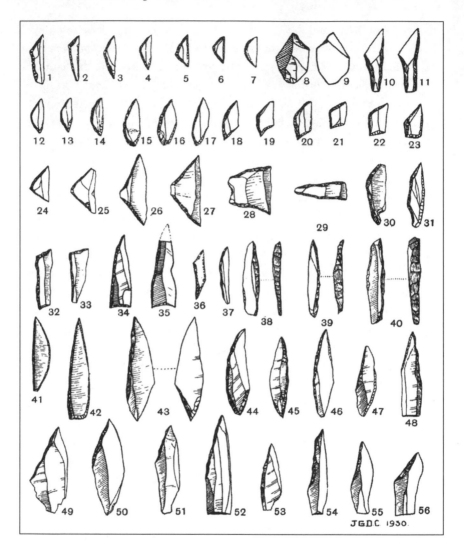

Figure 2.3   **Microliths from the Wangford-Lakenheath area of east-ern England. An illustration drawn by Clark for *The Mesolithic Age in Britain* [Figure 15]. Scale: Actual size. Courtesy Cambridge University Press.**

microlith-based Tardenoisian of France, first identified by Gabriel de Mortillet, it resulted from migrations and cultural influences from the already well-known microlithic Capsian culture of French North Africa, which brought the "microburin and microlithic derivatives, the gravette

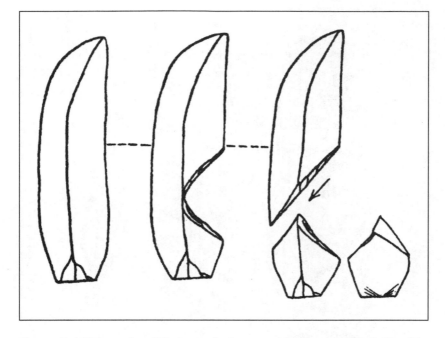

Figure 2.4 **The microburin technique, as drawn by Clark for** *The Mesolithic Age* **[Figure d]. The stoneworker selected a small bladelet, blunted one side and notched it, then snapped off the thicker base, creating a microlith (shown at two-thirds size). Courtesy Cambridge University Press.**

point, and second the trapeze [-shaped microlith]."[11] Grahame noted evidence for local cultures in Europe at the end of the Ice Age, among them the Azilian culture of northern Spain, derived from the Magdalenian, but felt that Tardenoisian influences "intervened" throughout western Europe.

From microlithic industries, Clark now turned to a second element of European Mesolithic culture, the "roughly chipped axes and picks of *tranchet* character" (Figure 2.5). (The tranchet referred to the working edge formed by a transverse sharpening blow across the base of the tool.) These artifacts were characteristic of the Maglemose culture, identified by Danish archaeologists along the shores of the Baltic Sea, "probably derived from some east European focus of the Upper Palaeolithic blade industries, and a strong bone tradition."[12] The Maglemose was a northern European culture, but "influences" from this culture reached eastern and southeastern England in later Mesolithic times.

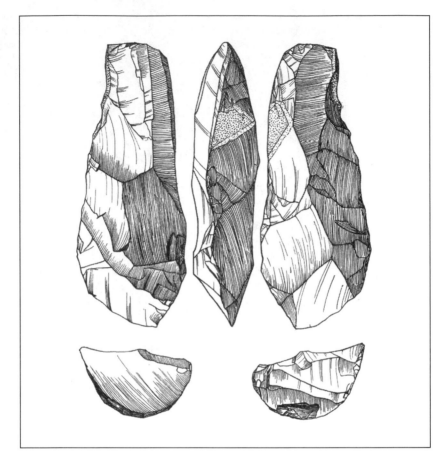

Figure 2.5 **Maglamose-type Mesolithic tranchet axe from the Horsham area, drawn by Clark for** *The Mesolithic Age* **[Figure 47]. Scale: Two-thirds size. Courtesy Cambridge University Press.**

A third element was the elaborate bone industries found in the Upper Palaeolithic Magdalenian culture of western France and in the Maglemose of the Scandinavian Mesolithic. Clark hypothesized that this technology had origins in Upper Palaeolithic cultures and was especially important not only in the Maglemose but also in the Kunda and Pernau cultures of the eastern Baltic coast, where bonework was all-important.[13] He showed that the Maglemose presence in Britain was greater than his predecessors had suspected.

Finally, Clark made a bold statement about the Mesolithic lifeway, which, he said, resulted from hunter-gatherers being driven by the spread of post glacial forests to the edges of lakes and sea coasts. He noted that Mesolithic shell middens were common throughout Europe. "The collection of shell-fish, fishing, and, on the sandy wastes, where the forests thinned out, the pursuit of small game, supplemented by the collection of roots and berries, were the only resources of the rather poverty-stricken folk of Western Europe in the Mesolithic Age." Like his contemporaries, he regarded Mesolithic peoples as "laggard" survivors of a "more primitive civilization in a backward region." Everyone believed that Neolithic farmers had entered ancient Europe, that the Mesolithic people whom they supplanted or who lived alongside them were "of the nature of survivals."[14]

As a result of his travels in Scandinavia, Clark had a particular interest in any Maglemose finds in Britain. Before embarking on the main body of his research, he described the few antler and bone harpoon finds known from the United Kingdom, among them flat "Azilian" harpoons from northwestern Britain and especially the characteristic Maglemose points found under a peat bed at Hornsea and Skipsea in northeast Yorkshire and at Holderness. There was, he wrote, "ample proof" of the existence of Maglemose societies in eastern England, a conclusion that was to prove prophetic.

Provinces A and B

Most of *The Mesolithic Age* is a detailed description of hundreds of Mesolithic flint assemblages, mainly surface collections found on sandy terrain. Like Garrod, Clark lamented the lack of stratigraphic information and poor preservation conditions, both of which militated against making sense of a maze of isolated finds. He divided Britain into two "divisions," using distribution maps, just as his younger contemporaries were doing for later cultures. Province A comprised most of the country outside a well-defined southeastern region, Province B, "in which the *tranchet* axe is common, *i.e.* the south-east of England" (see Figure 2.1).[15] At the time, when so little was known, this simplistic division made sense, for Clark was at pains to draw a clear distinction between those areas of the country that had come under Scandinavian influence and those that owed their microlithic technology to more southerly regions. The presence or absence of the tranchet axe seemed a convenient criterion, although grossly simplistic by today's standards.

Having established the technological provinces, Clark embarked immediately into a description of the sites and industries of Province A. He began in the Pennines with the finds made by amateur archaeologist Leslie Armstrong at Mother Grundy's Parlor Cave in Creswell Crags, where Mesolithic microliths lay atop sparse Upper Palaeolithic occupation. Here microburins "pointed to" the Tardenoisian. From the Pennines, Clark moved to the Huddersfield region, where concentrated patches of microliths and hearths lay on a north-south ridge at 380 to 460 meters (1250 to 1500 feet) above sea level. Here he distinguished between assemblages with nongeometric and geometric industries, the former symptomatic of the early Mesolithic, as they were across the North Sea in Belgium. This Pennines industry he believed to be one of the earliest in Britain, which "seems to represent the intrusion of a new culture from the continent, possibly from Belgium."[16] In this, he followed the thinking of the local amateur archaeologist Francis Buckley, who had already reached the same conclusion. On this, and many other occasions in *The Mesolithic Age*, one senses Clark's emerging broader vision of Postglacial Europe, his restlessness with the narrow provincialism of the collectors, whose finds formed much of the database for his dissertation.

After a brief excursion to describe "Tardenoisian" sites on the Isle of Man, Clark moved across to more familiar territory in the Lakenheath area of Suffolk, then to North Lincolnshire, where sandy areas had "proved attractive to Tardenois man." From there, he traveled to southwestern Britain and the Welsh borders. King Arthur's Cave at Ross-on-Wye provided stratigraphic evidence for microlithic artifacts lying between upper Palaeolithic and Neolithic occupation. A scatter of sites, large and small, notably in Cornwall, merely documented the widespread distribution of microlithic industries. So did locations in Wales and Scotland, where Clark identified shell limpet scoops that were in wide use in coastal regions. The seemingly endless catalog of microliths, scrapers, and surface collections is almost mind deadening but symptomatic of the great care Clark took to develop a comprehensive knowledge of what had been found, its stratigraphic associations, if any, and chronology. The resulting catalog represents a fair summary of what was known of Britain's microlithic industries at the time, but the virtual lack of stratigraphic sites made it effectively meaningless, as Clark was well aware.

Next, Clark turned his attention to his Province B, the "Microlithic and *Tranchet* Axe and Pick Industries of South-East Britain." Again, his summary consists of a site catalog, which begins with Kelling, a site on a gravel-capped plateau nineteen kilometers (12 miles) west of Cromer in Norfolk. The numerous flints included transversely flaked axes and burins, prompting Clark to assign the material to the Maglemose culture, so common on the other side of the North Sea. He passed quickly over other East Anglian sites, many of them little more than flint scatters, dwelling at some length on an industry found in gravels from the lower terrace of the Colne River. His predecessors had ascribed them to the Upper Palaeolithic, specifically to the Aurignacian. Clark firmly disagreed and ascribed the material to a Mesolithic tranchet and microlithic industry.[17] Two other sites, Lower Halstow in north Kent, and Thatcham in Berkshire, were deemed to have unusual importance. Lower Halstow yielded tranchet axes and other Mesolithic artifacts lying atop a marsh clay, dated to the early Atlantic period. Clark proclaimed the site to be contemporary with the "kitchen-midden culture" of Denmark and thus late Mesolithic, one of the first attempts to place a British Mesolithic site in a broader chronological and climatic context. The Thatcham Mesolithic level lay under a silt layer and atop a gravel horizon, and it contained tranchet axes as well as microliths and microburins, signs, Clark tells us, of "Tardenoisian admixture."

An entire chapter was devoted to extreme southeastern England, where numerous sites lay on the chalk downs and other sites on well-drained soils. Again, Clark described collection after dreary collection of flints from no less than thirty-eight assemblages, most of them in the hands of private collectors. He summarized the general artifact categories in a simple table, drawing attention to the widespread occurrence of microburins, abundant nongeometric microliths, and occasional transversely sharpened axes. "We suggest that we are dealing with a non-geometric industry of Tardenoisian character," he wrote, drawing attention to some analogies with equivalent assemblages in Belgium.[18] He also noted the close association between Mesolithic sites and more lightly vegetated, heathlike terrain, for "sandy regions were peculiarly adapted for the mode of life pursued by the folk who made the microlithic industries of Britain."[19] They had no need to clear dense forest, as did their Neolithic successors. In relating both Mesolithic and later prehistoric settlement to the underlying soils and geology, he was following in the footsteps of the simple settlement investigations carried out by Cyril Fox in the Cambridge region that had been part of his undergraduate reading.

Interpretation

In his conclusions, Clark lamented the unscientific conditions under which so many Mesolithic sites had been recovered. One had "to take account of the discoverer," he said with commendable understatement, and of the period when the find was made.[20] The British Mesolithic was much less well known than that of continental Europe, but the peripheral position of the United Kingdom meant that Britain received "initial impulses" from the Continent. Clark's interpretation of the Mesolithic was based on the assumption that both the Azilian of southwestern France and northern Spain and the Tardenoisian of France and Belgium arrived from across the Channel soon after the Ice Age. By the same token, there was not the considerable diversity of Mesolithic culture found in France and Scandinavia. An Early Tardenoisian was represented by the blade industries of the Pennine Hills. Later versions of the culture with finely made geometric microliths were absent from extreme southeastern England. The tranchet axe and nongeometric microliths characteristic of this area seemed to have arrived at about the same time as the Tardenoisan and may have resulted from Maglemose and much rarer "Champignian" influence, the latter being a Mesolithic industry with axes found in France and Belgium, still recognized as a local cultural group. Finally, Clark concluded that the Mesolithic overlapped with an incoming Neolithic in many areas, even if Windmill Hill and other causewayed camps yielded no microliths. Rather, there were signs of microlithic technology persisting into the Bronze Age, as if the Neolithic lasted but a brief period of time.

The Mesolithic Age is a short book, with only ninety-six pages of narrative and description and seven appendices. Six of these deal with stone artifacts and technology, including a fine description of the microburin technique. However, Appendix 7, added when the book was in press, marks a major sea change in both British Mesolithic research and Grahame Clark's subsequent thinking.

The Leman and Ower Harpoon

In 1931, the trawler *Colinda* working the North Sea's Leman and Ower bank hauled up a lump of peat ("moorlog") from a depth of eighteen meters (60 feet). The trawlermen cursed. Their nets routinely snagged and tore on waterlogged wood and mud lumps as they trawled for bottom fish. Wearily, they bent over to throw the dark fragment overboard. The lump split open and a brown, barbed object fell onto the deck, with some peat still adhering to it. Fortunately for science, the skipper was intrigued and brought the find back to port with his catch. The discovery came to the attention of the Norwich Museum, where it was identified as a classic example of a Mesolithic bone harpoon, identical to those made by the Maglemose people of Scandinavia (Figure 2.6). It was exhibited at a meeting of the Prehistoric Society of East Anglia at Norwich on February 29, 1932, just in time for Grahame to add a brief appendix to his book (which was being typed at the time), then formally described by Miles Burkitt.[21] Cambridge botanists Harry and Margaret Godwin agreed to analyze the pollen grains in similar peat to provide a more precise date for the specimen.

The chance find sparked high excitement, for the peat matrix came from a freshwater deposit deep under the North Sea. Godwin's analysis was not completed when *The Mesolithic Age* went to press, but Clark compared the specimen to Maglemose specimens from Scandinavia. "The harpoon would appear to date from the Ancylus lake phase of the Baltic, when Boreal conditions obtained," he concluded.[22] The find confirmed his thesis (which was actually nothing new) that southeastern Britain had been colonized from across the North Sea, at a time when a low-lying plain joined northwestern Europe to the higher ground of southern England.

This single discovery was a major turning point in Grahame Clark's career, for it brought home to him the potential of pollen analysis for studying major environmental change, and for dating the British Mesolithic, in areas like the Cambridgeshire flatlands in which swamps, marshes, and peat deposits abounded.[23] He believed the Mesolithic was not a cultural backwater but a vital period of adjustment to entirely new environmental circumstances. The problem was to document this with archaeological sites—and the best potential for such discoveries lay in wet locations. For the rest of his career, he argued for the importance of wet sites where organic remains and environmental data might be reasonably expected to occur, and, thanks to the work of the Fenland Research Committee, he was able to carry out such excavations himself. In a way, it is fitting that Leman and Ower is a final appendix to *The Mesolithic Age*, for this single harpoon and its associated peat changed Clark's career, even if he had little to do with the initial study of the discovery. (The find is

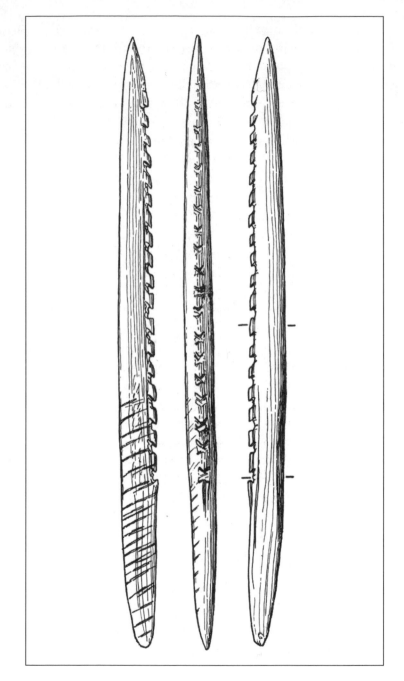

Figure 2.6 **The Leman and Ower harpoon. Scale: 2/3. Courtesy the Prehistoric Society.**

named after the location where it was found, albeit on the bed of the North Sea—common archaeological practice.)

Clark's first book was published to considerable acclaim, but it appeared at a time of major change in British archaeology. Reviewers praised it as the first detailed survey of Mesolithic Britain, the first attempt to bring order out of a confusing mass of surface finds and poorly documented archaeological sites. Gordon Childe, reviewing the book in the prestigious *Antiquaries Journal*, wrote: "for its exhaustive exposition and sound interpretation of the Mesolithic industries of Britain. . . . The book is indispensable and admirably fills a real gap." The German archaeologist Oswald Menghin, a scholar of the old school, remarked that the book "is distinguished by thorough working up of material, mature judgement, and a clear view of general aspects." He considered it of "fundamental importance" to any study of the Mesolithic cultures of Europe—high praise from a rigorous prehistorian with high standards.[24] It is still consulted by Mesolithic specialists to this day. However, *The Mesolithic Age* is a book in the older tradition of British archaeology, in the sense that it is almost entirely artifact based and is couched in the stylistic and typological language so popular in its day, with free use of words like "coup-de-poing" for hand axe, and such terms as "affinities," "influences," and "parallels" between small artifact collections on either side of the English Channel or North Sea. The book is a product of its time, for Grahame was working in an academic environment that was parochial at best, strongly artifact based, and obsessed with eoliths and the most minute details of stone tools. Clark himself was restless under this conservative regime, as witnessed by his constant references to the wider archaeological world beyond the narrow confines of Britain. However, he still attributed cultural change during the Mesolithic to invasion and migration, with environmental change being a very broad, almost deterministic backdrop to "developments of far reaching importance."[25] He was aware of the importance of environmental variables, but so far his own research experience had not made him aware of the importance of ecology in the study of the past.

Clark's Scandinavian travels of 1929 had left him with a lively appreciation of the complexities of Mesolithic cultures in northern Europe, and of the importance of finding and excavating sites associated with well-dated peat levels that could be placed within the now well-known vegetational sequence for Postglacial Europe developed by palynologist Baron de Geer and others. Unfortunately, only a few British sites had any stratigraphy at all. The Leman and Ower find convinced Clark (and others) that important Mesolithic sites could be found in the East Anglian lowlands that would place the dating of the "Tardenoisian" and other cultures on as firm a basis as the equivalent cultures in Europe.

"Impudent Puppy"

The Mesolithic Age years, 1929 to 1933, were busy years for Grahame, who traveled widely looking at museum collections while spending many days in the fens with Charles Phillips, and sometimes botanist Harry Godwin. Phillips had a "lofty old Austin" automobile, which carried them along remote country roads into the depths of a still remote rural landscape and allowed a bird's-eye view of the flat landscape. They would return in the evening to Phillips's lodgings on Chesterton Road, laden with stone tools and pottery, to dine on macaroni and cheese provided by Phillips's landlady, Mrs. Swayne, while the finds dried by the fire. Sometimes Stuart Piggott was among those present, adding another voice to already animated and far-ranging conversations not only about the fens but about the state of British archaeology as a whole. Another visitor was Christopher Hawkes, a young archaeologist with interests in Bronze Age and Iron Age archaeology, who remembered how more food was ordered with a sharp tap on the floor.[26] All four of the young scholars attended the meetings of the Society of Antiquaries in London, and those of the Prehistoric Society of East Anglia. They chafed against an archaeology dominated by dogmatic, provincial amateurs, who were long on trivial facts but weak on original ideas, often incapable of looking beyond the artifacts that obsessed them. New ideas fell on deaf, often hostile ears, for a new generation of professionals were leaving the old school behind. University vacations were spent in Sussex and Suffolk, where his Uncle Hugh rented a rough shoot and the pike fishing was deeply satisfying.

In his memoirs, Phillips recalled a meeting of the Prehistoric Society of East Anglia in 1932, when the venerable but troublesome A. Leslie Armstrong, a surveyor and long-established cave excavator of the old school, offered a paper on a novel form of flint point found on a sandy land surface near Scunthorpe in Lincolnshire. He boldly identified them as being of Upper Palaeolithic type. In the subsequent discussion,

Grahame brashly used his much wider perspective obtained from his research to argue that the points in question were identical to Maglemose specimens from Kunda in Estonia. After the session was over, a livid Armstrong strode up to young Clark, who was talking to Charles Phillips, and addressed him as "you impudent puppy!" Grahame and Phillips just looked at him in astounded silence. The incident was symptomatic of the tense undercurrents that lay just beneath the surface of British archaeology at the time.[27] Clark was unpopular with many because he tended to be extremely critical, even cruel at times. Miles Burkitt arranged for Grahame to be elected a fellow of the Society of Antiquaries on February 2, 1933, "before too many enemies were made."[28] Charles Phillips became a fellow on the same day.

At this point, Grahame met his future wife, Gwladys Maud (Mollie) White of Girton College. Mollie, also an archaeologist, was a graduate of Girton. She had read classics and classical archaeology and then took a fourth year to read for a diploma in archaeology and anthropology. After going down, she worked with the Welsh Commission on Historical Monuments. Grahame and Mollie first met in the main gallery of the University Museum of Archaeology and Ethnology. She had come with a question for Miles Burkitt about some Mesolithic artifact. Burkitt told her to "ask Grahame Clark about that." By chance, he was leaning over the balustrade of the upper gallery.[29] Romance soon burgeoned and the couple became inseparable. When Charles Phillips began excavations at a long barrow on Giant's Hill near Skendlebury, Lincolnshire, in June 1933, his party included Grahame and Mollie. The excavators stayed in George Hotel at Spilsby, commuted out to the site every day, and cleared a large section of the ditch, which was deeply cut into the underlying chalk. They found traces of Neolithic and Early Bronze Age visitation, even some broken wine bottles left by an eighteenth-century shooting party on their lunch break. (In 1934, Phillips returned for the actual barrow excavation and found evidence of communal Neolithic burial. The dig established his reputation as a serious archaeologist.)

By 1934, Clark and his contemporaries were becoming increasingly influential voices in British archaeology, despite their youth. While Piggott focused on the Neolithic, Clark increasingly turned his attention to the Mesolithic and the archaeology of the fens. It was here, he felt, that the best chance of finding stratigraphic evidence and perishable artifacts lay.

Dissertation

By this time, he had completed his doctoral dissertation, which was submitted on January 2, 1934. "The Mesolithic, Neolithic, and Early Metal Age Industries of Britain" is a mixture of already published work and some additional unpublished essays and contributions.[30] Clark also updated the dissertation in his own hand and with typescript inserts in an informal manner that would be unthinkable today. Symptomatic of his rapidly changing perspective are numerous references to botanist Harry Godwin.

Part 1, "The Mesolithic Age in Britain," consists of an unbound copy of *The Mesolithic Age* and four appendices. The first, Appendix A, is a letter to *Man* (December 13, 1932) describing the Mesolithic sites on the Burtle beds near Bridgewater in Somerset. Appendix B describes the Broxborne site and a classification of the axe and microlith industries of eastern Britain. The report is heavily artifact dominated, describing a five-yard-square squatting area sealed by peat, with evidence of fire. Broxborne is placed in Clark's southeast England group of industries with axes and nongeometric microliths. The report includes a chronological table assigning the Mesolithic to the Boreal (Maglemose harpoons and the Broxborne site), a time when rivers were cutting down, and the Atlantic, a time of "kitchen-midden cultures" in Scandinavia and the lower Halstow site in Britain, followed by the Sub-Boreal and the Neolithic. Appendix C describes the Tardenoisian of Horsham, also in Sussex, and includes a classification of microliths grouped by percentages. The fourth Mesolithic appendix, D, is a reprint of a paper published in *Sussex Archaeological Collections*, volume 73, "A Microlithic Flaking Site at West Heath, West Hastings." An otherwise undistinguished paper is marked by fine drawings that are executed in the characteristically simple style that adorned Clark's numerous Mesolithic papers and monographs in later years (Figure 2.7).

From the Mesolithic, Clark moved on to Part 2: "The Flint Industries of Neolithic and Early Metal Age Times in Britain (Ireland excluded)." No less than seven appendices adorn this section, which is very much an afterthought to the main body of the dissertation. A brief, rather stilted essay, written in the archaeological style of the day, gives a somewhat generalized impression of Clark's conclusions. The Windmill Hill and Peterborough groups, identified from pottery by Gordon Childe and Stuart Piggott, among others, are the starting point. "We may identify the Long Barrows

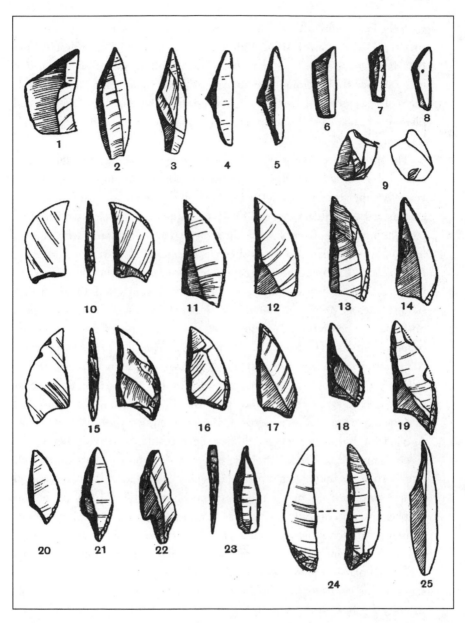

Figure 2.7 Microliths from West Heath, West Hastings. A fine example of Clark artistry. Scale: full size.

with the Windmill Hill folk," he writes, but admits that the issue is subject to debate. He compares the flint implements from Windmill Hill and Peterborough sites and confirms the already well-known observation that many surface tools belong in Metal Age contexts rather than Neolithic cultures. These included barbed and tanged arrowheads, flint daggers, and plano-convex knives. Stone technology remained in use long after metallurgy began.

The appendices are, for the most part, published papers, selected from a remarkable stream of minor publications produced during his dissertation years. A paper for *Antiquity* (1932–1933) on the age of British flint mines, coauthored with Stuart Piggott, forms one appendix, an essay on fifty-two curved flint sickles from various parts of England, compared with equivalents in Scandinavian and Swiss sites (*Proceedings of the Prehistoric Society of East Anglia* VII [1]) another. Perceptively, he identifies silica luster on the blades caused by cereal stalks, a phenomenon recently identified on flint sickle blades at Mount Carmel in Palestine by Dorothy Garrod. Two papers on Beakers, one on the Beaker invasion, a popular topic of the day, and the other on the pottery of this type from Ipswich Museum range more widely than stone tools, but the next three appendices return to polished flint knives, the dates of plano-convex knives, and derivatives of petit tranchet and transverse arrowheads in the late Mesolithic. By today's standards, all of these papers offer a very narrow perspective on the Neolithic and Bronze Age indeed, but his readers would have been comfortable with them.

Grahame Clark's dissertation is very much a product of its times and, like all such documents, is written in a genre and mode that would appeal to his examiners, among them Burkitt and Minns, and probably the ethnographer Darryl Forde. His mind was bursting with new ideas, but a solid, conservative monograph, combined with a series of published papers, provided an excellent dissertation for the day, which helped establish him as a serious scholar in the eyes of his older, and much more intellectually conservative, peers. Only the last appendix of all, a typescript ready for publication, reveals a new generation of research, which really entered Clark's mind with the finding of the Leman and Ower harpoon in 1931. The new archaeology lay in the fens, outside Cambridge, in a collaborative effort with botanists, geologists, and others. Appendix 7 describes an early Bronze Age site in the southeastern fenland, with the evidence for land movement in postglacial times afforded by the excavations and borings made at

Plantation Farm. Clark writes of researches by the newly formed Fenland Research Committee (see Chapter 3), which traced a scatter of prehistoric finds from a summit of a sand hill deep into a Lower Peat formed in Boreal times. The dissertation dwells little on Peacock's Farm, or the pollen researches that were to transform understanding of the British Mesolithic, but the report, tacked on at the end of the thesis, is a strong hint that intellectual change was in the air, indeed already under way.

Grahame Clark was awarded his doctorate of philosophy in 1934. One of his examiners, Thomas Kendrick, then director of the British Museum, examined Clark orally in one of the museum galleries. Grahame casually leaned on a case and broke the glass in the midst of the examination. But he still passed easily. By this time, his restless mind was already moving far beyond the staid world of artifact typology and microliths. He had already thrown himself into a new whirlwind of research and a restructuring of prehistoric archaeology in Britain that was ushering in a new intellectual era.

3

⟨≋⟩

The Fenland
Research Committee

*Too often one has the impression that archaeologists have so long breathed
the air of museum galleries as to have lost, if ever they possessed, a liking
for the open air of life.*[1]

T he discovery of the Leman and Ower harpoon in 1931 was a defining
moment in British Mesolithic archaeology and in Grahame Clark's
career. As we have seen, the well-preserved harpoon occupied a short
appendix in *The Mesolithic Age*, almost an afterthought to a work concerned
with flint assemblages and culture traits. Even before the book appeared,
Grahame had started a new phase of research that eventually revolutionized
his approach to archaeology. He had written in his monograph of "a great
geological and climatic divide" that separated the Upper Palaeolithic and
Mesolithic.[2] Leman and Ower inspired him, and others, to look for stratified Mesolithic sites in the peat levels of the East Anglian fenlands.

During his doctoral years, Clark had befriended botanists Harry and
Margaret Godwin, who were students and then colleagues of the ecologist
Sir A. G. Tansley, one of the first scientists to conceptualize and write about
ecosystems, organizations with numerous interrelated parts that remained
in a state of dynamic equilibrium. He formally introduced the ecosystem
concept to British science in a paper published in *Ecology* in 1935.[3] Tansley

had interested Harry and Margaret Godwin, originally plant physiologists, in plant ecology and recommended they study palynology (pollen analysis), a method of studying vegetational change through time pioneered by Swedish botanist Lennart von Post during World War I. He also suggested they use the method to study the history of the fens.[4] The Godwins had already become aware of pollen research, thanks to some articles in English written by Swedish botanist G. E. Erdtman, who had studied some British peat deposits. Encouraged by Tansley, they traveled to Scandinavia to learn pollen analysis. One of their first tasks on returning to England was to analyze the moorlog peat found with the Leman and Ower harpoon and assign it to the Boreal period of Postglacial time. They also convinced Clark that "it was time that British archaeology developed from the stage of surface collections of finds . . . to a stratigraphic approach."[5]

On June 7, 1932, Clark and the Godwins called a meeting in the Upper Parlor of Peterhouse and founded the Fenland Research Committee. About twelve people attended, among them Reid Moir, Charles Phillips, the amateur geologist Major G. E. Fowler of sugar beet factory fame (an expert on recognizing ancient waterways and an essential liaison to local farmers), O. T. Jones, the Woodwardian Professor of Geology, and a foraminifera expert, W. A. Macfadyen of the Sedgewick Museum of Geology. Miles Burkitt and Grahame Clark represented archaeology. Burkitt wrote in the *Antiquaries Journal*: "For some time past several people at Cambridge have felt that a research committee of experts in the various branches of science required should be formed to undertake a comprehensive study. . . . For a proper study of the fens, many different lines of investigation are required."[6] The committee was little more than a loose association that varied between twenty and forty-two specialist researchers in archaeology, biology, geography, and geology, who combined their efforts to unravel the complex history of the fens. Paleobotanist Sir Alfred Seward was elected president, Major Gordon Fowler vice president, and Grahame Clark honorary secretary.

The Fenland Research Committee held dinner meetings two or three times a year during the 1930s and twice during the 1940s as an independent entity with no formal institutional associations. Eventually the committee was dissolved, but reborn as the Subdepartment of Quaternary Research with Harry Godwin as director in 1948.[7] As Clark wrote many years later: "When it [the Committee] met it combined elements of a research seminar, a practical working committee and a con-vivial group which habitually dined together in one or other of the Cambridge colleges."[8]

Grahame was a driving force behind the Fenland Research Committee from the very beginning. As secretary, he cajoled, organized, raised funds, and ensured that talented people were closely involved. The committee invariably met for dinner either before or after conducting its business, a convenient way of encouraging informal discussion between members who did not see one another very often. Only a relatively small number of spe-cialists were closely involved in the committee's research. Clark was the most active of them all, organizing and conducting a series of vitally impor-tant excavations that were to change the course of much archaeological research in Britain. Altogether, he published no fewer than eight site reports and articles under the aegis of the committee between 1933 and 1940. In the process, his own definition of archaeology changed completely.

Plantation Farm

Clark had already begun work at a promising site buried under peat at Plantation Farm, Shippea Hill, eleven kilometers (7 miles) east-northeast of Ely. The few surface finds lay on a sandy ridge by the Little Ouse River. Apart from the crest of the rodden, the entire area was below modern sea level. (A rodden is a fenland term for a raised bank of silt, once a stream bed, now exposed as a ridge rather than a depression by the wastage of the upper peat.) There were many such long extinct waterways through the marshy landscape.

Mechanical core borings into the neighboring deposits reached a depth of eighty meters (260 feet) and revealed a sequence of natural layers formed against the rodden that once carried the waters of the Little Ouse to the North Sea. This, Clark realized, was the place he had been looking for, where there was a real prospect of finding artifacts in stratigraphic context. The committee's excavations into the peat layers were undertaken to study "post-glacial changes of environment in relation to man" and were ham-pered by continual flooding.[9] The sand hill had been occupied when it was a dry island in the midst of a swamp, identified by the Godwins from the aquatic plant pollen in the peat. Harry Godwin used a hand borer at the site to penetrate through the peat layers to the basal sand. A Lower Peat level had formed during the Late Boreal, at a time when the southern North Sea was low-lying fen. By remarkable coincidence, Godwin recovered a microlithic flake from the Lower Peat at a depth of 5.25 meters (17 feet). Following the formation of the Lower Peat, the land had subsided during the Atlantic phase, covering the site with estuarine silt. The land then rose slightly and the Upper Peat formed during the Sub-Boreal. The Early Bronze Age flints and potsherds from the site belonged to this period, their positions plotted between five and eighteen centimeters (2 and 7 inches) above the base of the Upper Peat.

The Plantation Farm excavation was of the highest importance, for it established a basic stratigraphy of the fenland found at many sites in later years—two peat series interrupted by a tidal silt. One should stress the word "basic," for more recent research has revealed a much more complex stratigraphic picture over a wide area. A small team of scientists collaborated on the site report, contributing studies of the foraminifera and pollen, also identifications of charcoals from the hearths. William Jackson of the Manchester Museum, an authority on ancient Egyptian cattle, contributed an analysis of the Bronze Age animal bones.

Plantation Farm was dug long before radiocarbon dating, which meant that the excavators had to place major reliance on precise relative dating. Fortunately, the Godwins were able to correlate the East Anglian site with the well-known vegetational zonation worked out for Scandinavia by von Post and his successors, dated, at least approximately, from retreating glaciers in northern Europe. The excavation was a giant leap forward and was followed by a second investigation, this time at Peacock's Farm, on the other side of the Shippea Hill rodden, during 1934. This time, Clark and Goodwin hoped to find Mesolithic occupation in the Lower Peat.

Peacock's Farm

On October 27, 1934, the minutes tell us, members of the Fenland Research Committee heard a preliminary report on the Peacock's Farm excavations "before dinner."[10] Clark and Godwin had sunk their trench well away from the sand ridge, employing a team of highly skilled local laborers with experience in diking and drainage work.[11] The trench was cut in steps, so that as large an area of the Lower Peat as possible could be exposed. They uncovered not only the Mesolithic level but a scatter of

Neolithic sherds about six meters (2 feet) above. The Peacock's Farm trench again revealed a stratified sequence in the Little Ouse river channel, which both amplified and refined the Plantation Farm observations. Early Bronze Age pottery and stone tools lay stratified above Neolithic A pottery and artifacts, in turn underlain by a handful of Tardenoisian microliths and other flint fragments, the latter associated with a well-marked black band below the Neolithic stratum.

A photograph famous in Cambridge and Mesolithic archaeology circles shows Grahame in Wellington boots standing on the sand of the channel bed, with Major Gordon Fowler sitting on the modern ground surface (Figure 3.1). Although the trench looks dry, it is difficult to keep intact because of the high water table. The Lower Peat overlies the sand, with Late Tardenoisian and Neolithic A levels clearly demarcated in white letters. Above lies a thick layer of fen clay, then the Upper Peat, with the Early Bronze Age level near its base. By fortunate happenstance, a cultural sequence from Mesolithic to Early Bronze Age came from a single site, and within the stratified context of changing environmental conditions (Figure 3.2). As for the Mesolithic industry, Clark concluded it was a "fairly advanced stage" of the Tardenoisian, the assemblage including both typical microburins and well-finished microliths. He thought it was late because he assumed that Mesolithic microliths evolved over time from simple to more refined. Meanwhile, the Godwins combined their pollen samples with A. S. Kennard and C. Oldham's mollusca studies to reconstruct climatic conditions through the periods of occupation. The Mesolithic inhabitants occupied a well-drained site surrounded by open water or swamp, with pine and ash in the vicinity. The areas may have been drier and warmer during Neolithic A times, with willows and reeds growing near the site in Early Bronze Age times.

The Peacock's Farm site, for all its scanty finds, was very important at the time. The single deep trench provided that rarity of rarities, a stratified sequence from the Mesolithic through the Bronze Age, which placed much of British prehistory within a broader environmental context for the first time. For the first time, a team of botanists, geologists, and prehistorians collaborated on the investigation of a British prehistoric site, a development that both set a trend for the future and provided a new direction for research. Peacock's Farm foreshadowed the dominant theme of Grahame's work in the decades that followed—the study of prehistoric

56

Figure 3.1 **The Peacock's Farm excavation. A famous picture of the trench, with Grahame Clark at the base of the cutting, Major Fowler sitting at the top.**

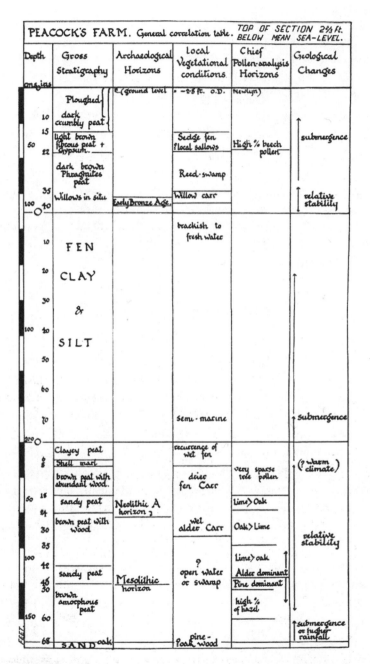

Figure 3.2 **The sequence from the Peacock's Farm excavations, showing cultural, geological, and vegetational stages.**

communities within their ecological settings. The published report was one of the first truly multidisciplinary archaeological studies to be published in Britain. The paper caused considerable interest among Stone Age specialists at home and on the Continent because of the direct association between vegetational changes and prehistoric artifacts, a rarity in an era when most Stone Age sites were little more than scatters of stone tools. Back in Cambridge, Clark used the excavation as a case study in his teaching, so a simple form of ecological archaeology entered undergraduate consciousness almost immediately.

Clark's emerging ecological approach was part of his growing awareness of the complex interrelationships between human culture and the natural environment. His other emerging interest was economic archaeology, which looked at the on-site evidence for subsistence and the ways in which people made a living.

A Crucible of Research

The pace of the committee's work continued unabated. In March 1935, Clark investigated a site on higher ground in Mildenhall fen to establish "a further correlation between the natural history and the human settlement of the fens."[12] With the help of undergraduate members of the newly formed Cambridge University Archaeology Field Club, he recovered later Bronze Age potsherds, with strong affinities with already well-known Deverel-Rimbury Late Bronze Age wares. However, the Mildenhall site lay on the periphery of the distribution of this pottery form, with one well-defined type so distinctive that he named it "Mildenhall Ware." The diversity of pottery designs suggested that the area saw contact between different Late Bronze Age peoples with, however, strong continuity with indigenous cultural traditions. By Late Bronze Age times, the farmers had been forced to abandon their settlements on the low-lying fen and had moved to higher ground like that at Mildenhall.

Clark and Godwin collaborated on another piece of Fenland Research Committee fieldwork, when an alderwood tub filled with bronze artifacts came to light at Stuntney Hall, near Ely. The find was a founder's hoard deposited near a wooden causeway that once joined Stuntney to the Isle of Ely, its contents "at first glance as of the Late Bronze Age."[13] Godwin placed the Late Bronze Age horizon "some distance over the surface of the Fen-

Clay," and assigned it to "a drier period, close to pollen zones VII-VIII [Sub Atlantic]." The hoard itself contained at least four types of ribbed palstave [axe], an artifact that Clark considered contemporary with the distinctive Late Bronze Age "carps-tongue swords" found over much of southeastern England. Using the same basic typological methods and distribution maps he had employed for years on stone tools, Clark correctly assigned the hoard to the second half of the Late Bronze Age.

The Fenland Research Committee was galvanized by Clark's efficient and dynamic leadership. He took care of administrative details, recorded the minutes, organized the logistics of the research, and made sure prominent scientists were kept appraised of new developments. Above all, the committee developed an enviable reputation for publishing its research promptly and in full. The archaeological research that formed part of this effort was very different from Grahame's earlier investigations of surface finds. All were excavations. All were designed to acquire stratigraphic and environmental data as part of the broader goal of studying the history of the fenland. Clark himself combined his multidisciplinary work with conventional typological analyses and distribution studies that were effectively identical to those he had employed in *The Mesolithic Age*. However, the focus of his research was shifting dramatically, away from his more traditional approach using artifacts and distribution maps. For a start, he was relying on selective excavation instead of surface collection, excavation that he made an integral part of his students' training. The University Archaeological Field Society was the instrument he used to introduce undergraduates to fieldwork. He was also shifting intellectual ground.

In *The Mesolithic Age*, Grahame had invoked environmental change as the reason for the major differences between Upper Palaeolithic and Mesolithic cultures. Invasion and migration were the major factors in cultural change. His views were now changing radically, as he began to appreciate the importance of changing ecosystems and local adaptations in shaping culture change. His new ecological approach to archaeology developed as a direct result of his experiences with the Fenland Research Committee. The committee was far more than a dining club or a research working group, it was an emerging community of younger archaeologists and colleagues in the natural sciences who were interested in ancient environments, as well as more rigorous excavation and analytical methods. The coterie of professional archaeologists was still narrow, even intellectually incestuous, in the

1930s. Grahame, Stuart Piggott, Charles Phillips, and Christopher Hawkes were all members of the committee. Many of the members drank morning tea together in the Museum of Archaeology and Anthropology, where field projects were hatched and artifacts and environmental data discussed. Prehistoric archaeology was a small, gossipy family of a mere handful of professionals or would-be professionals. Ideas flowed freely in a way that would have been impossible with a larger discipline.

Although much of the Fenland Research Committee's work was concerned with purely geological and botanical matters, its archaeological researches under Clark's capable direction changed the face of Mesolithic archaeology in Britain forever. Ultimately, they helped forge an entirely new ecological approach to archaeology that bridged the intellectual chasm between the old-style archaeology of the 1930s and the processual archaeology of the 1960s.

The Prehistoric Society

In the intervals between his fieldwork, Grahame was engaged in the affairs of the Prehistoric Society of East Anglia. By the time Clark started on his dissertation research in 1930, flint collecting was on the decline. Judging from the volume of flint-based papers published during the 1920s, this collecting was near mania, especially among professional men such as J. Reid Moir, the Ipswich tailor, and A. Leslie Armstrong, a government surveyor. The rising generation of young Turks, spearheaded by Grahame Clark, Charles Phillips, Stuart Piggott, and Christopher Hawkes, was in a suppressed state of rebellion over the conservative old ways.

The Prehistoric Society of East Anglia was founded on October 26, 1908, by a small group of amateur archaeologists, many of them little more than collectors, dedicated to the study of "all matters connected with prehistoric man in East Anglia."[14] By 1912, there were 148 amateur and professional members, among them the well-known American archaeologist Frederick W. Putnam of the Peabody Museum at Harvard University and prehistorian M. A. Rutot of the Musée Royal d'Histoire Naturelle de Belgique. The 1913 membership roll included many well-known scholars, including the biologist Ray Lankester, Professor William Ridgeway of Cambridge, then holder of the Disney Chair, and physical anthropologist Sir Arthur Keith of the Royal College of Surgeons, celebrated for his research on the Piltdown fossils. The society's reputation grew apace, its journal soon recognized as the leading vehicle for publishing British prehistory. By 1925, the society was national in all but name, to the point that a disclaimer was added to the *Proceedings* stating that the society "is not restricted either in membership or subject matter to the district from which it is named."[15] Only about a quarter of the membership was East Anglia-based. By 1934, the figure was 15 percent.

During the 1920s, the question of a name change for the society became a perennial topic at annual meetings. Matters came to a head in 1931, when the belligerent eolith advocate J. Reid Moir proposed that a special committee be set up to look into the society's "more efficient working." According to archives of minutes and correspondence preserved in the Ipswich Museum, the committee came about because of the persistent criticisms of Professor A. S. Barnes, former professor of electrical engineering at Manchester University, who had been active in the society's affairs since 1911. Barnes was vociferous in his criticisms of the older generation of members and especially of the editor of the *Proceedings*, Guy Maynard, curator of the Ipswich Museum, a quiet man whom Barnes considered inefficient. Above all, the overbearing Barnes was violently opposed to Reid Moir's eolith theories and said so to both Maynard and Moir in no uncertain terms. For years, Barnes argued for the dropping of the East Anglia title, an innovation that the special committee rejected at a council meeting on February 29, 1932, while making suggestions for more efficient operation of the *Proceedings*. Grahame Clark was elected to the council at this same meeting. Eight months later, on October 26, all the council members, including Clark, voted against Barnes's suggestion of a name change. The vote against the change may have been more of a diplomatic move than a real decision, a gesture of respect for Maynard, then general secretary.[16]

The next council meeting on May 24, 1933, saw Maynard stating that he wished to relinquish some of his responsibilities. "It was unanimously agreed on the proposal of Professor V. G. Childe, seconded by Reid Moir that . . . J.G.D. Clark be invited at once to relieve the General Secretary of the function of . . . Editor."[17] Grahame immediately took over the editorial reins as acting editor, quickly producing the 1933 and 1934 *Proceedings* on schedule. At the February 1934 council meeting, "Dr. J.G.D. Clark was congratulated on the quality of the *Proceedings* recently published."[18] He was made a permanent member of council and honorary editor, a post he held for thirty-five years. Thus began a lifetime of service to a society that became one of the passions of Clark's long career.

In February 1935, Clark suggested to the council that "the title of the Society shall be 'The Prehistoric Society.'"[19] This change, he argued, would allow the editor to solicit both national and international contributions to the society's *Proceedings*. On February 23, 1935, the matter was raised at the annual general meeting, deliberately convened at Norwich Castle Museum so that East Anglian members could attend. A postal ballot followed. Clark's proposal was carried by an overwhelming majority.

The transition was peaceful, with Maynard and Moir giving up their posts as secretary and treasurer in 1936. There were few resignations, and 135 new members joined in the first year. Charles Phillips became secretary and E. M. Alexander of the British Museum the treasurer. Meanwhile Clark worked hard to move the *Proceedings* away from endless papers on Stone Age flints to a new generation of archaeological research painted on a broad national and international canvas. He realized that the content of the first few issues would set the tone for *The Proceedings of the Prehistoric Society* (often referred to as *PPS*) for the future. Accordingly, he solicited contributions from his young friends, who were looking outward and stressing the importance of evidence obtained from other disciplines, especially the natural sciences.

In later years, all kinds of stories revolved around the demise of the Prehistoric Society of East Anglia, as if it had been a revolution triggered by a group of young prehistorians frustrated by the conservative ways of their elders. "It was a deliberate infiltration of the Young Turks headed by Grahame Clark," claimed Stuart Piggott in a memoir published in *Antiquity* in 1989. He recalled how he drove at high speed from Avebury to Norwich in Alexander Keillor's borrowed MG sports car to make the meeting. "We had the Society in our hands."[20] Although Grahame Clark is said to have referred with satisfaction to a coup in remarks to his students, later examination of the minute books and contemporary correspondence reveals a peaceful, logical transition, in which the very success of the society and its broadening membership played an important role.[21] However, there can be no doubt that Grahame Clark played a leading role in the change, sensing the precise moment to propose the change for a final time. It was no coincidence, either, that Professor Gordon Childe, an archaeologist of wide ranging-interests if ever there was one, was president of the society at the time. Piggott's memory of the excitement among his contemporaries is undoubtedly accurate, but he was not on the board and participated only peripherally in the discussions before the vote.

The first meeting of the new Prehistoric Society was held in the rooms of the Society of Antiquaries at Burlington House in London on May 2, 1935, with only nine members present. Clark was among six speakers on recent archaeological research. However, membership increased rapidly, growing from 353 members in that year to 668 in 1938.

Inevitably, the focus of the new society moved from Ipswich and Norwich to the new editorial offices at Cambridge, for the *Proceedings* soon became a mirror of new research in British archaeology and, to some extent, abroad as well. The first volume in 1935, printed by a new printer in Gloucester, carried Childe's presidential address, "Changing Methods and Aims in Prehistory," which set the tone for a broader interdisciplinary approach. Charles Phillips wrote on his excavations at Therfield Heath Long Barrow near Royston, while Stuart Piggott surveyed the relative chronology of long barrows as a whole. The old guard was represented by Moir and Sainty on stone tools, while Clark himself contributed a brief survey, "The Prehistory of the Isle of Man," a strongly artifact-based survey of major sites from the Mesolithic to Late Bronze Age. In it, he drew attention to the "Tardenoisian" industries on the island and to the relative isolation of the prehistoric societies that lived there. This paper laid the foundations for important research carried out by German archaeologist Gerhard Bersu while he was interned on the Isle of Man during World War II. The council authorized the printing of a thousand copies of the 1935 *Proceedings*, a bold step considering the small membership. The society's accounts showed a deficit of £179 2s. as a result. Given the economic stringency of the times, the extra print run showed remarkable confidence in the society's future and its editor.

The *Proceedings* for 1937 to 1939 continued to present an eclectic range of papers, a far cry from the narrow focus of earlier years. There was a survey of the Palaeolithic of the Lower Thames Valley by W. E. King and Kenneth Oakley of the British Museum, for river terrace archaeology was an emerging theme of Stone Age archaeology at the time. The younger generation was well represented. Piggott's 1938 article on the Early Bronze Age of Wessex with its discussion of possible Mycenaean connections was widely consulted by undergraduates for years, while Gerhard Bersu's first report on excavations at Little Woodbury, also published in 1938, was a model of innovative excavation methods, with its emphasis on large, open trenches designed to expose considerable areas and hut foundations. In the same year, Dorothy Garrod, fresh from her Mount Carmel excavations, published her classic paper "The Upper Palaeolithic in the Light of Recent Discovery," which argued for the spread of modern humans and Upper Palaeolithic culture from southwestern Asia into temperate Europe. Her essay was still required reading for undergraduates in the late 1950s. Glyn Daniel contributed an essay on the Transcepted Gallery Graves of France to the 1939 issue. The *Proceedings* became an important outlet for papers written as much by natural scientists as archaeologists, and achieved high visibility as a result.

Grahame himself was involved in three other important papers in these early volumes. In 1936, he was coauthor with a well-known amateur, S. Hazeldine Warren, Stuart Piggott, and the Godwins, of "The Archaeology of a Submerged Land-Surface of the Essex Coast," a widely cited study that compared the Stone Age industries of the coastal region of East Anglia with those from stratified contexts in the fenland.[22] The paper concluded that the ancient land surface submerged at high tide with its Late Mesolithic industries was of comparable age to the Lower Peat at the Shippea Hill site. In the same issue, Clark described "The Timber Monument at Arminghall and Its Affinities," a closely argued paper on henges (stone and wood ceremonial circles) that balanced several hypotheses and drew no conclusion in a somewhat magisterial way: "Fortunately this is not necessary; we are not writing one of those synthetic books wherein all difficulties must be resolved, and all questions answered."[23] Finally, he collaborated with amateur excavator W. F. Rankine in an important paper on the Mesolithic of the Horsham region.[24]

"A Congenial and Highly Educational Experience"

By 1935, the twenty-eight-year-old Clark had published a book and almost thirty papers, a remarkable academic output by any standard. His perspective had always been wider than that of most of his colleagues, but now his horizons were widening significantly. He had been elected to a Bye Fellowship at Peterhouse in 1932.[25] This three-year research appointment gave him the opportunity to carry out intensive research without any teaching obligations whatsoever. Many years later, he wrote: "Above all, membership of the High Table [the fellows' table in the dining hall at all Cambridge and Oxford colleges] gave me a congenial and highly educational experience of sharing in a community of scholars working in a wide range of different fields."[26] As a junior fellow, he had the task of introducing the French prehistorian Abbé Breuil at High Table in College. The two got on well, largely because they both agreed, like Dorothy Garrod, that Stone Age Europe was merely a northern extension of Africa and Asia and not the center of the prehistoric world, as so many prehistorians of the day wanted to believe. Grahame also widened his horizons far from the narrow confines of Britain in the *Proceedings*, with a new "Current Prehistory" section. In 1939, this described research in Bulgaria, Italy, South Africa, and Northern Rhodesia, the latter by his student J. Desmond Clark, newly appointed director of the Rhodes-Livingstone Museum.

Meanwhile, Grahame was being drawn more deeply into the Cambridge department. On July 19, 1935, the faculty board of archaeology and anthropology approved "an arrangement whereby Dr. Grahame Clark should give a course on geochronology and climatic history."[27] He was already doing many hours of lecturing and teaching on matters related to the Fenland Research Committee's activities. In 1936, he became a full-time, paid assistant lecturer in the Department of Archaeology and Anthropology, a direct recognition of his valuable contribution through lectures and "instruction on the practical side in fieldwork and excavation." His main responsibilities lay in teaching "Archaeology with the selected area Europe," one of three options in the tripos at the time. The board minutes praised him at a meeting on June 8 as "a capable and enthusiastic teacher whose value has been well appreciated by his students."[28]

The new lecturer was an immediate success. He was a mainstay of the European option to the point that Burkitt reported in the faculty board minutes for June 8, 1939: "Dr. Clark's subject is central to the work of the Archaeological side [of the tripos]."[29] Clark surrounded himself with young students and shared with them the starts and shifts of his rapidly moving research. He focused at first on honors undergraduates, for a first-rate undergraduate program was clearly the prerequisite for postgraduate research. The numbers of students taking Section A of the tripos increased sharply after his appointment, part of a general increase in enrollment during the 1930s. Many undergraduates were attracted to the African anthropology option, which was appealing to potential colonial administrators. Seventeen students had enrolled in Section A in 1928, 41 in 1934, no less than sixty in 1939. We do not know how many of them were in the archaeological option.

Clark trained a small coterie of undergraduates who graduated between 1935 and 1939 and went on to become exceptional and highly influential archaeologists immediately before, and after, World War II. Among them was Charles McBurney, who went on to become a prominent member of the Cambridge archaeological faculty for the rest of his career. In 1976, Charles McBurney recalled entering the department as a student in 1935: "The intellectual climate, as I recall it, was one of new ideas characterized everywhere by an atmosphere of excitement and optimism. Discussion and criticism indeed abounded . . . rendered fruitful by important new discoveries and often spectacular developments in method and theory."[30] He commented on how the work of the Fenland Research Committee featured prominently in Clark's lectures. McBurney himself trained a generation of Stone Age archaeologists between the 1940s and 1960s.

Three of Clark's early students went on to become prominent African archaeologists. Bernard Fagg became an internationally known West African prehistorian and an important pioneer in the study of Ife and Benin sculpture and West African art generally. J. Desmond Clark, who graduated with first class honors in 1937, was one of Grahame's earliest students. He wrote: "For me, Grahame's emphasis on paleo-ecology has been all important since, without an understanding of the habitat of any prehistoric group, it is impossible to begin to understand their behavior." He added: "Grahame gave us people, Miles instilled an interest in the artifacts."[31] Desmond Clark went on to become director of the new Rhodes-Livingstone Museum in Northern Rhodesia. Twenty-two years later, he was an internationally known professor of anthropology at the University of California–Berkeley. Thurstan Shaw worked in Nigeria, where he became professor of archaeology at Ibadan University and achieved fame for his meticulous excavations of the Iron Age Igbo-Ukwo royal burials.[32]

Clark himself had suffered from a lack of field training while an undergraduate. He acquired his excavation experience as a student on his own initiative, but now found he was the only Cambridge lecturer engaged in actual excavation and fieldwork. To correct this lamentable state of affairs, he proposed the formation of a Cambridge University Field Archaeological Society, run by undergraduates, to assist with excavations in the fens. In 1935, a number of student archaeologists put their signatures to an agreement with the Fenland Research Committee, among them Kenneth St. Joseph of Selwyn College, Rainbird Clarke of St. John's, and Terence Powell of Jesus, all destined to become well-known prehistorians in later years. A year later, the Board of Archaeology and Anthropology gave official recognition to the society. Clark served as honorary vice president, a position that put him in a good place to give advice and to steer undergraduate energies into his own projects. Much of the Mildenhall fen research was carried out by student excavators, several of whom contributed much to the published report.

By the late 1930s, Grahame Clark was an established member of the Cambridge faculty and an important member of a new, and younger, archaeological establishment in Britain. He was training a small number of talented archaeologists in his own mold, at a time when the board was becoming seriously concerned with space and expansion issues, especially for classrooms and the library. A shortage of teaching staff resulted in Glyn Daniel, who had graduated with a first in 1934 and a Ph.D. in 1938, being invited to give a course on the megalithic tombs of Europe. He soon became a permanent member of the faculty. The advent of World War II interrupted further development of the department until 1946.

By all accounts, the 1930s were an exciting period in Grahame's career, a time of growing intellectual maturity, when he completely changed his approach to the past and was one of the founders of a new, and infinitely more professional, archaeology. As Stuart Piggott put it in 1963: "Young and irreverent persons in Cambridge, with like-minded and contemporary friends and colleagues elsewhere were . . . making the first conscious and concerted effort to professionalize prehistory."[33] Much of this new professionalism came from the work of the Fenland Research Committee and from the efficient, intense, and intellectually ambitious archaeologist who was one of those responsible for its coming into being. At the same time, Grahame Clark was busy broadening his contacts in Europe, as well as teaching the aims and methods of archaeology. In the highly productive years of the late 1930s, he still found time for extensive European travel and to write two of his most important and influential books, which provide telling insights into his intellectual development. We discuss *The Mesolithic Settlement of Northern Europe* (1936) and *Archaeology and Society* (1939) in the next two chapters.

4

⌘

The Mesolithic Settlement of Northern Europe

*One of the points I most wanted to make was the need to pursue
archaeological research in the context of total ecosystems. A second was to
emphasize the advantage of concentrating on the types of sites where the
residues of organic substances were most likely to survive.*

"A Path to Prehistory"

Walking on the ancient Litorina Sea shoreline of the Baltic Sea in the
summer of 1929 was an epiphanic moment for Grahame at the
threshold of his career. He realized firsthand the magnitude of the environmental changes in northern Europe at the end of the Ice Age, and the
remarkable cultural adjustments required of Mesolithic groups occupying
hitherto uninhabited lands once covered by Ice Age glaciers. This may have
been the moment too, when the idea of writing a synthesis of Mesolithic
settlement over all of northern Europe first entered his mind. Grahame
Clark was both self-confident and ambitious enough to undertake a task
that would have been daunting to a scholar of many more years. He had the
example of Gordon Childe to encourage him, for Childe had written *The
Dawn of European Civilization* before he was thirty years old.

The three years of the Bye Fellowship at Peterhouse from 1932 to 1935
gave Grahame a unique opportunity to carry out the necessary research as

a sequel to his British project. The research fellowship freed him from teaching responsibilities and provided continual opportunities to interact with colleagues from many disciplines. Clark's later preoccupation with multidisciplinary research had its roots both in the Fenland Research Committee and in the give-and-take of Peterhouse life, where he met scholars whom, under normal circumstances, he would never have encountered. Herein lies one of the strengths of the Cambridge and Oxford college system and Grahame took full advantage of it.

Grahame had come a long way since his memorable walk along the Litorina shoreline. The Fenland Research Committee and continual interaction with the Godwins had made him aware of the well-established climatic and vegetational sequence for the Postglacial Baltic region developed by Scandinavian botanists. (The outline sequence is summarized in Figure 4.2.) His first visit to Denmark and Sweden had given him a tantalizing exposure to the potential of waterlogged sites, where organic remains were preserved, offering a far more complete portrait of Mesolithic culture than the plethora of stone tool scatters from Britain. It remained to examine key sites and museum collections at first hand, to make closer contacts with Scandinavian colleagues. The Bye Fellowship gave him the time to travel extensively.

He began his travels in Holland in 1933, bicycling over the Overyssel heaths to inspect microlithic sites found by "Herr Butter of Deventer."[1] From Deventer, he traveled to Kiel in northern Germany, where he studied the Maglemosian artifacts recovered by Professor Gustav Schwantes from a site of Boreal age at Duvensee. Schwantes, who disapproved of the Nazis, became a friend and close colleague (Figure 4.1).

In Denmark, Grahame returned to the National Museum, which he had first visited five years earlier looking for perforated bronze axes. Now he returned to examine the rich finds from the Maglemose-type site and other waterlogged Mesolithic sites. This time, he had a chance to appreciate the full range of organic remains that had come from the rich Danish sites and to study the distinctive art styles that adorned Maglemose artifacts, largely unknown outside Denmark. He met more fieldworkers, too—Erik Westerby, who was excavating a coastal site at Klampenborg, and "Herr Winther at Rudkøbing on Langeland Island," who had excavated a nearby megalithic tomb and settlement at Troldebjerg. In Berlin, Grahame found his plans to examine microlith collections at the Museum für Volkekunde

Figure 4.1 **Map showing European Late Glacial, Mesolithic, and Neolithic sites mentioned in the text. Some later sites are also included.**

cut short by an enormous military parade. He traveled on to Franconia and Bavaria to see the Tardenoisian collections from Ensdorf rockshelter, most of them housed in a monastery at Ansbach, where he spent the night.

The year 1934 found Grahame in northwestern Germany, where he sought out Mesolithic collections in museums at Bielefeld, Halle, Hanover, and Münster. Then he headed south to the Federsee, where he examined some remarkable finds from a Late Glacial settlement at Stellmoor, also Tardenoisian sites excavated by Hans Reinerth.

Clark's 1933–1934 travels heightened his interest in wet sites and ancient environments. He developed a particular interest in the Maglemose culture, partly because he was convinced it was a more important presence in Britain than had hitherto been suspected. Prophetically, he also believed it was a matter of time before a waterlogged Maglemose site came to light on the western side of the North Sea. During his journeys, he came in contact with three archaeologists who exercised a strong influence on his thinking. Therkel Mathiassen was deeply involved in Mesolithic waterlogged sites; he was also an expert on Canadian arctic cultures. He had carried out seminal research in modern-day Inuit societies as well as on Thule prehistoric sites dating to A.D. 1000 and later across the Canadian archipelago. His influence on arctic anthropology is still felt today. Mathiassen alerted Clark, once again, to the importance of ethnography as a way of interpreting archaeological data. He had thought about the significance of ancient environments, as had J. Troels-Smith, who was busy refining pollen analysis, and Gudmund Hatt, a respected pioneer in the study of early Scandinavian agriculture. Clark visited all three in the field and observed their ecological approaches firsthand in the field. His intellectual relationships with these three scholars endured for many years and were a catalyst for his subsequent research into European economic prehistory in the 1940s and 1950s.

The Mesolithic Settlement of Northern Europe

Back in Cambridge, Clark read everything he could find on Mesolithic archaeology in northern Europe. Once again, his thinking resembled that of Gordon Childe, who used cultures to write a form of history distilled from material remains. We see the same use of distribution maps, artifact assemblages, and chronological markers as in Childe's *Dawn*. But there are major differences. The treatment is more detailed and covers a smaller area. Above all, Clark placed a major emphasis on environmental change (something that Childe eschewed for all his career) and on detailed cultural analysis.

The resulting synthesis appeared as *The Mesolithic Settlement of Northern Europe* under the Cambridge University Press imprint (1936). It was, wrote its young author, an attempt "to present the findings of archaeology in the context of Quaternary Research."[2] In this Grahame succeeded brilliantly, pointing out that the archaeological research needed to be conducted "in the context of the total ecosystem," a revolutionary notion in British archaeology at the time. After his experience with *The Mesolithic Age* and its serried rows of flint artifacts, and then the opportunity to examine rich Maglemose collections on the Continent, Clark also stressed the importance of concentrating on sites where organic remains were most likely to survive. Peacock's Farm had merely whetted his appetite for finding a much richer site with superb organic preservation. More than ten years were to pass before he had the opportunity to investigate such a Mesolithic settlement.

Mesolithic Settlement is a distinguished book, a dramatic contrast to its more conservative predecessor, with a range of vision and depth of learning unusual in such a young scholar. The introduction lays out the basic thesis: that the post–Ice Age environment of northern Europe "has undergone changes in the last few thousand years so profound as to alter its influence on cultural development and so rapid as to afford a natural time-scale for the dating and synchronizing of human cultures."[3] Clark also attributed the origins of the Mesolithic to these environmental changes. The dominant theme of The *Mesolithic Settlement* was ecological and environmental.

Postglacial Environmental Change

Chapter 1 provides a multidisciplinary survey of Postglacial environmental change. Clark's synthesis was the first available to archaeologists in English and stood as the standard account for beginners and general readers until the 1960s. He began by correlating what was then known of the retreat stages of the Alpine and Scandinavian glaciers. The position of these ice sheets had a direct relevance to such difficult archaeological problems as dating rock engravings, many of which were at sites once buried under deep ice. From glaciers, he moved on to the little-known varve dating method developed by Baron de Geer in the late nineteenth century, then to the complex interactions between sea level rises and land movements.[4] Chapter 1 also lays out the history of the Baltic Sea, from its beginnings as the "Baltic Ice-dammed Lake" in about 8300 B.C. to its various iterations as seas and lakes, culminating in the Litorina Sea, which reached its maximum extent in about 4500 to 4000 B.C.

Clark lamented how little was known of the history of the North Sea, except for some core borings and studies of the "moorlog" on the Dogger bank, already famous for the Leman and Ower harpoon find of 1931. He concluded: "There is good reason for believing that the coast of the old mainland between east Yorkshire and north Jutland must have been especially favorable for settlement; the influence of the Gulf Stream must have served to temper in the coastal regions the still cold climate. . . ."[5]

Chapter 1 then discusses climate and vegetational changes since the Ice Age. By today's standards, the zonation based on pollen analysis and peat bog stratigraphy is extremely crude, but Clark placed it in a broader context of environmental change, including evidence from macrofossils such as the hazelnut, even the modern and ancient distributions of the common tortoise. "The development of the post-glacial forests was neither catastrophic nor disorderly," he wrote.[6] He gave a succinct description of palynology, with the caution that "at least 150 grains" were needed per sample. North Sea moorlog samples allowed him to date the submergence of the land bridge that once connected Britain and Europe to the Boreal and Atlantic, an event he considered to have taken place within a short period of time.

From vegetational zones, he moved on to direct pollen associations with archaeological sites, not only obvious examples, such as Bronze Age barrows in northern Germany buried under sub-Atlantic peat, but important Maglemose settlements. Such sites, like Mullerup in Denmark, were seasonal camps on well-drained islands or peninsulas in marshes or swamps. He quoted Peacock's Farm as an excellent example where Postglacial stratigraphy and human occupation occurred within the same site. On the Continent, "the co-operative work of Dr. Reinerth and of the botanist Karl Bertsch on the Federsee . . . has produced very complete and beautiful results."[7] In the 1930s a small lake, the Federsee, had shrunk progressively since the Ice Age, with archaeological sites and peat deposits on receding shorelines that documented both the changing environment and the human

prehistory of the area. Here Clark summarized research that was to influence his own excavations at the Mesolithic site of Star Carr fifteen years
later (see Chapter 8). A wooden causeway near Oedenbühl at the southeastern corner of the Federsee could not be dated from its design or with
artifacts. So the excavators used pollen and careful stratigraphic observation
to tie the feature into the Late Bronze Age, when beech trees abounded in
the area. He also stressed another advantage of palynology: its ability to provide relative dates from tiny samples adhering to artifacts, like a fragment
of woven cloth from a peat deposit near Ottersberg, east of Bremen. The
find had been made as long ago as 1879, yet a tiny pollen sample assigned
the fabric to the Early Iron Age.

The pollen data assigned the northern European Mesolithic into three
broad divisions:

Period I (Pre-Boreal). Cold-loving trees like willow, birch,
and pine predominated. Early Mesolithic.

Period II (Boreal). Temperatures rose and mixed oak forest
rose to dominance over older, cooler trees. Pine and hazel were
especially common. Maglemose and Tardenoisian cultures.

Period III (Atlantic). The climatic optimum, when temperatures were highest and warmth-loving trees predominated. Mixed
oak forest was widespread. Late Mesolithic and Ertebølle cultures and the first farmers.

From vegetation, Clark turned to fauna, to the major changes in animal
populations from Late Glacial times onward. Period I saw forest forms like
pig, also red and roe deer, coming into prominence, while reindeer still
flourished. During Period II, Maglemose settlements yielded forest mammals, especially red deer and pig, while beavers were also common, along
with elk and the formidable aurochs (the primordial Ice Age wild ox, which
survived in Poland until 1627). Birds and fish, including pike and cranes,
were abundant, representing a considerable shift in hunting practices from
earlier Ice Age times. Clark describes the bones of young cranes and the
fully developed roe deer antlers, evidence for summer occupation. He
applied similar methods for identifying seasonal occupation at Star Carr.
The Scandinavians were already using them by 1900. Period III sites lay, for

	CLIMATE		VEGETATION	FAUNA	POLLEN	ECONOMY		LAND/SEA	
POST-GLACIAL	SUB-ATLANTIC Deterioration: wetter, colder —c.500 B.C.—	IX	Pine reverience Beech (Grenz)	Domestic sheep preponderate over swine	FOREST	Settled agriculture, pastoral activities, marine + inland hunting + fishing	IRON	BALTIC SEA	LITORINA SEA
	SUB-BOREAL Drier, more continental —c.2500 B.C.—	VIII	Spread of grasses + ling Oak forest Introduction of cereals + weeds of cultivation	Tame horse Red + roe deer, wild pig etc.; domesticated ox, pig, sheep, dog		←Forest clearance Shifting agriculture, pastoral activities, marine + inland hunting + fishing	NEOLITHIC / BRONZE	TRS.4 TRS.3	
	ATLANTIC Warmth max.; moist, oceanic —c.5000 B.C.—	VII	Mixed-oak forest (oak, elm, lime) and alder	Aurochs, red + roe deer; wild pig etc.; dog		Hunting, gathering, fowling, fishing + strand-looping	MESOLITHIC	TRS.2 TRS.1	
	BOREAL Rising temp. continental	VI	Pine/hazel; beg. mixed-oak forest	Aurochs, elk, red + roe deer; wild pig, beaver, bear; dog				ANCYLUS LAKE	
	—c.6800 B.C.—	V	Pine/birch forest						
	PRE-BOREAL Slow rise of temperature —c.8000 B.C.—	IV	Birch forest	Aurochs, elk Reindeer, bison — Wild horse	OPEN VEGETATION	Hunting, gathering, fowling + fishing	UPPER PALAEOLITHIC	YOLDIA SEA	
LATE GLACIAL	YOUNGER DRYAS Sub-arctic	III	Tundra / Park tundra	Reindeer, bison, alpine hare				BALTIC	
	ALLERØD Osc. warmer —c.10,000 B.C.—	II	Park tundra / Birch forest	Giant Irish deer, elk, beaver, bear				ICE-DAMMED	
	OLDER DRYAS Sub-arctic	Ic	Tundra	Reindeer				LAKE	
	BØLLING Osc. warmer	Ib	Park tundra						
	OLDEST DRYAS Arctic	Ia	Tundra	Reindeer					

J.G.D.C. 1950

Figure 4.2 **Chronological table with vegetational sequence and glacial retreat events from** *The Mesolithic Settlement of Northern Europe* **(Table A). Courtesy: Cambridge University Press.**

the most part, on the shores of the Litorina Sea, where forest animals accompanied large numbers of marine species, including four seal species, whales, and a wide variety of birds and fish. The bones suggested that many Ertebølle sites were occupied year-round.

At the end of chapter 1 is found a general correlation table of Peacock's Farm that links glacial episodes, Baltic Sea history, vegetation and climatic phases, fauna, and archaeology into a single correlated sequence (Figure

4.2). The chronology in calendar years is crude by today's standards, the relative chronology comparatively unrefined, but the Mesolithic settlement of northern Europe lies within an explicit, well-researched environmental framework. Although such correlations were routine to a small number of Scandinavian, especially Danish, scholars, they were startling for many archaeologists in Britain and elsewhere in Europe. Chapter 1 displays Clark's remarkable ability to pull together widely diverse forms of evidence into a single learned synthesis. At the time, he had few rivals in the art. Chapter 1, in a real sense, represented his approach to prehistory at the time.

Late Glacial Cultures

Chapter 2 is the first of four predominantly archaeological chapters that explore the Mesolithic sequence of northern Europe in considerable detail. "The Tanged-Point Cultures" surveys a series of Late Glacial societies, which, at the time, were still little known—and nonexistent—in Britain. Clark argued that a group of "flake cultures, characterized by tanged points and simple forms of microliths" flourished over the northern European plain from Belgium to the Ukraine during Period I and was also associated with the first settlement of many deglaciated areas of northern Scandinavia. The roots of these cultures lay firmly in the Upper Palaeolithic: "The immediate origins are to be found in cultures, contemporary with and perhaps in part later than the Magdalenian of France, the remains of which are found in open stations in northern Germany and in northern Holland."[8] Clark boldly compared the tanged points to Gravettian Font Robert points from southwestern France of considerably higher antiquity. More importantly, he drew attention to the Hamburgian culture sites at Meindorf and Stellendorf, where tanged points were found. He described the Stellmoor site, excavated by the German archaeologist Alfred Rust, whom he had not yet met in person, "a veritable hunting station of the Hamburg people, in which large quantities of organic remains have survived intact." The artifacts and bones of the camp lay in a layer of freshwater mud under a peat bed. The fauna included reindeer, wild horse, glutton, birds, and pike. There were no forest animals at Stellmoor, with a birch tree cover characteristic of the early Pre-Boreal. Stellmoor yielded reindeer antler artifacts and "suitable splinters" removed from young antlers "presumably with burins" to make barbed points. This is the "groove and splinter" technique for making antler artifacts, which Clark was to find at Star Carr fifteen years later. The Hamburgian he considered slightly later than the classic Magdalenian of southwestern France, but earlier than the tanged-point cultures, "to which it is probably ancestral."[9] The Stellmoor finds had a strong influence on Clark's thinking about the potential of sites where organic remains were preserved.

Chapter 3 describes the first signs of adaptation to more forested conditions. Grahame identified the Lyngby culture from the distribution of characteristic reindeer antler axes found over southern Sweden, Denmark, the north German plain, and further east into Poland. At the time southern Sweden and Denmark were joined by a land bridge associated with the Yoldia Sea phase of the Baltic's history. The axes themselves had been compared to American Indian clubs by Sophus Müller and Gustav Schwantes. Clark followed Schwantes in considering them "as marking a transition between clubs and the specialized forms of axes and adze, and in this they are of very great significance."[10] They were the prototypes for the flint axes and adzes that marked Maglemose culture in Period II.

The Maglemose Culture

The discussion of the amorphus Lyngby culture passes into the central theme of *The Mesolithic Settlement*, a long essay on the Maglemose culture of the northern European plain, "a rich culture adapted to the environment of the forest." For a generation, Clark's account of the Maglemose was the definitive synthesis for English-speaking readers and for many Scandinavians as well. He began by surveying the terminological labels used to describe this remarkable culture, rejected several more local labels, and pushed for the term "Maglemose," which signifies "big bog" in Danish. He wrote: "The term seems worth retaining because it expresses an important aspect of the culture, the most typical sites of which are, in fact, found in bogs and other low-lying places."[11]

The core of the Maglemose culture lay in Denmark and southern Sweden, with outliers in northern Germany as far as Poland, and across the southern North Sea into southeastern England. Clark argued on the basis of the Leman and Ower harpoon that the southern North Sea was "relatively well settled," for he believed that fen conditions held "peculiar attractions" to Maglemose people. Above all, the Maglemose people were "specially attracted by rivers, lakes, and fens, which suggests that fishing and fowling played an important part in their economy."[12] He reported instances of barbed bone spear points impaled in pike skulls and numerous edible waterbirds, including swans. Forest animals were of importance, among them elk and deer. The find of a virtually complete aurochs from Vig in Denmark, with a microlith embedded in its bones and evidence of a fatal wound to the lung, showed that hunters were not afraid to tackle formidable prey, even if the dying animal eluded its pursuers in a marsh. Grahame regarded the Vig find as of crucial importance, providing evidence for the use of composite, microlith-armed weapons in the chase.

Clark stressed the unique nature of Maglemose sites in boggy areas. "It implies, on the one hand the possibility of widespread pollen-analytical investigation, and on the other the survival of perishable objects of wood, bone, and antler."[13] He believed that many sites were occupied seasonally, with little variation in the material culture from one time of the year to another. Thus dwellings were temporary, leaving little trace in the archaeological record. At the Duvensee site south of Lübeck, the people settled on a slight eminence in a bog, only habitable in the dry season. They laid down a floor of birch and pine bark on the peat, bringing in small areas of sand and clay for their hearths. At least five superimposed floors came from the same location, suggesting that it was used year after year. He knew of no large Maglemose settlements, logical for people who appeared to live "in small social groups, to have migrated seasonally, and to have lived on hunting, fishing, fowling and collecting."[14]

Clark described Maglemose culture under broad headings based on raw materials. Simple, and clearly argued, it remains an excellent summary of classic Mesolithic technology. He began with flint, with microliths manufactured with the microburin technique, and with much standardization over a huge area from Britain to northern Germany. He argued that blunt-backed microliths were designed for insertion into the soft wooden shafts of spears and arrows, the blunting combined with resin adhesive helping to lock the tiny barb into the wood. Numerous varieties of burins were used to groove and splinter antler, also for engraving. Flaked adzes and axes were a fundamental part of Maglemose culture, a reflection of their forested environment. Clark was among the first to recognize the transverse axe sharpening flakes, used to rejuvenate a blunt axe with a quick sideward blow. The flint industry was supplemented with a range of pebble axes, perforated mace heads, and rubbers.

Many of the Maglemose wooden artifacts described in *Mesolithic Settlement* came from the Holmegaard site in Zealand. They included fire-hardened pointed sticks, possible throwing sticks, and perforated wooden sleeves for holding stone axes. Clark illustrated wooden canoe paddles, probably used with dugout canoes, described a fishing net (often called the Andrea net) found at Korpilahti in Finland, found in some recently drained meadows, lying on pale gray mud. The double-threaded plant bast cord net itself had decayed, but the sink-stones and eighteen pine-bark floats survived, together with traces of the fiber binding that once attached them to the net. The find dated to Period II and Maglemose times.

Antler and bone were of vital technological importance. Clark describes antler sleeves for adzes and axes and illustrates one from Svaerdborg in Denmark with the stone adze blade still in place. There were decorated and perforated antlers, antler axes and adzes, and barbless bone fishhooks, as well as net-making tools. He devoted much care to the classification of the most important antler and bone artifact: the barbed point, "perhaps the most important type fossil of the Maglemose culture."[15] Here he applied the methodology of distribution maps, describing most of the known finds as fish spears, some of them parts of two- and three-pronged leister (barbed fishing spears) (Figure 4.3). He divided the points into plain, notched and barbed, also tanged and slotted forms. His typology was quite elaborate. Single-barbed points formed seven distinct types, slotted forms five. He was more interested in their potential uses, perhaps as eel spears or as fish spears, drawing attention to an ethnographic specimen of a leister from Hudson's Bay, Canada, in the Copenhagen Museum. *The Mesolithic Settlement* is notable for its occasional use of ethnographic and folk analogy in creative ways, to support an argument, or to amplify an interpretation of an artifact, a hint of the direction in which Clark's interests in studying ancient economies were moving at the time, to come to full flower a decade later.

Dating the Maglemosan culture in general terms proved relatively easy, thanks to the abundance of environmental evidence. Clark argued for a date in Period II, on the basis of the Leman and Ower harpoon from the bed of the North Sea, and artifacts dredged from Danish fjords. He also pointed out that more research would enable the subdivision of the Maglemose, as

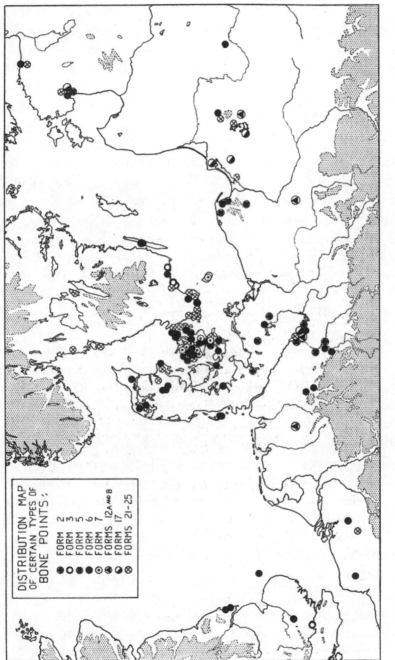

Figure 4.3 A classic Grahame Clark distribution map showing Mesolithic bone points. From *The Mesolithic Settlement of Northern Europe* (Figure 47). Courtesy: Cambridge University Press.

has happened with the advent of radiocarbon dating and much more refined palynological methods. As to its origins, he traced "certain elements" to the Upper Palaeolithic, whereas "others were called forth to meet the exigencies of the new environment of the Mesolithic period."[16] Stone axes, fishing equipment, and "drilling apparatus" were Mesolithic innovations.

The Ertebølle Culture

The Maglemose flourished during Period II, pressing northward into new exposed lands as time went on. Period III saw the emergence of the Ertebølle culture in Denmark and Schleswig Holstein. Clark himself proposed the term "Ertebølle" as the cultural label to replace the older term "kitchen-midden," which he had used in *The Mesolithic Age*.[17] Many sites came from sea levels slightly higher than modern ones, formed by the rise of the Litorina Sea, making many sites easier of access, while others in areas with lesser water transgression lay below the shallows of the Baltic. More ocean oriented than the Maglemose with its forest hunting, the Ertebølle people occupied year-round sites on the coast, pursuing sea birds, sea mammals, and fish. Clark focused more on occupation sites associated with pollen-bearing levels than on shell middens, which provided only limited information.

In terms of material culture, the Maglemose and Ertebølle shared many resemblances, but with fewer flaked stone axes and a predominance of transverse, trapezoid arrowheads in the later culture (Figure 4.4). Clark theorized that these "petit tranchets," some attached to wooden shafts with fiber and sinew bindings, were used for bird hunting. He also noted the presence of numerous burins in Ertebølle settlements, and end-of-blade scrapers unlike the horseshoe-like forms used by Maglemose folk. Organic deposits at Brabrand Sø and elsewhere yielded wooden throwing sticks, handles, wooden arrow shafts, and a possible club. By far the most important innovation was crude pottery, simple vessels fabricated from a gritty clay, using the coil method, as much as forty-six centimeters (18 inches) high. One common form had a pointed base and out-turned rim, presumably so it would stand in sand or soft earth and hold liquids.

Clay vessels were not characteristic of Mesolithic cultures, and their appearance in Ertebølle sites was puzzling. Clark rejected any thought of diffusion of ceramics from local farming peoples. He theorized that the idea

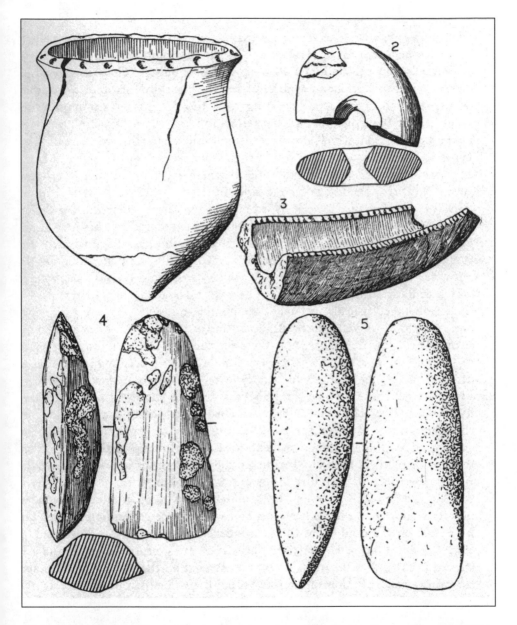

Figure 4.4 **Ertebølle artifacts from various locations. From** *The Mesolithic Settlement of Northern Europe* **(Figure 53). Scale: 1/2 to 3/4 full size. Courtesy: Cambridge University Press.**

spread from the south or southeast, from areas where farming was established considerably earlier.

After Ertebølle, Clark briefly surveyed equivalent cultures in Sweden and the so-called Lower Halstow culture of southeastern England, known from a site on the Medway river estuary. He linked all of these to the Ertebølle tradition and then argued that Period III cultures tended to display more regional variation than earlier Maglemose culture. This, he said, reflected contemporary geographical changes caused by rising sea levels, which brought an emphasis on coastal settlement. In turn, Ertebølle formed the basis of the Arctic culture of northern Scandinavia, which flourished long after farmers settled to the south.

Maglemose Art

The Mesolithic Settlement mainly focuses on the Maglemose culture and reflects another of Clark's emerging interests—prehistoric and, eventually, modern art. He devoted an entire chapter to Maglemose art, a tradition based almost entirely on the engraving of small objects such as antler hafts, axes, adzes, and points. Like his description of the culture itself, his discussion of the art remained a standard account for a generation.

Maglemose art was executed by incision, pricking, and drilling, the former achieved with a fine flint edge, sometimes so finely as to be practically invisible (Figure 4.5). Clark was especially fascinated by the pricking and drilling, the latter producing small holes of regular size made by rotating a pointed object. He agreed with Sophus Müller that a bow drill was probably used to produce such regular holes and drew attention to a bone rib with notches and a natural curvature from the Mullerup site, which could indeed have been such an artifact.

The art styles ranged from improvements of natural cracks to a variety of geometric motifs, of which Clark identified no less than twenty-four. He analyzed these "as an objective study of the patterns as culture fossils."[18] Distribution maps, another classic Clark method, revealed an indiscriminate distribution of the different designs, which ranged from fishnet styles to rows of triangles and cross-hatching. Biomorphic styles included some stylized human figures and animal forms, the most famous being the perforated antler haft from Ystad he had examined years earlier, with two cervids placed back to back, looking in different directions. The animals are angu-

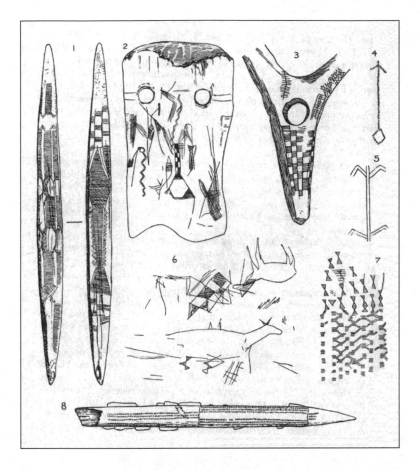

Figure 4.5 **Maglemose art objects from various Scandinavian locations. From *The Mesolithic Settlement of Northern Europe* (Figure 61). Scales: 25% to 35%. Courtesy: Cambridge University Press.**

lar and reasonably naturalistic and clearly contemporary with the checkered patterns on the same artifact. Clark prized this object as a special example of Maglemose art and remembered the opportunity to handle it as a special moment in his early career.[19]

"An art is characteristic of a culture and betrays individual features peculiar to itself," Grahame wrote. Despite this observation, he looked for the origins of the tradition in the engraved bone and antler artifacts of the Upper Palaeolithic. Since the western Upper Palaeolithic art traditions were more naturalistic than those of eastern Europe, he looked to that region but observed no potential artistic links whatsoever. Palaeolithic art experts such as Henri Breuil and Miles Burkitt had noted more emphasis on geometric motifs in later Upper Palaeolithic art. A fair number of the motifs found in Maglemose sites were found on Magdalenian objects, so Clark argued for an origin from western art traditions. He observed that the fishnet and, to a lesser extent, the checkered pattern of the Maglemose did not occur in the earlier tradition. This, he hypothesized, was because fishing became of importance in the Maglemose, a bold hypothesis, even in an era of bold theories.

Finally, he looked for connections between the Maglemose artistic tradition and the art of the Arctic cultures of northern Scandinavia, rejecting a common theory of the day that the Arctic tradition had roots in the Upper Palaeolithic, perhaps as far back as the Aurignacian. "It looks to us extremely unlikely," he remarked in his best magisterial style. He argued for connections with sculptures found over a wide area from Sweden to Russia, most of the art dating to Period III.

Tardenoisian Culture

Chapter 5, "The Microlithic Cultures of the Sand Areas and the Highlands," discusses the Tardenoisian in northern Europe. Tardenoisian sites were concentrated in his familiar British stamping grounds and also in northern France, the Low Countries, and the southern border of the north German plain. Almost all sites were confined to sandy areas or to higher ground, to areas like the Pennines of northern England or on sandstone plateaus in southern Germany. By settling in open areas or near lakes, the Tardenoisians avoided heavily forested terrain. Furthermore, they lived in areas where agriculture was impracticable and may have survived long after the arrival of the first farmers on the nearby loess lands of central Europe.

The stratigraphic position of the Tardenoisian was established from cave and rockshelter stratigraphy, but most sites were in the open, some with "pit dwellings." Clark describes one such dwelling from Eyb near Ansbach in southern Germany, a sandstone pit lined with blocks with a hearth area in the center. Unfortunately, no diagnostic artifacts were found inside. He summarized: "Tardenoisian man constructed dwellings for himself, sometimes mere wind-breaks, but where practicable huts with branch frames covered with reeds or wattle and daub, as well as occupying various natural shelters."[20] Except for a few bone artifacts, almost all Tardenoisian material culture was in flint, a function of its sandy context.

Clark drew attention to the common use of microliths fabricated from narrow blades by the microburin technique. The finished artifacts were commonly blunted down one edge and were triangles or trapezes. He stressed the virtual absence of axes and adzes, as if the Tardenoisians never exploited forested environments. Their material culture was remarkably uniform over the entire area, except that late versions of the Tardenoisian with its many trapeze-shaped microliths were absent in Britain, a function Clark believed to be the result of the drowning of the North Sea. He described three stratified stages of the culture from Belgium and called on the peat layers of Peacock's Farm with their handful of microliths to date most of the Tardenoisian to Period II, to the Boreal period, with later stages of the culture spilling over into Period III, making it contemporary with the classic Maglemose and much of the Ertebølle of the Baltic region. The Tardenoisian's links with earlier tanged point cultures was unknown, but there were important common elements with Maglemose culture. Clark argued that "although the indigenous population contributed locally to the new civilization, it was due primarily to ethnic movement under stress of the new climatic changes which characterized the post-glacial period."[21] Like other Mesolithic scholars of the day, he was firmly convinced that the Tardenoisian with its microliths spread northward into western Europe as a result of desiccation at the end of the Ice Age.

Reviews and Reactions

The Mesolithic Settlement of Northern Europe appeared in 1936 and immediately established Grahame Clark at the forefront of Mesolithic archaeologists. W. F. Grimes, writing in the *Proceedings*, praised the clarity of the writing, "a vivid picture of post-palaeolithic life over the whole lowland of northern Europe, in which the activities of man may be studied against an ever-changing environment."[22]

The book is a fascinating mix of traditional culture history and a new approach that stressed adaptation to local conditions and rapidly changing environmental conditions. The culture history evolves directly from Clark's earlier work in Britain, with its similar emphasis on typology and the minutiae of stone technology and the use of distribution maps. Like other archaeologists of the time, he uses characteristic "type fossils" as indicators of technology change and identity. At the same time, he is not afraid to indulge in the kinds of sweeping generalizations that characterized Stone Age archaeology in the 1930s: Dorothy Garrod's migration of very early Upper Palaeolithic people from southwestern Asia, the French theory that derived the Tardenoisian with its microliths from an increasingly arid North Africa, Gordon Childe's hypotheses that farming and other innovations spread from southwestern Asia into temperate Europe. Clark saw the Mesolithic settlement of northern Europe as a fusion of ancient ideas with new ones resulting from Postglacial climatic change and from the new challenges of exploiting forests, lakes, and seashores. The backdrop was environmental change and the ingenuity of Mesolithic people in adapting to an increasingly diverse and rapidly changing world of rising sea levels and temperatures, new vegetation patterns, and entirely new animal and vegetable forms.

By the mid-1930s, none of this was particularly new, especially to the Scandinavians. What made *The Mesolithic Settlement* so important was Clark's brilliant gift at separating the intellectual wood from the trees, his ability to focus on the broad issues, the major rather than the minor changes, while still teasing highly detailed information from seemingly unspectacular archaeological sites. The book is simply laid out, closely argued, at times almost magisterial in its tone, both deeply conservative and innovative. Young Clark had spent years traveling, examining collections, visiting sites, and reading an enormous and often obscure literature. He achieved his synthesis by developing an international network of academic colleagues who sent him reprints and talked to him at conferences. Grahame absorbed and synthesized data with almost single-minded intensity wherever he went. His archives are crammed with heavily annotated Scandinavian papers, with his notes on obscure sites and artifacts, on perceived connections between different art styles and objects. This collection of impressions and annotations formed one of the foundations of *The Mesolithic Settlement*, as did his own excavations at Peacock's Farm and elsewhere. Above all, he learned the preeminent importance of waterlogged sites for the wealth of environmental and cultural information that could be gleaned from them. His dream was to find and excavate such a site on British soil.

The Mesolithic Settlement of Northern Europe was hailed at the time as an important and trendsetting book. A. J. Armstrong reflected widely held opinion when he wrote in *Man* that the account was "immensely strengthened by the synchronization of independent researches by geologists, biologists, archaeologists, and botanists."[23] For the first time, the remarkable Mesolithic cultures of the north were accessible to general archaeological readers. Generations of students learned about the Mesolithic from its pages. For years it was the definitive account of the Maglemose culture in the English language. Now outdated by years of more detailed and fine-grained archaeological and environmental research, it remains a landmark book in twentieth-century archaeology. *The Mesolithic Settlement* was a remarkable piece of scholarship for an archaeologist in his late twenties and set an entirely new tone for later Stone Age archaeology in Europe and much further afield. Few prehistorians of the day had the single-minded intensity, comparative knowledge, and practical experience to write such a book. With this work, Clark stood out from his contemporaries as a Stone Age archaeologist of the first order.

As he corrected the proofs, he was already contemplating a quite different and even more ambitious book—about archaeology and the society of which it was a part.

5

◈

Archaeology and Society

The standing of archaeology within a society is one index of its degree of civilization.

Archaeology and Society

s *The Mesolithic Settlement of Northern Europe* was in press, Grahame
Clark married Mollie White in St. Peter's Church opposite Chichester
Cathedral in the summer of 1936. Although his salary as an assistant lecturer was a mere £150 a year and he had a minuscule private income, Mollie
gave up her post on the Royal Commission for Ancient and Historical
Monuments without a qualm. "I want a quiet background," he said to her,
and through their long, very happy marriage, Mollie provided just that.[1]
They spent their honeymoon traveling through Norway and central Sweden
visiting Arctic rock carvings, which "gave so graphic an insight into the
mentality of the Stone Age Scandinavians." Many of the sites were very close
to the water, the Nämnforsen group in Ångermanland "on a rocky inlet
among foaming falls and rapids." They photographed the pecked outlines by
applying chalk to the engravings or by shining a flashlight at an oblique angle
across the rock surface (Figure 5.1). Near Oslo, they were lucky, for the
rock glistened after a shower of rain. "When we returned home we earned
a few pounds by supplying a brief illustrated article to *Antiquity*."[2] Following
their honeymoon excursion, they made their first public appearance as husband and wife at the second Congress of Pre- and Protohistoric Sciences in

Figure 5.1 Rock engravings from Rødoy, Norland, Norway, delineated with chalk by Clark for photographic purposes, 1936.

Oslo. Then, as now, such meetings were an excellent place for younger scholars to make contacts with colleagues elsewhere, visit sites, and learn of new discoveries.

The same year, they set off again, this time in the company of Charles Phillips, who owned a comfortable Ford V-8. Grahame was particularly anxious to meet a German archaeologist named Alfred Rust, who was working on important Late Glacial sites in northern Germany. They visited the Schleswig Museum, where they spent three days with archaeologist Gustav Schwantes, examining the famous fourth-century votive boat from Nydam on Als and walking over the Danevirke, a Dark Ages and medieval earthwork that closed Jutland off from the rest of Europe. They also inspected a half-moon-shaped earthwork, the Hedeby, once a major trading center on the shores of Schleswig fjord at the east end of the defensive line.

Schwantes escorted them to Alfred Rust's excavations at Meiendorf, "among swamps and little lakes teeming with a large population of frogs, newts, snakes, and all kinds of waterfowl."[3] Clark and Rust took to each other at once, for they were both independent-minded, determined men with a fanatical devotion to archaeology. Rust was of Clark's age but had lacked the financial resources to attend university. Instead, he rode his bicycle from Germany to Syria, where he found other archaeologists and eventually ended up directing an important Upper Palaeolithic cave excavation at Jabrud. Then he had returned to Germany and excavated the Late Glacial reindeer hunting site at Stellmoor, which Clark had admired on a previous visit. By 1937, Rust had acquired a Ph.D. and a violent antipathy to Nazis, like his colleague and friend Schwantes. The Ahrensburg and Meiendorf sites interested Clark profoundly because of their Late Glacial materials and well-defined climatic evidence. He and Rust were to remain in touch for many years.

Next they traveled to the ancient Hanseatic city of Lübeck, where Phillips remembered the dairy and cheese shops giving off an appalling stench. On their way to Denmark, they spent a night in Kiel, where Phillips and Clark rented a small rowing boat to explore the harbor. They rowed around the new battleship *Scharnhorst* as seamen leaned on the rail idly watching. Wrote Phillips: "This was rather extraordinary, for one would have expected that such a proceeding would be instantly stopped, but we completed our circuit and went back to our hotel." Four years later, both of them were working in a wartime aerial photographic unit and tracked the battleship until it sank in 1943. They left Germany with relief through an

unfriendly frontier post adorned with a large portrait of Adolf Hitler, visited an Ertebølle shell midden in Jutland (a rarity, since many of them were
removed to make shell manure in the nineteenth century), and walked
fields near the Gudenaa River picking up flints. Unfortunately, three kilometers (2 miles) outside the town of Randers, their car collided with a large
farm truck, which had turned out from a farm entrance without someone
in front to direct it onto the main road, a legal requirement at the time.
Phillips was only shaken up, but the others sustained slight concussions, and
one of Grahame's toe phalanges was broken. The Clarks were in hospital for
three weeks. Phillips was fined £2 for exceeding the speed limit of twenty
miles per hour, the truck driver considerably more.

"The Kind of Archaeology Promoted by Museum Curators"

Back in Cambridge, Grahame threw himself into the important business of
undergraduate teaching. Mollie and he bought a house on Barton Road,
close to where the Godwins lived. He could now indulge his many archaeological interests in the classroom on a regular basis between expeditions
into the fens and a heavy investment in the affairs of the Prehistoric Society.
He taught courses on the human settlement of Scandinavia "from the with-
drawal of the Pleistocene ice-sheet to the spread of farming economy," using
The Mesolithic Settlement as his primary text. Here he emphasized the importance of the relationship between ecological and economic change, a very
different approach from that taken by Miles Burkitt, who had advanced but
little from his type fossil/stratigraphic approach drawn directly from his
experiences with Breuil, Obermaier, and others before World War I. He
also taught a more general course on prehistoric archaeology, in which he
argued that "the prime objective of prehistoric archaeology was not only to
classify and date artifacts so much as to throw light on the life of the communities that made and used them."[4]

Clark had a strong background in history and anthropology, which had
leavened his narrow archaeological training to the point that "I was concerned to attack . . . the kind of archaeology promoted by museum curators." He railed against the preoccupation of many of his colleagues with artifact classification, chronology, and cultural groups, stemming directly from

Danish archaeologist Christian Jurgensen Thomsen's Three Age System, which had been used to put the National Museum in Copenhagen in order in the early nineteenth century.[5] Archaeology, he said, was both history and anthropology, a discipline in which artifact assemblages should be studied for the information they revealed about "the societies that produced them." Grahame rightly gave credit for his perspective to Gordon Childe, whose *Dawn of European Civilization* had been one of the first books he purchased as a student. Like Childe, Clark had a thorough schooling in typological methods and had worked hard to acquire comparative, firsthand knowledge of collections and sites. Like Childe, he used material remains to argue what he called "historical hypotheses." Such an approach required an anthropological, ecological, and historical perspective.[6]

Clark's general courses drew on his Scandinavian experience—remarkable waterlogged sites excavated by his Danish colleagues—where they could study the full range of Maglemose and Ertebølle material culture. Organic sites hold the most promise, he repeatedly told his students. However, to his frustration, no such locations came his way. By this time, Harry Godwin was turning his attention away from the fens to the waterlogged Somerset Levels with its Neolithic trackways. Clark was encouraged to join them but elected instead to excavate a Mesolithic site at Farnham near London, where there were no peat deposits. But he readily acknowledged his debt to his botanist friends. Godwin and his colleagues gave Grahame the chance to "study prehistoric archery rather than prehistoric arrowheads."[7] He longed to excavate his own waterlogged settlement that would amplify the arid landscape of microliths that represented the British Mesolithic.

The Farnham excavations were the source of considerable intellectual frustration. Grahame worked in collaboration with amateur archaeologist W. F. Rankine during the long vacation of 1937–1938. Although the excavators used a scraping technique borrowed from the Danes for exposing occupation surfaces, the dig yielded no ecological data, precious little information on structures, and nothing more than a plethora of microliths and other stone artifacts, enough to demonstrate ties with both Maglemose and Tardenoisian cultural traditions (Figure 5.2). The report, which included a review of evidence for Mesolithic structures, appeared in the *Proceedings* for 1939, but only after vigorous arguments with Rankine, who wanted a longer report.[8] Grahame and Mollie consoled themselves by flying to Paris and then on to Milan, Herculaneum, Pompeii, and Rome.

Figure 5.2   **A Mesolithic living surface at the Farnham Mesolithic site, with Mollie Clark giving the scale.**

Archaeology and Society

Clark was a competitive personality, an archaeologist who craved recognition and an international reputation. But his cravings came as much from a single-minded focus on archaeology as from personal ambition. He was frustrated by both the conservatism of many of his colleagues and the elusiveness of organic sites. There was a strong missionary quality in Grahame Clark. He considered it imperative that British archaeologists study wetland sites and pay careful attention to environmental change. He also believed passionately that archaeology had potentially important contributions to make to modern society. His Cambridge courses and the experience and perspective gained from writing *The Mesolithic Settlement* gave him both the impetus and the background to write a different kind of book about archaeology, aimed fairly and squarely at the general public.

Methuen and Company published *Archaeology and Society* in 1939, a wide-ranging essay on the uses, limitations, and importance of scientific archaeology. Most popular archaeology books of the day dealt with serried rows of cultural periods and artifacts. Clark's little textbook was a survey of how one went about doing archaeology to study communities and the ways they made a living. The book, a success, was revised in 1947 and again in 1952, and was widely read by archaeologists and their students as far afield as China and New Zealand. Judging from the many references to its pages in American archaeological literature, *Society* was one of the most widely read of Clark's books in the United States, probably because it offered an accessible, short account of what at the time would have been considered a "new" environmental archaeology, not to be confused with the so-called New Archaeology of the 1960s, capital *N* and capital *A*. Today, the book seems somewhat old-fashioned and provincial, but at the time it represented a true intellectual cutting edge. It begins with a simple definition of archaeology: "the study of how men lived in the past." In other words, the full range of preserved archaeological evidence could be used to study not only many aspects of ancient human cultures but also their ecological interrelationships. The book ends with a forthright statement: "One may end by reflecting that the standing of archaeology within a society is one index of its degree of civilization."[9]

Archaeology and Society is among the more important of Clark's books, for it lays out his approach to the past in some detail and explains much about his approach to later work.

A Discipline Free from "Fallible Defects"

Chapter 1 is a general introduction to archaeology. It argues that although archaeologists may be preoccupied with objects "often in themselves unattractive," they are really concerned with people. Clark likened archaeologists to criminologists whose powers are limited by the data. "For all his powers of detection he [the archaeologist] is for ever cut off from a knowledge of individuals; he can track men down, but they remain anonymous. Yet, how often would a knowledge of some dynamic personality solve problems of prehistoric archaeology yet unexplained." History, he wrote, is "an art," whereas archaeology with its flints and potsherds is free "from all those defects of fallible humanity which impair the value of documentary evidence." Herein lay the appeal of prehistory. It was a young science and a popular one, with news value in the press. There has been "a veritable revolution in the public attitude toward archaeology."[10]

Why then, Grahame asked, are people more interested in archaeology now than they were in the more leisured days of recent centuries? He looked for answers not in the Industrial Revolution but in the history of archaeology itself, in the watershed between an amateur pursuit and an emerging science that came with recognition of the antiquity of humankind in 1859. The theory of evolution sparked widespread scientific interest, as well as fascination among the general public. "So human and intimate were the questions involved, that it could hardly have been otherwise." The general idea of growth and progress were phenomena of time as well as place. One could not understand the present without understanding the past. So, "conscious of the weight of the towering edifice of his creations in the material world, modern man has been anxious to deepen the foundations of his civilization in the past." The Victorians had embraced progress as a direct offspring of biological evolution and thus archaeology as well, which provided evidence for "the ascent of humanity." "It is true that today we do not regard the progress of mankind with quite the assurance of our Victorian forebears, and it may be that we are more ready to acknowledge dips and even troughs in the general upward curve," Clark wrote. "But the broad fact of technical progress when viewed from the dawn of the Stone Age is undeniable."[11] Progress in its various forms was a theme to which Clark returned again and again during his career.

The Basics

Archaeology and Society was written as a textbook, so the next four chapters reflect a need to cover many of the basics. In chapter 2, "Discovery": How Do Archaeologists Discover Sites? Clark discusses finds made by natural processes or human activities, citing the coastal erosion at Clacton in Essex, which revealed Stone Age artifacts and the Vinca Bronze Age site in Serbia, exposed by the waters of the Danube River. Wind erosion at sandy locations allowed Clark to mention Mesolithic sites in one of his stamping grounds— Lincolnshire—and the nineteenth-century storm that swept away the sand dunes that covered the Stone Age village at Skara Brae in the Orkney Islands. The Swiss lake dwellings were an example of waterlogged sites exposed by low lake levels. Discovery as a result of human activities included plowing, for plowed land was a favorite haunt of the collectors Clark had known in his youth. He quoted the example of the Adam's Head long barrow in Lincolnshire, once plowed for wheat, then potatoes, which did not grow. So the superstitious farmer abandoned his new field, but a later owner overcame his prejudices and plowed it flat. Clark inevitably covered peat cutting in the fens, Scandinavia, and northern Germany, with its potential for organic finds, even the discovery of wrecks under the Mediterranean, where bronzes survived a couple of thousand years beneath the sea without the slightest ill effects.

From rural settings, Clark turned to industrial activity, to the archaeology under London streets and the finds made during public works. "The deep excavations required for gasometers have sometimes been fruitful," he wrote, citing the Maglemose harpoons from Holderness in northeastern England, found during such construction work.[12] Sewage farms were frequently built on well-drained gravel soils also favored by Stone Age people. The Mesolithic site at Farnham, with its semisubterranean houses, was one example. Clark ranged over road construction work, quarrying, harbor dredging, even war. He cited the example of a standing order on the German side of the western front in World War I, which required all archaeological finds to be reported to general headquarters. Clark recorded an instance from the more casual British side, where Captain Francis Buckley, later to become an important amateur investigator of Mesolithic sites in the Pennines, collected Levallois artifacts from trench parapets near Arras in northern France. He also described pioneer efforts at aerial photography of archaeological sites by Royal Air Force and German observers, which revealed hundreds of sites during the Great War.

Clark had spent much of his earlier years looking for surface indications of archaeological sites. His discussion of "Surface Indications" reflects long experience and the influence of Cyril Fox, when he writes of a highland and lowland zone in Britain. The discussion is heavily skewed toward British sites, for he was, after all, writing for a predominantly British audience. "With the shadows long in early morning or evening sites of low relief are to be seen to their best advantage," he wrote. Snow was useful for showing up low-lying field system boundaries—and to Therkel Mathiassen in tracking old Eskimo house ruins in the Hudson's Bay region of Canada. He strongly advocated the use of aerial photography, even on well-known sites, such as the Trundle, where the Neolithic causewayed camp of his youthful excavation days had been first detected from the air. He discussed crop and soil marks, the first textbook to do so, and drew attention to the importance of overlying vegetation for locating sites. Again an example came from the Arctic, from western Greenland, where different types of growth covered ancient Norse sites of different ages. The chapter ends with a discourse on other sources for finding sites: Schliemann's discovery of Troy through Homer's writings, the works of pioneer fieldworkers such as the antiquarian William Stukeley at Avebury and Stonehenge, place-names, and the clues to be gleaned from large-scale maps. "The apparently irrational behaviour of a field boundary may give the clue to an archaeological site, whose presence caused deviations to be made at the time of the enclosures." Finally, he discusses the celebrated dragons' teeth divination bones, which led to the discovery of the Shang civilization in northern China.[13]

Preservation, the topic of chapter 3, was a subject close to Clark's heart. He made a fundamental distinction between organic and inorganic remains, then discussed the role of climate: warm and moist, very dry, and temperate conditions. His examples were revealing of Clark's broadening interests. He took his readers to the Maya rain forest, where vegetation overwhelmed "even the strongest masonry" and preservation was very poor. "Excavations have habitually disclosed a bewildering variety of burnt clay and stone objects, including masks, crystal skulls, and flints worked to the most fantastic shapes; not a trace of the woodwork." His dry climate examples include Egyptian papyri, the tomb of Tutankhamun, and the granaries of the Desert Fayum, where Gertrude Caton-Thompson had found early farming settlements in the 1920s. He wrote wistfully: "Any archaeologist digging in England would give his head to find grave-furniture in anything approaching such a state of preservation as that in the young pharaoh's tomb." In Central Asia, he described Aurel Stein's discoveries in the Taklamakan desert, where he found dwellings with timber foundations and matting walls, together with the "gaunt and desiccated remains of gardens, drives with their rush fences, avenues and arbours of poplar trees and orchards of peach, plum, apricot and mulberry." The possessions of the inhabitants lay where they had been abandoned to the wind and sand: an office complete with pens and a hammock, weapons, felt and cotton fabrics, even a wooden mousetrap. There were tattered rugs. "It is, indeed, difficult to believe that the pale blues and greens and the dull Chinese reds were delighting the people of Niya more than a century before the Roman legions left the shores of Britain. . . . It is a chastening thought that in a temperate climate not one of the documents, none of the textiles and little of the wooden structures and their furnishings would have survived more than a few years."[14]

From Chinese Turkestan, the reader traveled to the dry Basketmaker caves of the North American Southwest, where Clark discoursed on the hairstyles of the dead and a dog burial, where the flies accompanying the corpse were still intact. The Andean mummies of Pachamac and other coastal cemeteries receive brief mention, Clark drawing attention to the tattoos of bird and fish on limb and leg and the magnificent basketry and textiles in brightly colored hues.

In temperate environments, we cover familiar ground: the Swiss lake dwellings, which "have given us more tangible evidence of the perishable aspects of the material culture of Neolithic man than all the 'dry land' sites of Europe put together," the Glastonbury and Meare villages in Britain, and the oak coffin burials under northern European Early Bronze Age barrows. Bog finds receive a mere nine lines, which is surprising, given the author's recent preoccupation with Scandinavian Mesolithic sites and their rich organic contents. "The most perfect climatic conditions for preservation" were in the circumpolar regions, where Clark covers the Bereskova mammoth from Siberia, whose flesh was so fresh that the discoverer's dogs ate it; Thule sites in the Canadian arctic excavated by his Scandinavian friends Therkel Mathiassen and Kaj Birket-Smith; and Scythian tombs in the Altai, with their elaborate horse burials, complete with textiles, felt items, and rectangular chambers. The burial at Pazyryk moved Clark to lyrical expression: "We can see in our mind's eye the dead leader borne on an ox-drawn cart . . . to the traditional burial-place of his forebears high up on the mountain slope. We can almost assist at the building of his tomb and smell the timber as those who fashioned from it the coffin and the double chamber. The funeral hangings, the horses harnessed for the pleasure of the great one in the next world, we can see them all, so fresh that, as their excavator remarked, it seems incredible that it all happened some 2,000 years ago."[15]

Burial sites, wrote Clark, gave archaeology a "flying start." But settlements offered the most promising avenue of research for future years. He ended his preservation chapter with a brief discussion of how people's behavior affects the survival of material culture. He concluded, "It is through death and destruction that generations of men remote beyond the verges of history have come to life again in the consciousness of humanity, and it is the spoiling hands of the archaeologists that confer immortality upon them."[16]

Chapter 4 covers excavation, "an essential link between discovery and interpretation."[17] Clark urged against rigid adherence to a theoretical "excavation technique," perhaps a subtle dig at Sir Mortimer Wheeler's rigorous methods, which were widely in use by the late 1930s. Careful conservation in the ground and after excavating are constant themes, consistent with Grahame's strong interest in the potential of organic objects. Ghost sites receive careful attention, not only spectacular examples like the plaster casts of victims at Pompeii and the famous Ur wooden lyre box but also posthole discolorations, timber structures like those on the banks of the Federsee, and loess sites like the Bandkeramik settlement at Köln-Lindenthal, Germany. The excavation chapter reflects Grahame's broad experience and constant traveling in Europe, for such methods as the "shaving" technique used to expose house postholes in Germany's loess country were almost unknown in Britain. The Sutton Hoo excavations also weighed heavily on his experience. He quotes with approval the excavation of the Ladby Viking ship in Denmark, where the excavator exposed the iron bolts still in position, although the planks had vanished, and the metal ornamentation around the prow. "As for the wooden and textile furnishings of the ship, these must be restored in the imagination nourished with memories of the Oseberg and other ships found under happier conditions."[18]

Stratigraphic observation is handled with specific examples, from the northern Spanish rockshelter at Castillo, the occupation sequence at Ur in Iraq, and coastal mound sites in northern Holland and Germany. Barrows, megalithic tombs, and cemeteries receive cursory discussion, which informs the reader of little but the most basic principles. Finally, Clark moves on to "Henges," and to Stonehenge in particular, where he laments "an immense, 'learned' and essentially vapid literature [which] enshrines the speculations—and let it be confessed, the pompous nonsense—to which it has given rise."[19] Serious excavation reports were minimal. Unfortunately, he does little more than list the major features such as the stone circles in their perceived stratigraphic order. There is no substantive discussion either of the site or of the ideal excavation methods needed to investigate the complex sequence of events at the stone circle. *Archaeology and Society* treats excavation by example and does little to explore the nuances of excavation methods.

Chapter 5, "Chronology," is a fascinating excursion into the dating methods of an archaeological world before radiocarbon dating (announced in 1949). In the late 1930s, prehistoric archaeologists relied heavily on relative dating methods, especially on artifact typologies. As Clark himself put it: "It is tactless to insist too strongly on a date in years for your find." He added in rationalization: "The difference between relative and absolute dates is less one of kind than degree, of the degree of attainable precision." Finally, a prophetic remark: "Nevertheless there is every reason to think that prehistory would gain immensely in definition if its chronological apparatus was more precise."[20] Clark himself was to be in the forefront of using that increased precision.

Hardly surprisingly, Clark placed major emphasis on traditional typology, of La Tène brooches and the processes by which artifact styles evolved, citing Victorian archaeologist John Evans's classic exposition on the devolution of the Macedonian *stater*. He covers by then routine ground: the value of hoards and other sealed finds, and sites at which stratigraphy and typological change can be combined, as was the case with the recently published Mount Carmel caves from southwestern Asia. But he comes into his own with the discussion of Holocene climatic change, peat stratigraphy, and postglacial relative chronology and the familiar Blytt and Sernander sequence of pollen zones for northern Europe. Here he drew on his own travels to the Federsee and throughout Scandinavia, on sites and sequences already discussed in *The Mesolithic Settlement of Northern Europe* three years earlier. The relative chronology section ends with a discussion of synchronism and site distributions as ways of establishing sequences and tracing trade routes.

Modern-day archaeology textbooks allocate much space to absolute dating methods, whereas *Archaeology and Society* covers the subject in just over thirteen pages. There were few methods to describe: geochronology and the newfangled Milankovitch solar radiation chronology for the Pleistocene, much promoted by geochronologist Frederick Zeuner of the University of London; the varve chronologies for northern Europe developed by Baron de Geer; and dendrochronology, used mainly in the American Southwest and tried experimentally on oak trees in northern Europe.[21] Clark's hope that the nascent and incomplete European tree-ring sequences would one day form an accurate timescale has come to pass in recent years with a timescale going back more than 8,000 years. Then there were historical records and cross-dating, a brief discussion remarkable for the comment that "the Chinese were too well bred to vaunt the antiquity of their early kings in the manner of the later-day Babylonian priests."[22]

"The Economic Basis"

Chapter 6, "Interpretation," begins with a statement that proclaims Clark's bias from the beginning: "The ultimate aim of all his [the archaeologist's] digging and delving, his piecing together and his reconstruction is to find out how people lived." Then follows one of the most famous of Clark's diagrams, which depicts "the structure of a society, so as to make clear the interrelations of its different aspects" (Figure 5.3). This version is a simple one, elaborated over about fifteen years with the addition of habitat and biome as the twin foundations below subsistence. As far as one can tell, this is the first diagram that linked human culture with environmental conditions in a single schema. Many years later, Clark remarked that "with that figure as a basis I could do anything."[23] The diagram is a simple system in which population density interacts with food supply, "the economic basis," and with "social organization and behavior." "Art and Religion," "Form of Settlement and Houses," "Living Area," and "Material Culture" are major sections in a chapter that was one of the first theoretical formulations of its type to appear in a general book in archaeology.

Clark placed food supply and what he called the "economic basis" at the front of his interpretative concerns. Were the people food producers or foragers? If the latter, were they predominantly hunters or fishers and fowlers, or did plant foods play an important role in subsistence? What about seasonal activities, the survival of old food-getting practices, and methods of preparing food and drink. "When the archaeologists of the future come to study the stratification of London, it may be that the rise of the tea-cup and the relative decline of the beer-bottle will be regarded as marking a decisive stage in the history of the British Empire."[24] However, beyond a brief discussion of the potential of animal bones, shells, and plants, there is little specific discussion of methods. He expresses the prophetic hope that "the more intensive application of biochemistry to archaeology" will reveal more information on ancient diet, now a major specialty within the field.

From food supply, we move on to living areas, a cursory discussion of environment and settlement patterns, and then to houses and settlements, again a very superficial survey, which goes little further than the obvious. In discussing material culture, Clark urges maximizing the potential of well-preserved sites, such as wet locations, using rock art for interpretative purposes, as well as ethnographic analogy. "It is desirable to select parallels

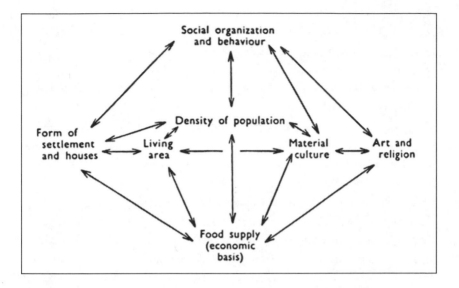

Figure 5.3   **The famous habitat, economy, and biome diagram from** *Archaeology and Society* **(1939).**

from cultures which do not differ too profoundly in environment and general cultural level," we are cautioned, and cultures showing not too remote links.[25] Clark advocated the use of folk survivals in the same area, an approach used with success in northern Germany and elsewhere, which formed one of the major foundations of his economic synthesis of European prehistory fifteen years later. Art and religion receive brief attention, with the major emphasis on rock art and its interpretation. "In the presence of phenomena for which he is unable to advance any rational explanation the archaeologist is almost as prone as early man himself to resort to 'religion'." "Caution in these matters is golden," he admonishes us, lest the "fair garden" of archaeology be overrun by "hordes of fertility and sun-worshippers."[26] The subsequent discussion is a superficial journey through fertility, sun worship, and burial customs.

"Population" discusses the difficult problem of estimating ancient populations and population growth, as much a matter of informed guesswork then as it is today. Clark himself used aboriginal population densities from North America to arrive at an Upper Palaeolithic population of Britain of some 250 people. "The entire population of Britain during Upper Palaeolithic times

could have been comfortably accommodated in four or five buses."[27] He estimated 3,000 to 4,000 inhabitants for Mesolithic Britain, with the population
increasing a hundredfold between Mesolithic and late Iron Age times. The
age structure of the population was also important, with life expectancy
being much shorter than today. A section of Chapter 6 entitled "Social
Organization and Behavior" also caused Clark to raise his hands in despair,
eking out inferences based on cautious ethnographic analogy. Estimating the
size of small social groups could be reasonably straightforward, evidence
from social stratification being obtained from burials and, sometimes, canni-
balistic remains.

After pages of cautious discussion, he warned against complacency.
"Although always ready to proclaim the youthfulness and vitality of their
subject, prehistorians are sometimes prone to behave as if it was mature."
The finest artifacts of the ancients may look magnificent when displayed in
a museum or illustrated in a textbook, but of themselves Clark considered
them of little more value than a collection of postage stamps. "They only
have meaning in relation to what had perished, and material culture has
meaning only in relation to society."[28]

Archaeology in Contemporary Society

Chapter 7, "Archaeology and Society," became the most quoted part of
the book and gave it its name. In it Grahame asked a question that engages
archaeologists to this day: "To what extent, and how, can archaeology sub-
serve a social purpose?" He believed its main application was in providing
"sentiments needful to the stability and, indeed, to the very existence of
society." Archaeology, he wrote, "multiplies and strengthens the links
which bind us to the past." With a touch of classic Clark elitism, he added:
"There can be no doubt that archaeology owes much of its appeal to its
power of satisfying sentiments based in the final analysis on the primitive
herd instincts, which nevertheless underlie human society." He drew
attention to early antiquarian studies such as William Camden's *Britannia,*
which appealed to nationalist sentiment, to King Henry VIII's appointment of John Leland as king's antiquary, and to recent archaeological
researches by the Irish government sponsored to draw attention to prehistoric times. He praised other nations such as China, Estonia, and
Turkey for their enlightened interest in their ancient heritage. As the

shadows of World War II lengthened over Europe, he castigated the exploitation of archaeology for "odious and predatory aims" by the fascist regimes of Germany and Italy. Mussolini's extravagant excavations in Rome of the 1930s prompted the remark: "It is as though the monuments of ancient Rome had been left unveiled to stand as silent witnesses to the pomp of the pinchbeck Second Empire."[29]

Mussolini's work paled beside the efforts of Nazi Germany to reconstruct the history of "early Germanic times." Clark quoted Heinrich Himmler: "Prehistory is the doctrine of the eminence of the Germans at the dawn of civilization," then castigated the theories of the notorious philologist Gustaf Kossina, who had devoted his career to demonstrating the superiority of the German people by, among other things, inflating the chronology of central European prehistory. Clark inveighed against the moral bankruptcy of a scholarship that was aimed at giving Germans, through cultural superiority, their right to dominate and exterminate inferior neighbors. He called it "diseased nationalism." On the other hand, archaeology had a modest role to play in evolving a world order that was a force for peace and in promoting notions of human unity. "In the dim but immense vistas of unrecorded time, the history of nations fades into the prehistory of man."[30]

Clark also argued for a closer relationship between archaeology and the natural sciences, especially in the area of human ecology, for prehistoric archaeology provided a good way of examining the interrelationships between ancient humans and their environments. As such, "archaeology has established itself as an integral part of the edifice of knowledge, an edifice which, if not continually extended and maintained, would collapse and in its turn destroy the basis of civilized life. The maintenance of learning and research at the highest level is no luxury, but a necessary condition for the existence of the modern community."[31]

The chapter ends with a passionate attack on archaeology in the Communist world. Clark did not consider the Soviet Union's archaeological activities a model for such activity, where archaeology, like the other sciences, primarily served society's aims and its political and economic theories. The task of a scholar in a totalitarian society was to interpret the past in the light of already established verities, while living at the mercy of suddenly changing political theories and established orthodoxies. Research was controlled from the stage of fieldwork to its ultimate popularization. In contrast, Western scholars spent their careers "for the most part assessing shades of grey; only rarely do flecks of black and white allow him to discern with comparative ease the contours of the truth."[32]

"It may be concluded that archaeology deserves to be cultivated in a free society first and foremost as an end in itself. . . . to enlarge and deepen man's knowledge of his own development."[33] Archaeologists should devote themselves to more than acquiring knowledge, even if some of it serves noble social ends, free from any ties to the requirements of states or dictatorial regimes. As for the state, it was a provider of basic services, like maps, and there were opportunities for archaeologists to work in such public agencies. But, in the final analysis, the standing of archaeology within a society was an index of "its degree of civilization."

Grahame Clark never deviated from this belief through the remainder of his long career. *Archaeology and Society* remains an eloquent statement of his approach to the prehistoric past. In 1939, he was on the cutting edge of archaeological thinking, with ideas that foreshadowed some of the theoretical furor of the 1960s, for which Clark had little respect. His approach to the past, clearly laid out in *Archaeology and Society*, was to remain virtually unchanged for over fifty years.

6

⊗⊗⊗

The War Years

I venture to think that Palaeolithic Man has more meaning than the Greeks. . . . Dig up Pekin Man and his crude implements and you establish ground of common interest to educated men of every race, something which concerns them all equally as men.

"Education and the Study of Man" [1]

By the outbreak of World War II in September 1939, Grahame Clark had become a widely respected archaeologist with three books and many significant papers to his credit. *Archaeology and Society* had been well reviewed. Gordon Childe, writing in *Antiquity*, praised the author's "philosophical depth and a breadth of vision quite exceptional among archaeologists." He proclaimed it a book for reading "in long dark evenings of isolation and alarm." In the *Archaeological Journal*, Jacquetta Hawkes said that the author exemplified "the modern trend in prehistory at its best." Stuart Piggott wrote perceptively that "the book . . . should brilliantly justify the author's claim that his subject has now been lifted from the lush but fever-stricken valleys of amateurish guessing, and is now finding its true haven in the bright cold air of at least the foothills of the scientific mountain range." He had also written *Prehistoric Britain*, a popular summary of prehistoric times, which took much the same approach and focused on activities as much as cultural sequences. [2]

Grahame's reputation extended into Germany and Scandinavia, thanks to his books and papers as well as his editorship of the *Proceedings of the Prehistoric Society*. He was in demand as a lecturer and was consulted about important excavations, thoroughly enjoying the experience of visiting the Sutton Hoo Anglo-Saxon ship burial excavations as the shadows of war gathered.[3] Under normal circumstances, his career would have unfolded smoothly, with perhaps an opportunity for a lectureship at another university as a stepping-stone to a chair. But the war intervened and a promising career went on hold.

A Paper on Wik Monkan

Grahame himself was still contemplating more work on the Mesolithic and Neolithic of the Fenland. In so doing, he had been influenced by a paper describing the seasonal round of the Aborigines of the Cape York region in northern Australia by anthropologist David Thomson, which had appeared in the *Proceedings* for 1939.[4] Thomson's essay foreshadows the ethnoarchaeological studies in the 1960s and 1970s of Australians, southern African San, and other hunter-gatherer groups which sought to use studies of living societies as a way of acquiring data for interpreting archaeological sites abandoned by ancient hunter-gatherers. He pointed out that the Cape York people recognized seasonal differences in their adaptations and classified their territory in reference to such important criteria as food resources and raw materials. The paper describes the seasonal round of the Wik Monkan people and points out how few material remains would be left for an archaeologist to study even if one passed the same way a few days later. The most durable structures were ovens made in shallow hollows, where fires were lit and stones or ant bed fragments laid atop the blaze, which heated the meat when the wood collapsed. Thomson concluded: "Remains of such cooking places will long remain to mark the places where the Aborigines have hunted in Northern Australia."[5]

Grahame was deeply impressed by this elegant but now largely forgotten paper, which linked ethnography and archaeology in real terms. It vindicated his perception that stone tools and debris alone were a totally inadequate archaeological signature for interpreting Mesolithic cultures. He readily admitted its influence on him for the rest of his career. Thomson's work was at the back of his mind during his Australian travels during the

1960s. Nearly thirty years earlier, Thomson's research turned Clark's thoughts even more toward economic and environmental issues. His planned fenland fieldwork for 1940 would have tested Thomson's seasonal theories close to home.

Clark was an inveterate note taker and reader. His editorship meant that he became familiar with research in many areas of archaeology. By 1939, he had assembled a substantial body of information on prehistoric subsistence, which followed the Scandinavian and German models of drawing on folklore and ethnography as well as organic finds from northern lakes and marshes. Where these notes would have carried him had not the war intervened, we do not know, but there is no question that environment and subsistence bore heavily on his thinking during the war years. In many ways, the involuntary pause in fieldwork and teaching was beneficial. For the first time, Grahame had some leisure to develop his ideas about environmental archaeology and ancient subsistence more thoroughly than might otherwise have been the case.

Aerial Intelligence

At first, young university teachers found themselves in a reserved occupation, so Clark was at loose ends while awaiting his call-up. *Archaeology and Society* had given him the impetus to learn more about Russian prehistory. Together with an archaeological colleague, Tom Patterson, Grahame passed the time by taking Russian lessons from the recently retired Professor Ellis Minns, with the objective of being able to read Soviet periodical literature. This proved somewhat easier than he had anticipated, owing to the extensive borrowing of Western archaeological terminology. Their last lesson proved the Rubicon. Minns gleefully confronted them with Pushkin, which humbled his young pupils and taught them just how far they had to go.

In due time, Clark was drafted into the Royal Air Force Volunteer reserve as a pilot officer and posted to the Central Interpretation Unit at Royal Air Force Medmenham in the Thames Valley, where, like many other archaeologists, he served in the aerial photograph interpretation unit. Medmenham was a hive of prehistorians who had worked together frequently in prewar years, among them Glyn Daniel, Dorothy Garrod (just appointed to the Disney Chair), Charles McBurney, and Stuart Piggott. Charles Phillips became station security officer. When the buildup to D-Day began, Old World prehistorian Hallam Movius of Harvard University also arrived. The work was demanding and required long hours, but at least there was a chance to talk shop and maintain some intellectual continuity, a bonus at a time when normal archaeological activity went into hibernation.

Clark seems to have kept his own counsel. According to Claire Wilson, who worked at Medmenham when he was there, Grahame was "polite but remote, with little small talk."[6] Most of the archaeologists were soon posted abroad. Glyn Daniel and Stuart Piggott were sent to India, where Daniel displayed a considerable talent for military administration.[7] Piggott served as an army officer in India from 1942 to 1945. During those years he traveled widely and saw the collections in the major Indian museums. His perceptive synthesis, *Prehistoric India,* owed much to his firsthand experience of field conditions and collections.[8] Charles McBurney was sent to Cyrenaica in North Africa, where he used his excursions during the Libyan campaign of 1942–1943 to search for Stone Age sites over a 1,200-mile length of the North African coast between Alexandria and Tripoli. Although Piggott never returned to India, McBurney mounted five more expeditions to Libya and spent three seasons excavating the huge cave at Haua Fteah, which provided an important Middle and Upper Palaeolithic sequence for a hitherto virtually unknown region. Several generations of Cambridge undergraduates learned artifact typology and animal bone identification from the Haua collections.[9]

Grahame remained in Britain because of a low health classification, which he always believed was the result of an attack of dysentery in earlier life. He was able to live with his family in a small, isolated house at Little Marlow in the Thames Valley until 1944, when he was transferred to the Air Historical branch based at Westminster in Central London. The Clarks and their children, a son and a daughter, reestablished their home on Barton Road in Cambridge.[10] He commuted to London every day, writing and editing articles for the *Proceedings* on the train. This habit continued after the war, when he would edit much of the *Proceedings* while traveling to committee meetings and lectures at the Prehistoric Society, the Society of Antiquaries, and elsewhere.

Throughout the war, Clark was determined to maintain the publishing activities of the Prehistoric Society despite acute paper shortages. The president, the redoubtable Gertrude Caton Thompson of Fayum and Great Zimbabwe fame, recommended to the council that they suspend all meetings but keep their publication program going as the best way of holding the society together.[11] The strategy worked remarkably well. The society ended the war with over six hundred members and a healthy balance sheet, largely because paper rationing kept the *Proceedings* short. Much of the credit for this should go to Grahame, who managed to produce a thin volume for each year of the war. The standard for papers remained remarkably high, notably a 1940 article on the dual nature of megaliths by Glyn Daniel, together with the first of a long series of articles on the petrological analysis of Neolithic stone axes. Grahame himself contributed an article on the first settlement of the Americas that drew attention to recent Clovis and Folsom finds and concluded that the first settlers enjoyed some form of Mesolithic culture and that their cultural roots were in northeast Asia. Only a trickle of articles on British archaeology appeared during the war, the most notable a survey of a barrow group in the New Forest threatened by frenzied wartime building. The most important articles described research overseas, including Dorothy Garrod's 1928 excavations in the Shukbah cave in Palestine (1942), Thurstan Shaw's important researches in the Late Stone Age Bosumpra rockshelter in the Gold Coast (now Ghana) (1943), still an important cultural sequence for the region, and Bernard Fagg's description of a microlithic industry recovered from the Rop shelter in Nigeria.

As soon as the war ended, Clark commissioned short articles from colleagues in Europe to describe archaeological researches that had taken place during the German occupation. Raymond Lanthier of the National Museum of Antiquities in Paris reported on a surprising amount of archaeological research, the appearance of *Gallia*, a new periodical for reporting excavations, and the dramatic Upper Palaeolithic cave art from Lascaux. A parallel article by Johannes Brøndsted on Denmark described numerous finds made during extensive peat digging in a time of fuel shortages.

Grahame's major contribution to the war effort was to keep the Prehistoric Society alive, so that it could take giant strides ahead when hostilities ended.

The London posting gave Clark some leisure time, which he spent visiting art galleries. He became friends with Arthur Baxendale, keeper of modern art at the National Gallery in Edinburgh, who kindled his interest in the subject. In later years, Grahame was an avid collector of up-and-coming artists under Baxendale's expert tutelage. In August 1943 he attended the

Future of Archaeology Conference held at the Institute of Archaeology in Regent's Park, where he delivered the introductory address.

The Future of Archaeology

The Future of Archaeology Conference was an informal gathering attended by a remarkable number of archaeologists, given the large number of their colleagues serving abroad at the time. The meeting revolved around twenty-nine delivered papers and included summaries of the present state of prehistoric, Romano-British, and medieval archaeology in Britain, with attempts to predict what issues would be important after the war. The atmosphere was informal and unusually freewheeling, making the transcripts of the discussions unusually interesting.

Kathleen Kenyon, a Mortimer Wheeler protégé who later became famous for her Jericho excavations, stressed the need for good basic training in excavation, artifact analysis, and interpretation. The issue of professionalism was on many delegates' minds, for at the time amateurs shouldered a considerable burden of excavation and fieldwork while making their living at the same time. There were calls for licensing excavators, a familiar issue even today. Cyril Fox advocated the National Artefact Card Index, while others urged the writing of archaeological guidebooks. Museums, overseas schools, and expeditionary funds, as well as the importance of archaeology for education at all levels, were predictable subjects.

It was business as usual, with one important exception. The pace of fieldwork and publication had slowed to a crawl, many archaeologists were otherwise engaged (many of them working in government bureaucracies), and there was time to step back and look at the state of British archaeology from a distance. Clark had written of Nazi misuses of archaeology in 1939, and the full extent of German atrocities and extreme nationalism were on the minds of many. It was no coincidence that much of the conference revolved around the issue of the relationship between archaeologists and the state, for Britain lacked the cohesive state archaeological organizations found in many other European countries. There were few coordinated research programs such as that of the Fenland Research Committee. Archaeology was still very largely an amateur discipline, with very few professionals on the ground, especially in universities. Many delegates expressed discontent with civil bureaucracy, much of it from firsthand war experience. Oxford archaeologist John Myres argued that the state's task was to preserve the past, not to sponsor and carry out research—the task of local and national archaeological societies. Clark strongly agreed: "I think that all of us have had experience of Government or Service Departments during the last few years and I feel very doubtful whether this experience has made us more enthusiastic for further contact." Others violently disagreed, among them Jacquetta Hawkes, who was spending the war with the Ministry of Information: "Archaeologists seem to be a flock of sheep flying before the big bad wolf of State Aid."[12] W. F. Grimes, then an archaeologist with the Office of Works, urged the formation of a government excavation grants board and careful control of excavation, which until then had been a matter for individual initiative, with very patchy results.

Much discussion centered around the organization of archaeology, based on statements about the frameworks used in France and Germany. Most speakers were concerned with the national interest, but Grahame returned to a theme of his introductory address: "Many speakers have stressed the National interest, but I would stress rather International interest." He expressed his admiration of "exceedingly far advanced" German research methods. "Card indexing, record, and so on are all magnificent. We are years behind, but where has it led Germany and where would it lead us?"[13]

Fear of state control ran deep among an archaeological community of individualists. Many feared imposing professionalism on amateur societies. Grahame came to the issue from a somewhat different perspective—a fear of totalitarianism and nationalism gone mad. Back in the 1930s, he had traveled widely while researching *The Mesolithic Settlement of Northern Europe,* made friends with German colleagues, and developed a warm admiration for their thorough methods, especially with organic sites and artifact typologies. At the time, he and other professional archaeologists were trying to give archaeology in Britain more national visibility and had pointed to the organization of German archaeology as a model. But he had also seen National Socialism and its political oratory firsthand and had followed the Nazis' prostitution of archaeology for nationalist ends, so his endorsement was a qualified one. By the time of the Future of Archaeology Conference, he was denouncing state control as a development with a potential for evil and arguing that "the solidarity of civilized men" had been undermined by the excesses of nationalism. Much more important were "world allegiance" and the commonalities of humanity. Archaeology was an international discipline that transcended all national boundaries and was a potential key-stone for the education of the future.

"Human Well-Being"

Grahame's introductory address to the Future of Archaeology Conference appeared in *Antiquity* and is among the most radical of his publications.[14] The meeting brought to the fore his years of thinking about archaeology's role in education, at a time when public debate about postwar schools was on the rise. He argued that "human well-being" should be the overriding aim of education rather than preparation for a career and achieving com-petitiveness in an increasingly competitive world. Education, he wrote, should be "anthropomorphic," aimed at helping people understand them-selves and humankind. What was needed in an increasingly global world in which nationalism was bankrupt was an approach to education that was based "fundamentally on the biological unity and cultural inheritance of mankind."[15] Science had examined astronomy, the structure of the earth, and other natural phenomena long before it turned its attention to humankind. The narrow shackles of theological dogma, which proclaimed that humans were created in God's image, stood in the way until the publi-cation of *The Origin of Species* in 1859. Since then, science had revealed an extraordinary chronicle of human achievement, which was largely neglect-ed by "educationists," just as scientists of the preevolutionary era did.

Warming to his theme, Grahame quoted the pioneer anthropologist Edward Tylor, who countered arguments that the educational curriculum was already too crowded to accommodate archaeology with the statement that "the science of Man and Civilization . . . connects to a more manage-able whole the scattered subjects of an ordinary education." Anthropology and prehistory had much to offer in this regard, especially in view of the remarkable advances of the past twenty or thirty years. Education in schools was a "parody of knowledge," Clark argued cogently, "graded bands of intellectual pabulum done up in conventional packets; at worst they are degraded into media for the acquisition of marks in competitive examina-tions. . . . Such education breeds barbarians possessed of a little knowl-edge in restricted fields, but unaware of its relation to life in human soci-ety, individuals fit only for regimentation by bureaucrats, themselves among the most accomplished and therefore the most deplorable products of the system."[16] Anthropology and prehistory focus on humanity. They and they alone of all academic disciplines can bridge the gaps between the arts and the sciences.

Anthropology and prehistory were so all-embracing that they should permeate all education, even provide a framework to learn about humanity's place in nature and about the development of human society and civilization. Education's primary goal should be to train people to live in the world as human beings, rather than as individuals or members of different societies. Thinking in a world of vastly improved communications must be global and based on tradition, our common past. Education should be based in the "common experience of humanity, its emergence from the world of beasts, its age-long struggle for betterment." Grahame attacked scholars who thought of education as merely Christian or Hellenistic, based on the concepts of their remote youths. "I venture to think that Palaeolithic Man has more meaning than the Greeks. . . . Excavate Pekin Man and his crude implements and you establish common ground of interest to educated men of every race, something which concerns them all equally as men."[17]

What, then, would such a curriculum embrace? First, "the relation of man to the universe, stages in his evolution, the definition of his principal varieties," in other words, human diversity. Second, "the outlines of world prehistory from the earliest times to the period of the discoveries basic to civilization." Then one could also introduce the natural sciences and many humanist disciplines as natural and necessary extensions of "life at large." Once this common basis of understanding is laid, then "comes the time for building an edifice in accordance with whatever cultural tradition prevails in the society concerned." Among the priorities, Clark listed human cultural diversity, the notion that people's roots go deeper than their own community, a strategy that would militate against the narrow tribalism of nationalisms and other strident agendas. Grahame argued that modern history and cultural affairs should be reserved for "the closing stages of secondary or even for higher and adult education." "There is much to be said for school history books stopping short at 1789, provided that further instruction is forthcoming either at the university or in the course of some extension learning." Such a curriculum would treat the "childhood of the race" in elementary school, the "birth and growth of his own peculiar civilization" in secondary school, modern history later.

Clark was careful to emphasize that he had nothing against the diversity of history or the "cultivation of diverse traditions." But societies as a whole should be concerned with the earliest human history, which forms a heritage of incalculable value to individuals, societies, and the "One World." In a prophetic statement, he remarked that "no amount of political or economic well-being can compensate for lack of appreciation of, and sympathy for, native culture." He urged a diversity of education in people's indigenous histories, a conscious step back from the standardized schooling and training of an increasingly homogeneous and industrialized world, in which we "draw inspiration from the traditions and achievements of the race." Humans differed from animals in the possession of culture. We were cultural beings capable of leading full and satisfying lives. But we had forgotten what culture is, the "'cultural barbarians', who proliferate in our great cities, constitute, like the infiltrating barbarians of antiquity, a fifth column of portentous dimensions."[18] Humans must be reacquainted with their heritage as cultural beings.

Grahame Clark's passionate advocacy of the value of archaeology in education reveals his ardently international view of human prehistory. His interest in "world prehistory," a phrase he used deliberately in the *Antiquity* paper, went back to his very early career. He was always engaged with the wider picture of his research, whether a fenland excavation or a survey of Mesolithic Britain. His concerns were with changes in human cultures that resulted from migration or, increasingly in his later writings, from environmental change and adaptation. Such perspectives, his interest in organic sites, and the long tradition at Cambridge of training undergraduates for a career in the Colonial Service, meant that intellectually he jumped national boundaries as part of his own specialized research. Another catalyst was the editorship of the *Proceedings of the Prehistoric Society*, as he pursued a policy of publishing papers on topics far outside the narrow confines of Britain and Europe. As early as 1937, the *Proceedings* boasted of a research report section that covered briefly discoveries made in many parts of the world. During the war years, *PPS* published an extraordinary range of overseas papers, which would have had little interest for most members of the Prehistoric Society but Grahame published them anyway because he considered them important. Long before *Archaeology and Society,* with its many international examples, and years before the Future of Archaeology Conference, Grahame Clark was thinking of world prehistory as a viable intellectual prospect.

Clark's introductory address to the conference had deep roots in the increasingly eclectic archaeology at Cambridge, and in his growing revulsion for state-controlled archaeology and nationalist contortion of the past. By the time the meeting convened, he had reevaluated his initial attraction to state control in what he perceived as a rapidly changing archaeological world of much easier communication and constant global interchange. His paper writes of a "world prehistory," but it would be naive to think that the notion of a truly global archaeological perspective divorced from notions of linear human progress was Clark's alone. As another Cambridge archaeologist, Christopher Evans, has pointed out, to some degree world prehistory was a product of the momentous changes wrought by World War II—improved communications, the global perspectives and international future thinking engendered by the formation of the United Nations in 1945, major advances and faith in the potential of science, and a resurgence of postwar idealism.[19] But the conference was a catalyst for Grahame Clark, as he saw clearly the consequences of prewar archaeology and firmly embraced world prehistory as a long-term goal, but a prehistory firmly based on notions of the biological unity of humankind and human responses to changing environments. This global perspective, albeit firmly anchored in Cambridge, permeated much of Clark's work after 1943.

Economic Prehistory

Archaeology and Society sold well and a second edition appeared two years after the war, in 1947. While researching the book, Clark began accumulating a large body of information on the economies of prehistoric Europe, much of it stemming from his work for the *Mesolithic Settlement of Northern Europe*. The outbreak of hostilities brought this long-term research to a standstill but did not prevent him from refining his ideas on a new approach to archaeology based not on artifact typologies, stone tools, and other inorganic finds, but on organic remains and environmental data.

Clark's economic prehistory came from diverse intellectual strands—from his multidisciplinary fenland experience and extensive travels through northern Europe, where organic sites were commonplace, from wide reading in European anthropology, history, and folklore, and from an unrivaled knowledge of Mesolithic and Neolithic museum collections. Above all, it came from his unique breadth of vision, which rose above local detail to grasp broad issues and long-term trends, the interplays between patterns of human settlement and changing environmental conditions. He realized that finding artifacts in deposits that could be linked to Postglacial climatic changes gave archaeologists a unique opportunity to study the ways people adapted to their environments and made a living. Economic prehistory was closely linked to environment and ecology.

Few scholars, except perhaps some Scandinavians, could imagine writing the steady stream of papers that appeared under his name between 1942 and 1948 on such diverse and obscure topics as bees, water, seals, whale hunting, sheep, fishing, and fowling. By no means were all the ideas Clark's, for he read omnivorously and made notes on even the most obscure papers. His ability lay in his gift of sensing which approaches were important in the wider world of archaeology. In 1944, for example, Harry Godwin drew his attention to a paper by the Danish palynologist Johannes Iversen published by the Danish Geological Survey in 1941.[20] Iversen had analyzed pollen cores from Ordrup marsh, where he managed to identify sudden drops in tree cover at the moment when traces of Neolithic settlement appeared. At the same time, domesticated cereal pollens and cultivation weeds like *Plantago lanceolata* appeared for the first time. Clark was electrified by the Iversen paper, which demonstrated the potential of palynology for the study of the spread of agriculture across Europe. He developed this theme in a paper at a conference at the London Institute of Archaeology in 1944.[21]

Clark's first substantive excursion into economic prehistory came with an *Antiquity* paper, "Bees in Antiquity," published in 1942.[22] The article was a survey of what was known about a neglected subject archaeologically. "They serve to point a moral," wrote Clark. "The tendency has all too frequently been to concentrate on those aspects of ancient cultures which lend themselves most readily to classification." He urged an approach that studied how people had lived in society, of how they exerted themselves within their society to satisfy their wants. From this perspective, a way in which people gratified their taste for sweets "merits as least as much attention as current fashions in safety-pins and other topics beloved of 'museologists.'"[23]

That said, Grahame surveyed the extraction of beet sugar and cane sugar, the latter having considerable antiquity in India, then spreading widely with the expansion of Islam and during the European Age of Discovery. Before sugar, honey was the main source of sweetness, eagerly sought by prehistoric and living hunter-gatherer peoples, witness rock

Figure 6.1   **"Raiding the wild bees' nest. A scene from rock-paintings at La Cuevas de la Arāna, Valencia, Spain." An illustration from "Bees in Antiquity" (Figure 1). Courtesy, The** *Antiquity* **Trust.**

paintings of ancient honey collectors from southeastern Spain and Donald Thomson's Aborigines from the Cape York region of northern Australia (Figure 6.1). Grahame pointed out that pliant rods and bark receptacles used by the Aborigines to collect honey would never survive in the archaeological record. We learn that the ancient Egyptians domesticated bees and that beekeepers were a recognized profession. They placed a high premium on honey for sweetening food, as an element in perfume, and as an intoxicant, sometimes mixed with wine. Clark reported a Bronze Age concoction of honey, myrtle, and cranberry wine from Denmark and explored the early history of mead in Europe, a liquor obtained by boiling drained honeycombs and "still consumed among some of the Finno-Ougrian peoples." He stressed the importance of beeswax for modeling the features of Egyptian mummies, ancestral wax masks fabricated by the Romans, Renaissance medallions, and the originals for some Wedgwood pottery designs. Above all, prehistoric Europeans made use of it for *cire-perdue* casts in metalworking. A clay model of a metal artifact or ornament was encased in a clay mold, then heated so that the wax flowed out, to be replaced by molten ore.

Clark was unable to establish whether prehistoric European farmers had practiced beekeeping or whether they merely collected wild honey, but he believed apiculture to be of high antiquity. So he turned to folklore to describe Finno-Ougrian peoples in the Volga region, who both collected wild honey and "improved" woodpecker holes with perforated boards to make them attractive to bees. The collector would then remove a board and collect the honey with ease. Some communities even developed "bee-gardens," clusters of boarded trunk holes close to human settlements. He describes the ways in which individuals marked bees' nests as their personal property, a practice that was widespread in medieval Europe and was the subject of frequent lawsuits. Europe, he wrote, was a place with extensive flower-bearing pasture, a land, like biblical Palestine, "flowing with milk and honey." He recalled an old European saying that where there was good wool, there would be good honey and theorized that the pastoral economies of Bronze Age Europe favored beekeeping. "Which tell us more, the bees or the bronzes?" he asked. "A question-begging question. In the study of any society, past or present, no aspect can be safely omitted, for all are interdependent."[24]

This seemingly obscure paper might seem, on the face of it, to be exploring an esoteric byway of the past, but it was the first article in which Grahame explicitly espoused economic prehistory as an alternative to traditional culture history. "Bees in Antiquity" married archaeology, historical sources, and folk culture in an effortless, wide-ranging synthesis that expanded the frontiers of archaeological knowledge about the subject without exceeding the bounds of reasonable inference. This approach became a Clark trademark, and he employed it in papers on an eclectic range of economic topics.

In 1944, he returned to the pages of *Antiquity* once more with "Water in Antiquity," exploring a neglected factor in prehistoric settlement and ritual life, and a substance that had done much to preserve organic remains of the past.[25] Clark reviewed the potential of Pleistocene geology for studying changes in Stone Age settlement, citing the recently completed fieldwork by Gertrude Caton Thompson in Egypt's Kharga oasis, where she found Acheulian hand axes in association with fossil spring deposits. He then turned his attention to ways of securing water by improving natural spring sites with boulders or hollow tree trunks to enable the dipping of containers. He cited examples from Bronze Age Denmark, where votive offerings of bronze ornaments were found in the bubbling water, and described divination rituals at English holy wells and cites the offerings at the St. Moritz spring in the Swiss Alps, which was an important place of pilgrimage because of its healing springs as early as medieval times and, judging from Bronze Age offerings in its waters, even earlier.

The artificial well was a major invention, probably associated with the rise of cities, cut into rock subsoil or lined with bricks as at Mohenjodaro on the Indus River, layers of bricks being added as the city mound accumulated. The Romans used stone or timber to line wells, some of the largest being the stepped wells on the Saalburg frontier station in Central Europe, where they dug no less than ninety-eight, only about three being in use at one time. It is they who introduced well technology to Europe.

From wells, we move on to lifting devices, the simple rope and bucket, the ancient Egyptian lever-like *shaduf*, and the many variations on the same theme throughout the world, and Roman aqueducts and pumps. Clark describes pipes and channels for moving water, reservoirs and cisterns for collecting rainwater, as much for industrial purposes as for drinking, even baths and drainage systems. Irrigation agriculture was a catalyst for many developments in water-lifting technology such as the water wheels of Babylon and the screw pumps devised by Archimedes of Syracuse for draining mine shafts. Finally, he emphasizes the importance of water mills powered by flowing water that were such a vital element in European feudal agriculture. "So, from the Stone Age to the 20th century has water reflected the image of society," he concluded, remarking that the harnessing of water power requires collective rather than individual activity. Not such a distinguished paper as "bees," perhaps, but, again, a broad-ranging survey that showed no hesitation in moving from one period to another, often remote in time and place in the interests of discussing a critical reality in ancient and modern human life.

Grahame's war years were far from wasted intellectually, for he had time to think about issues that had been at the back of his mind for some time. Relieved of the distractions of fieldwork and teaching, he maintained *PPS* with one hand and nurtured two intellectual concerns—economic archaeology and world prehistory—with the other. Both dominated Grahame's thinking in his highly productive postwar years.

7

⟨≋⟩

The Economic Basis

Whatever the ultimate inspiration or the intermediate cause, it was by
their hands that the early Europeans dragged themselves out of the
primeval mire of savagery, struggled up the long and undulating slopes of
barbarism and ultimately attained to some kind of civilization.

Prehistoric Europe: The Economic Basis [1]

G rahame Clark had been an assistant lecturer in the Department of
Archaeology and Anthropology at Cambridge since 1935, his career
frozen for the duration of the war years. Demobilized in 1946, he was
appointed a full lecturer at a moment when the returning Dorothy Garrod
began to give substance to a much wider vision of prehistory than that
taught under the Minns regime before the war. Quiet and retiring, Garrod
enjoyed a stellar reputation for her Mount Carmel research in Palestine,
which had completely redefined the study of the origins of modern humanity in Europe. Fortunately, she found herself with a returning faculty
unscathed by hostilities. With Glyn Daniel, Charles McBurney, and
Grahame Clark, she had in place a team who were well aware of the wider
archaeological world. Within two years, Garrod designed and implement-
ed a Part II tripos in archaeology and anthropology, which gave undergraduates a much wider range of choices.[2] The tripos continued to marry
archaeology and anthropology and drew on classical and Oriental language

as well, creating a broadly based curriculum that allowed a student to explore specialized options from the second year onward. The Part II organization put in place by Garrod was remarkably effective and trained an entire generation of professional archaeologists in fields as diverse as Stone Age prehistory and medieval archaeology. It survives, albeit in considerably modified form, to this day.

The department was built on a foundation of Miles Burkitt's lectures to Part I students, which helped attract many undergraduates to archaeology until his retirement in 1958. Garrod also recruited Americanist Geoffrey Bushnell as curator of the Haddon Museum. A geologist by training, Bushnell started his career as an oil executive in Ecuador, became interested in Andean archaeology, and obtained his Ph.D. in archaeology for work on the Santa Elena cemetery in the southwest of the country. He added a useful dimension to an increasingly international department, in which method and theory in archaeology was now a compulsory course topic for Part II students, who could choose from various options obtained by combining courses from several departments. Theoretically, one could take Part II in Egyptology, Mediterranean archaeology, or Indian archaeology, but most focused on prehistory and relied on the training given by the faculty in the department. One option covered the Palaeolithic and Mesolithic of Europe and the Mediterranean area, involving course work by Clark, Garrod, and McBurney. Another dealt with the later prehistory of Europe, taught mainly by Daniel, a third with the archaeology and protohistory of northwestern Europe.

Clark was itching to do fieldwork, for he and his colleagues regarded this as an essential part of the curriculum. During the long (summer) vacation of 1947, Grahame led a team of undergraduates on an excavation at Bullock's Haste on the Car Dyke at Cottenham, close to Cambridge. A cross-section through the dyke revealed early Roman occupation and suggested it might have served as a canal.[3] No less than 350 man-hours of excavation went into the fieldwork. Among those taking part was John D. Evans, later to become a Mediterranean archaeologist and director of the London Institute of Archaeology after Gordon Childe. Many of the students on the dig were members of the newly resurrected Cambridge Archaeology Field Club. As before, the club served as a means of training undergraduates in field methods, as well as attracting outside lecturers to Cambridge. Clark had also reopened his Scandinavian connections directly after the war. Three Swedish students, all of whom later became professional scholars, worked on the Car Dyke excavation for a week under the auspices of the British Council.

The end of the war found the Prehistoric Society in surprisingly good fettle, with over six hundred members in good standing, a budget surplus in the bank, and the *Proceedings* published continuously through the war years. The society geared up for an expansion of its activities, electing a keen amateur archaeologist and experienced administrator, Sir Lindsay Scott, as president for a special four-year term to oversee the rebuilding process. At the same time, the council appointed four vice presidents to serve for variable periods to assist with the work and provide continuity. Grahame lobbied for editorial assistants and was able to persuade Stuart Piggott and the Stone Age archaeologist Kenneth Oakley of the British Museum to serve in this capacity.

The first issue of the *Proceedings* after the war was nearly three times longer than its predecessors. The lead article was by the wartime president, Gertrude Caton Thompson, who wrote about the Levallois industries of North Africa in a paper that was an important baseline for future field seasons by Charles McBurney and others.[4] The tradition of survey papers on archaeology during the war years continued with a paper by Professor Sean O'Riordan of University College, Dublin, on research in Ireland from 1937 to 1943. Here also, archaeology had come to a virtual standstill, largely because the government had stopped sending laborers on excavations to reduce unemployment, redeploying them to food production and peat digging for fuel. Harry Godwin contributed an important paper on the relationships between bog stratigraphy, climate, and archaeology, which summarized his thinking on these themes since the Fenland work of the late 1930s. This stellar volume and its immediate successors helped establish the *Proceedings of the Prehistoric Society* as one of the leading archaeological journals in the postwar world.

Few people realize just how much time and energy Grahame Clark lavished on the Prehistoric Society and its *Proceedings* throughout his career. He attended virtually every council meeting, lecture, and conference for years, editing, and often rewriting, papers on the Cambridge to London train, the pages scattered on carriage seats and sometimes on the floor. His editorship and appreciation of archaeology in distant lands fostered the development of world prehistory as a practical and intellectual concept in many inconspicuous ways.

Travels in Norway and Finland

Grahame also continued his research on prehistoric subsistence. He obtained a Leverhulme Fellowship in 1947 and 1948, which enabled him to travel extensively in northwestern and central Europe.[5] During the 1947 long vacation, he traveled "light with a rucksack" across Scandinavia and explored environments known only to him from the literature. He called on Danish prehistorian Johannes Brøndsted, director of the National Museum in Copenhagen. In Bergen, he made contact with Professor Knut Faegri, a leading authority on pollen analysis, and "enjoyed sea bathing with Professor Johs Bøe, who held the chair of archaeology at Bergen." He then traveled by small boat up the Norwegian coast as far as Trømso. The boat called in at small ports and remote fishing villages, bringing mail and provisions. Grahame would go ashore for milk and food, where he observed firsthand the complete dependence of small communities on fishing and the ways in which they preserved catches for use during the winter. Both cod fishing and drying methods had changed little since ancient times. "Peat-stacks on the higher ground, small-wheeled carts carried it down to the township," he wrote of the town of Rörvik in his travel notes. The boat took them through ancient Stone Age fishing grounds, where he was intrigued to see that the same kinds of timber frames were still used to dry fish and hay. He was fascinated to learn that fishmeal was fed to cattle, "signs that as in prehistoric times hunting and fishing economies were still being practiced side by side." He studied flint collections in Trømso ("depressing in the rain") and Narvik, journeying between them by bus, observing with interest that "the hay was already partly gathered into the wooden stores. The drying racks here made almost all of wood—on the coast usually wooden uprights and wire horizontals." Leaving bomb-damaged Narvik, he traveled by train across Lapland as far as Harparanda at the head of the Gulf of Bosnia.

A short walk took him across the border into Finland. He boarded a train in a forest clearing bound for Helsinki, which was packed with drunken soldiers and refugees from the Soviet Union. When the soldiers became too intoxicated, they were slung unceremoniously off the train into the forest. The journey was "incredibly uncomfortable, slow, bumpy, smoke-laden and crowded." He stayed in a good hotel in Helsinki but found himself sleeping on paper sheets and drinking coffee brewed from parched grain, so austere were the measures taken by the Finns to pay off wartime reparations imposed by the Soviets. He called on Dr. C. A. Nordmann, director of the museum, a fellow Mesolithic specialist, and paid careful attention to the artifacts of the Stone Age coastal cultures of the region. He also spent hours talking to Dr. T. I. Ikonen about Finno-Ougrian (or Finno-Ugrian) folk culture and was struck by his host's Finno-Ougrian features. In Stockholm, he "re-entered the Nordic zone with a vengeance," called on old friends and colleagues, and examined hunting and traveling artifacts in the Nordisk Museum.[6] Some of the Leverhulme money also allowed him to visit Switzerland to inspect the organic finds from the Swiss Lake Dwellings at the Landesmuseum in Zurich and elsewhere. All these travels gave him a vivid impression of the folk culture and ecology of regions on the northern and southern margin of the temperate zone, and a chance to examine archaeological sites and collections.

Wherever Clark traveled, he experienced firsthand the traditional economic practices of both coastal and inland communities that were flourishing before industrial agriculture and the Common Market. He reveled in the rich folk culture of the northlands, in the wide use of simple organic materials like saplings and fiber nets for fishing, and he saw endless opportunities for profitable analogy between past and present economic practice. Of all Grahame's travels, this, and a journey to Australia in 1964 (Chapter 11), probably exercised the most pervasive influence on his archaeological thinking about economic prehistory.

He had already assembled a considerable body of information from the European literature, enough to write his wartime papers on bees and water for *Antiquity* and to develop a major paper on seal hunting for the 1946 *Proceedings*.

Seal and Whale Hunting

"The research, on which the present paper is based, is part of a programme to further knowledge of prehistoric times by the study of social activities," Clark announced at the outset. "The more we discover about any human activity the more fitted we become to interpret correctly the material objects or structures associated with it." His research was not based on archaeology alone, but on biological taxonomies and the observations of Scandinavian biologists in the field, "which enabled us to visualize the

opportunities open to the old hunters." Apart from vital stratigraphic dat-
ings by Quaternary geologists, his research was also "guided by the light of
ethnology," as well as more telling "analogies drawn from the folk culture of
northern Europe, whether still or recently extant, or whether recorded by
earlier observers."[7] Grahame quoted approvingly from a paper by the
Scandinavian archaeologist A. W. Brøgger in *Antiquity* for 1940: "To be able
to approach any understanding at all of the culture of antiquity, it is
absolutely necessary to begin with what we know today—to know the elements in peasant culture still found in Norway and Sweden some 50 to 100
years ago; to know something of life along the coast and at sea, in the forests
and amid the mountains, on the land, the fields, the pastures, the hinterland
and the mountain farms" (Figure 7.1).[8]

The study began with a description of the distribution and habits of the
four main species of seal hunted by Stone Age hunters in northern
Europe. From there, he moved on to the evidence for prehistoric seal
hunting, the earliest coming from Upper Palaeolithic sites in southwestern France, mainly quarry taken as hunters pursued salmon far up rivers.
Rising sea levels had buried Late Glacial sites, so the coastlines of the
Litorina Sea, dating to Boreal times, yielded the first plentiful evidence of
Mesolithic seal hunting. Here Clark used the simple narrative of sites, find
spots, and distribution maps perfected in his earlier Mesolithic researches to build up a picture of a hunting activity that persisted into the
Neolithic and later, complete with isolated finds of seal skeletons associated with barbed elk bone harpoons in Litorina Sea clays—kills lost by
hunters in deep water.

After a brief consideration of different seal prey, Clark turned his attention to hunting methods, where he let his fascination with Scandinavian
folklore come into full play. He ranged effortlessly over a staggering array
of sources. We learn of horsehair seal nets and clubbing forays in the
Western Isles of Scotland: "A savage slaughter with clubs and staves
becomes the order of the day, or rather of the night."[9] The Finns used nets
to trap seals leaping from rocks into the sea or swimming through ice-free
leads through ice floes. He included a 1539 map by Olaus Magnus depicting black clad seal hunters kneeling on ice floes, tethered to their boats full
of their victims. We learn that a version of the Eskimo *máupoq* method flourished in Sweden, where white-clad ice hunters would wait for hours to harpoon a seal through a tiny breathing hole.

Figure 7.1 Olaus Magnus (1539): Seal-Hunting at the Head of the Gulf of Bothnia. This drawing appeared in Clark's "Seal-Hunting in the Stone Age" [Figure 10].

What relevance did these observations have to Stone Age seal hunting? Here Clark faced problems "inherent in the nature of the evidence," which he sought to overcome by the doctrine of reasonable supposition. For example, he argued for the use of clubs, unknown in the archaeological record, since we knew that Stone Age hunters slaughtered large numbers of seals at favored locations. Nets too were a possibility, since Mesolithic and Neolithic fisherfolk used them. Only harpoons survived with certainty, which Clark described in some detail, including specimens found in male graves, "which only confirms that seal-hunting was, as might have been expected, a masculine occupation."[10] He argued for the possible use of dogs in seal hunting, "in modern Finland dogs were used to scent out the breathing holes of seals," and assumed that the hunters used skin boats for taking their prey on open water, citing rock engravings of putative skin boats in Norway.

Seals had many economic uses for Stone Age peoples, again elaborated from folk culture sources. Simple chemical analyses of the residues in stone lamps showed that seal blubber was used for lighting and heating, known for certain to have been used in Ertebølle clay lamps, the skins for clothing, and many other items of equipment, including skin boats. According to the medieval Norse lord Othere, seal hide ropes were used at sea and on land, while the Scottish islanders used them to haul plows. Seal bone made good harpoon heads, while seal flesh was commonly eaten, the flippers being considered a special delicacy.

Seal hunting assumed considerable importance in Scandinavia with the appearance of Neolithic farming cultures in neighboring areas. A flourishing trade in seal oil and skins developed, with beef and grain being taken in exchange in a form of symbiosis that survived until modern times. Clark cited the seal-hunting islands of Kihnu and Ruhnu in the eastern Baltic's Gulf of Riga, whose inhabitants traded such commodities for corn, salt, iron, and other goods from the Estonian mainland right into the twentieth century.

"Seal hunting in the Stone Age" became a model for a certain genre of Clark papers, which appeared at intervals over the following years. The formula varied but little: a survey of archaeological data, sites, and distribution maps, combined with a discussion of often esoteric folklore sources that provided a context for discussing a particular prehistoric economic activity. Such require a unique blend of a broad, synthetic vision and a detailed command of the basic data and sources, a combination rare in any scholar and especially in archaeologists of Clark's, or any, generation. The French historian Emmanuel Le Roy Ladurie once remarked that there were two kinds of historians: parachutists and truffle hunters. The parachutist observes the past from afar, slowly floating down to earth, while the truffle hunter, fascinated by treasures in the soil, keeps a nose close to the ground.[11] Some of us are by temperament parachutists in everyday life. Others are truffle hunters, with fine minds for detail. Ladurie's characterization can be applied to archaeologists with equal facility. Grahame Clark combined the best qualities of a parachutist with a remarkable grasp of detail, much of it acquired from reading literature in several languages and still more from far-flung travels to sites and museums.

He followed his seal hunting article with another important survey, this time of whaling, which appeared in *Antiquity* in 1947. "Whales as an economic factor in prehistoric Europe" followed the same pattern as the sealing paper.[12] He began with a description of the various whale species found in European waters, some of which were never pursued until historic times owing to their habitats near pack ice, their speed, or their lack of buoyancy. The Biscay Right whale, porpoises, pilot whales, and other dolphins could have been taken with simple methods or could have been exploited when they stranded. Clark recalled that strandings were important events, meticulously recorded because almost invariably disputes arose over ownership of such an economically valuable resource. We learn that the tongues of whales stranded in the Chichester bishopric were the property of the monarch, of Olaus Magnus's calculation that a single whale's blubber, bones, and meat could fill between 250 and 300 wagons, of quarrels over a stranded rorqual in which rivals came to blows with lumps of blubber. From historical events, we move on to a valuable survey of known prehistoric strandings, notably in Scotland's Firth of Forth, there associated with Stone Age antler picks and other artifacts, and a Stone Age example on a beach of the Litorina Sea in Jutland. Then we proceed to archaeological occurrences of whale bones, especially from Scandinavia, with a distribution map showing whale forms and recorded sites (Figure 7.2). Finally, Clark reminded the reader of depictions of cetaceans on Arctic rock engravings.

Regarding the economic uses of whales, he remarked on their importance as sources of heat and light, indulging his fondness for folklore with a description of the consumption of porpoises at the court of King James V of Scotland and of Basque whale markets. Whale meat was also consumed in prehistoric times, while the bones fulfilled a multitude of uses and were used for house construction and even fuel. Clark noted that stranded or slaughtered whales would normally leave almost no trace in the archaeological record, except when their bones were used for artifacts or as fuel or housing materials.

The seal and whale papers, as well as others on forest clearance, were eye openers to British prehistorians, once again. Their use of folk culture and historical sources gave a fresh slant to the archaeological evidence. Each displayed a formidable array of scholarship. Such papers were hard to write even in the 1940s, when there was much less data to play with. Today, they would be almost impossible to carry off, given the huge mass of informa-

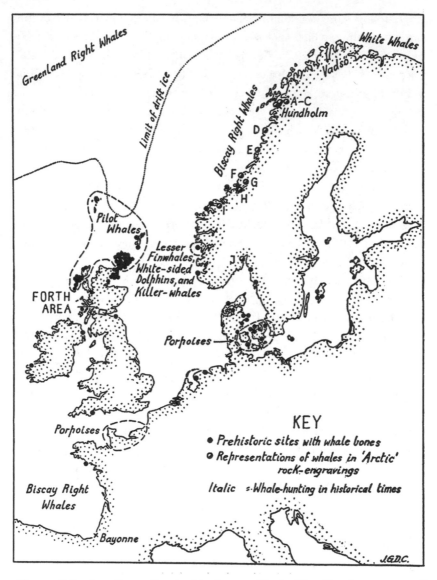

Figure 7.2 Another classic Grahame Clark distribution map, of whale bones found at prehistoric sites, from "Whales in Prehistoric Europe" [Figure 6].

tion that has come out of the ground in the past half century. At the time, they were a breath of fresh air in a world of European archaeology still preoccupied with artifacts.

Archaeology and Folk Culture

In 1950, Clark was elected to a fellowship at Peterhouse, an appointment he held for forty-five years, including seven years as master (1973 to 1980). The fellowship exposed him to a broad range of academic disciplines and to some remarkable scholars, among them the economic historian Michael Postan, lecturer, then professor of economic history as well as a fellow of the college (since 1935). Postan was perhaps the most important economic historian of his generation, one of the first scholars to make use of such sources as monastic records to look at medieval subsistence agriculture. His *Historical Methods in the Social Sciences*, published in 1939, introduced his approach to a wider audience, but it was his studies of medieval agriculture that stimulated Grahame to take another look at Neolithic farming. He had done little on the subject since writing a paper on the spread of agriculture into Europe in 1945, but Postan's quantitative studies on the dynamics of subsistence farming, subsequently published in his classic *The Medieval Economy and Society*, rekindled Clark's interest in farming and folk culture.[13]

For many years, Clark and Postan were close colleagues who bounced ideas off each other at college dinners and on other occasions. Michael Postan was an inconspicuous but important cornerstone of the new economic prehistory, for he alerted his archaeological colleague to the realities and hazards of subsistence agriculture in early historic Europe, which were little changed from much earlier prehistoric times.

Folk culture dominated much of Clark's thinking during the late 1940s, partly because of his Leverhulme travels in Scandinavia, but also because of his abiding concern with prehistoric subsistence and economic life. In 1951, he contributed an article on folk culture to a volume of essays in honor of O. G. S. Crawford, the founding Editor of *Antiquity*. He paid tribute to Crawford's concern with the unity of humankind, to his efforts to "restore the flesh and blood and to make the past a reality to the present generation."[14] These efforts recalled the writings of Sven Nilsson, the first scholar to formulate an economic model of hunting, then pastoralism and agriculture, using ethnographic observations. Sir John Lubbock, a

Victorian archaeologist, had also remarked that "if we wish clearly to understand the antiquities of Europe, we must compare them with the rude implements and weapons still, or until lately, used by savage races in other parts of the world." Grahame cautioned against doctrines of universal stages of human evolution and against uncritical analogy: "The greatest caution is needed in using existing savages as sources for reconstructing prehistoric savagery." Yet much could be learned by judicious use of the comparative method, especially when there was a continuous historical sequence between prehistory and modern times and environmental conditions had not changed significantly.

Clark argued that the "Folk-Culture of the highly civilized parts of Europe" offered potential for such comparative research. By folk culture he meant the culture of "those who are mainly outside the currents of urban culture and systematic education." At the core of such research was the demonstration of historical continuity for the "rural substratum which preserves continuity with the prehistoric past." In Europe, such evidence had survived best in areas least touched by the Industrial Revolution, such as "the Celtic fringe of Britain, the Scandinavian countries, the Alps, the Balkans and the Mediterranean Basin."[15]

After citing some notable research on organic sites such as the Swiss Lake Dwellings and the brilliant excavations on the Iron Age settlement at Little Woodbury by Gerhard Bersu, Grahame warmed to his central theme. Folk culture could tell us much about ancient subsistence, and especially prehistoric farming practices. He pointed to Scandinavia, where people living on the margins of farming areas continued their traditional hunting and fishing practices alongside subsistence farming. "Here the same rhythm of ploughing, sowing and harvesting, interspersed with hunting and catching the same land and sea mammals, the same fowls and fishes, has persisted since prehistoric times."[16] His seal and whaling papers offered some idea of the potential that folk culture approaches offered.

Folk culture even gave insights into the ways people domesticated plants. Grahame cites examples from eastern Europe and Scandinavia, where it was possible to study the "different stages between the gathering of the wild form and its domestication." Swiss farmers would fence off wild alpine sorrel to preserve it as fodder for their cattle. In places where it would not grow naturally, the farmers would plant it deliberately. "The symbiosis between men and plants . . . may well explain how domestication devel-

Figure 7.3 Under the Yoke: Burning the Brushwood. Oil on canvas painting by Finnish artist Eero Järnefelt (1863–1937), painted in 1893 near Lapinlahti in eastern Finland. Järnefelt was a major artist during the so-called golden age of Finnish painting. *Under the Yoke* was one of his major works. Grahame Clark published the painting in *Prehistoric Europe* to epitomize traditional European slash-and-burn agriculture. Reproduced with the kind permission of the Ateneum Art Museum, Helsinki, in whose collections the painting resides.

oped by easy transition from collecting," he wrote. In a clear thrust at Gordon Childe's Neolithic revolution, he wrote: "The lack of any clear demarcation between the gathering and cultivation of plants and the hunting and herding of animals, which appears when real life is studied, should not only make us critical of dogmatic writing on the subject of 'economic revolutions' in the remote past."[17] He drew attention to some of the practices that awaited systematic research: slash-and-burn agriculture among the Finno-Ougrians and wooden plows that were still in use in many areas of Europe. Even the technology of skis and sledges offered opportunities for folk culture analogy (Figure 7.3).

He ended the essay by stressing that folk culture demonstrated just how vestigial the archaeological record could be. Even if research on organic sites and new recovery methods were developed, the problems of interpreting the material remains of the past would become even more challenging. Many conventional assumptions based on artifact "type fossils" were false indeed unless checked against other sources. He quoted the example of Jutland's black handmade pottery, which was distributed as far afield as Holland and Vienna by packhorse and canal barge in the late eighteenth and early nineteenth centuries. An archaeologist confronted with such a potsherd distribution alone would assume that the diffusion of the ware had come in prosperous times. In fact, black ware was manufactured and traded widely at a time of deep agricultural depression purely as a survival strategy for hungry village farmers to raise cash. When prosperity returned after 1864, Jutland's handmade wares rapidly declined into virtual extinction. Thus any study of ancient economies must be undertaken in the context of the beliefs and cultural values that determined its long-term behavior. "Observation of living communities stresses not only the complexity of economic life, but also its limitations as a source of information about prehistoric times."[18]

"Folk-Culture and the Study of European Prehistory" ranks among Grahame's more important papers, for the principles behind it formed the basis for a stream of articles that came from his pen between 1942 and 1948. He surveyed such topics as sheep and swine, prehistoric European fishing, and fowling in a series of authoritative studies that appeared in his regular publishing outlets: *Antiquaries Journal, Antiquity,* and *Proceedings of the Prehistoric Society*. Each paper followed the same general format, each relied on folk culture analogies, and each was an archaeological synthesis revealing an astounding reservoir of knowledge on the part of the author and a seemingly effortless command of such esoteric information as the feathering of arrows, the qualities of light plows, and slash-and-burn agriculture. All this research culminated in the publication of an important book, *Prehistoric Europe: The Economic Basis* (1952).

Prehistoric Europe: The Economic Basis

Gordon Childe resigned as Abercromby Professor of Archaeology at Edinburgh University in 1948 to take a new chair in European prehistory at the Institute of Archaeology in London. Grahame was among those who applied for this prestigious chair, but to his chagrin the electors appointed Stuart Piggott. This disappointment came at a time when Clark was considering bringing together his ideas on economic prehistory within the compass of a single volume. The newly elected Piggott promptly invited Grahame to give the prestigious Munro Lectures at Edinburgh in 1949. The invitation provided the incentive for him to write *Prehistoric Europe: The Economic Basis*, arguably the most influential of all Clark's books. Years later, Clark himself described the book as "essentially an act of propaganda." He wrote it "to show how much more information about prehistoric economy could be gleaned from the archaeological evidence even of the quality then available, and by inference how much more could be learned by making purposeful investigations in the future."[19] In fact, the book was far more than that, representing a train of thought that had been unfolding in Clark's mind since the writing of *The Mesolithic Settlement of Northern Europe* before the war. The war years had been a crucible, giving Grahame the breathing time to think deeply about what he had learned and, above all, about the multidisciplinary perspective that ecological and economic prehistory required. He brought all these threads together in *Prehistoric Europe*, the first book to "view this vast subject as it were stereoscopically by bringing into focus two distinct lines of vision, those of the natural scientist and of the historian."[20] *The Economic Basis* (the title most commonly used to refer to the book) was quite unlike any other synthesis of European prehistory, all of which were modeled, usually unsuccessfully, on Gordon Childe's *Dawn*.

After a brief statement of his methodology, familiar to anyone who had read his seal-hunting and whaling papers, Clark devoted chapter 1 to what he called "ecological zones and economic stages." He avowed an explicitly ecological approach, with the assumption that human societies operated within ecological systems and were in a state of equilibrium within them. There were periods, of course, when they were in a state of disequilibrium, "when the pattern of life changed, at times drastically and often quite rapidly."[21] To study these changes required taking into account environmental changes after the Ice Age, shifting cultural and economic needs and requirements, and the changes in the environment caused by human activity, epitomized by Johannes Iversen's pollen research into forest clearance by farmers in northern Europe. Plant ecology in particular was of vital importance for studying prehistoric culture change.

From a general statement of the ecological perspective, Clark moved on to the vegetational zoning and ecological changes that unfolded after the Ice Age, topics familiar to readers of *The Mesolithic Settlement*, even if the text figures were now more refined. In an ambitious table, he summarized general cultural developments in Europe with those of the wider Mediterranean world, for he argued that one could not understand cultural change in temperate zones without reference to the momentous changes unfolding to the south and east, where agriculture and metalworking, for example, first developed. The cultural framework was one of inevitable progress. Clark classified European society into three main progressive stages: "savagery" (hunting and gathering), "barbarism" (farming and stock raising), and, later, urban civilization. The Mediterranean civilizations exploited the environmental potential of their homelands to their full potential. In Europe, the environment set tighter limits, which prevented European "barbarians" from developing cities or literate civilizations. "It needed all the power of Rome to break through the boundaries established by ecology and to incorporate within the sphere of the Empire a substantial area of deciduous forest."[22]

The nine chapters that followed did not carve a chronological path. They were in the genre of his earlier articles, covering broad economic topics reflected in such titles as: "Catching and Gathering: Inland" and "Farming: Crops and Livestock." Two chapters discussed technology, another was entitled "Houses and Settlements," a third, "Trade." Each embraced a tried-and-true formula, a meld of archaeology, ecology, and folklore that synthesized across cultural boundaries and ranged from the Upper Palaeolithic to the Iron Age. The technology chapters are particularly strong, with their emphases on the importance of identifying sources of tool-making stone and metal ores, and the useful, and unusual, survey of organic materials used in toolmaking. Clark left his readers in no doubt of the importance of technology to all archaeologists, for this was the device Europeans had used to drag themselves "out of the primeval mire of savagery . . . up the long and undulating slopes of barbarism and ultimately . . . to some kind of civilization."[23] His was a magisterial perspective, clearly based on notions of evolution, technological innovation, and human progress, but one shared by many archaeologists at the time.

Prehistoric Europe did not display any particular theoretical or analytical sophistication, but it drew attention to the potential of economic prehistory. Nor was the volume an integrated synthesis. Rather, it was something between a collection of (unpublished) papers and a broad survey of economic data. Each chapter stood alone; each chapter cut boldly across cultural lines, even if the focus was mainly northern European; each had a multidisciplinary perspective and was an important statement on an aspect of economic prehistory in its own right. Clark firmly believed in proselytizing by the written word, and this *Prehistoric Europe* achieved.

The book was reviewed by the Swiss prehistorian Emil Vogt in *Antiquity* in March 1953. He gave it only a lukewarm welcome. He criticized Clark for taking the easy way out, for not starting with "the great culture groups" and emphasizing their common elements, and, more importantly, the differences in their economic structure. Vogt commented on the strong northern European emphasis of the book and on the importance Clark placed on distribution maps. But he praised the comprehensive biography, often culled from obscure sources.[24] Gordon Childe wrote in the *Antiquaries Journal* that the book was "a new interpretation of archaeological data—or perhaps we should say revives a mode of interpretation familiar last century, but with far richer material . . . and profounder vision." Clark conceived of culture "as action, not as the fossilized results of action." As Clark himself once admitted, Gordon Childe said to him after reading the book: "Yes, Grahame, but what have you done about Society?" Grahame spent much of his later years thinking about this very question.

Grahame's long-term intellectual adversary Christopher Hawkes felt the book had serious limitations. He praised it as "a fine example of this kind of work, and a wonderful compendium of knowledge. But its logic is simple, and need never be anything but straightforward." He pointed out that there was nothing in "North American ecology, by itself, to compel either Iroquois institutions . . . or the Constitution of the United States." Clark and Hawkes disagreed sharply about archaeological theory, with Hawkes considering the ecological approach "self-fulfilling" and ahistorical.[25]

In some respects, the conservative, culture history–bound Vogt was correct. *Prehistoric Europe* is not a synthesis of the broad sweep of European prehistory or even an integrated analysis of the economic prehistory of the region. The book is a set of essays derived from lectures on different aspects of ancient economic life. Each chapter stands alone, in the format of a journal article that integrates environmental background, folk culture, and archaeological information. *Prehistoric Europe* ends abruptly with a chapter entitled "Travel and Transport," as if the author ran out of topics to survey. Grahame never pulled the diverse strands of Europe's economic basis together in the kind of broad-brushed synthesis at which he was such a consummate master. One sometimes suspects that Grahame was more comfortable with folk culture than archaeology, simply because it offered more potential for interpretation of the nonmaterial aspects of prehistoric culture. His Leverhulme journey to northern Norway and Finland in 1947 had brought him into direct contact with what today would be called "living prehistory" or "ethno-archaeology." The experience was something of an intellectual epiphany, just as encounters with Australian Aborigines were to be nearly twenty years later.

For its day, *Prehistoric Europe* was a remarkable advance. Fifteen years of research and diligent tunneling into folk literature came together in a set of essays that are still invaluable as basic statements about the economic prehistory of Europe. But, as Vogt pointed out in his *Antiquity* review, the surveys tend to be superficial and selective, as if directed to a more general archaeological audience than fellow specialists. They were also strongly functionalist. Nevertheless, the book displays a remarkable breadth of reading and multidisciplinary scholarship that was unique among archaeologists of the day and would be exceptionally difficult to write today, with the explosion in economic data of recent years.

Many believe that *Prehistoric Europe* was Grahame Clark's finest contribution to archaeology, for its pages have an authoritative quality that set the book aside from many others. The essays are written with a cool self-assurance that was a mark of Clark's pursuit of archaeology. The book's eclectic approach and emphasis on subsistence practices helped put economic prehistory in the intellectual map, just as Clark had hoped it would.

Prehistoric Europe sold widely and was translated into several languages, including Russian. It was one of the first of Clark's book to be published in the United States, where his work was still almost unknown. In Britain, an entire generation of Cambridge students were strongly influenced by the book's ecological and economic perspective. Many of them became professional archaeologists in areas like Africa and Australia, where opportunities for ethnographic analogy abounded.

At the time when *Prehistoric Europe* appeared, Grahame was deeply involved in a wider pedagogical agenda at Cambridge University, which owed as much to Dorothy Garrod as it did to his own efforts. Garrod had been appointed to the Disney Chair on the basis of her superb research at Mount Carmel in Palestine, an experience that distanced her from the avowedly Eurocentric perspectives of many of her Stone Age contemporaries. By 1937, the parochial vision of the past that had been popular between the two world wars was already an anachronism, thanks to the work of Louis Leakey in East Africa, Gertrude Caton Thompson in Egypt's Kharga oasis, Tom Patterson in India, and Garrod herself. Such local visions were even more out of date in the late 1940s, when Garrod firmly labeled her basic survey course on archaeology "World Prehistory." The perspective was still relatively narrow by modern standards, being confined in the main to France, Africa, and southwestern Asia, but it was very different from the narrow focus on northern and western Europe characteristic of earlier curricula. The more global perspective made use of V. Gordon Childe's now widely available syntheses of European and southwestern Asian prehistory such as *New Light on the Most Ancient East*, published in 1934, where he first introduced his notions of a Neolithic and Urban revolution that soon gained wide acceptance and were widely quoted in popular world histories of the day.

The new emphasis on world prehistory was entirely appropriate for an academic department based on a museum that was internationally famous for its ethnographic and archaeological collections. But the Department of Archaeology and Anthropology was still minuscule by university standards and grew slowly, for the university authorities took careful account of faculty-student ratios in its departments. This meant that the main burden of teaching fell on very few people, all of whom had different perspectives. Clark was perhaps the most ardent internationalist of all, in part because of a natural intellectual predilection, but also because of his editorship of the *Proceedings*, which brought him a steady stream of important papers from overseas.

In 1952, Dorothy Garrod retired from the Disney Chair to pursue her research in France, and Grahame Clark achieved his ultimate personal ambition. He was elected to the preeminent chair in prehistoric archaeology in the world in her place, apparently without serious opposition.

8

⬡

Star Carr

The Star Carr excavations have opened up rather than closed a field of prehistoric research.

Excavations at Star Carr[1]

The research for *Prehistoric Europe* and several other economic papers occupied much of Grahame's time during the late 1940s, but he never abandoned his hope of finding a Mesolithic settlement with well-preserved organic remains, which would give Britain an equivalent to the rich, waterlogged Maglemose sites of northern Europe. The Farnham excavations in 1937–1938 had been an attempt to locate such a site, but without success.[2] Heavily engaged in teaching and writing, Clark had little time for active survey work in the fens, and Harry Godwin had shifted his attention to the waterlogged Somerset Levels in southwestern England, where prehistoric wooden trackways were to be found. But Grahame's interest in such a site never flagged, for he knew that knowledge of the British Mesolithic would not advance significantly until such a location added a new dimension to the dreary stone tool typologies he had studied in the 1930s. Given his heavy teaching load and ambitious writing schedule, he could do little more than hope that something would come along.

Discovery

In 1948, fate played into his hands. Grahame received a letter from a Mr. Gwatkin, curator of the Scarborough Museum, informing him that a local amateur archaeologist named John Moore of Irton near Flixton in northeastern Yorkshire had found a scatter of Mesolithic microliths in peaty deposits.[3] Grahame got in touch with Moore at once, for Irton was not far distant from Holderness, where some well-preserved Maglemose harpoons had come to light before the war. Moore had made his original discoveries in the summer of 1947, when he observed a flint blade exposed in the side of a field ditch cut through a low gravel mound. He subsequently excavated the exposure and collected a small artifact assemblage, which included some flint core axes, which appeared to be of Maglemose form. Clark asked him if he had found any bones, so he returned and found some fragments sticking out of the deposits.[4] In late 1948, Moore found additional traces of occupation on a neighboring hillock, including wild horse bones, a shouldered flint point, and a broken flint blade. He also identified several other locations, among them a site named Star Carr, and attempted by trial borings through the surrounding peat and mud to establish the stratigraphy of what he correctly recognized as a long dried-up glacial lake, now known to scientists as Lake Pickering. By this time, and quite independently, Harry Godwin had made extensive Hiller core borings through the peat and subjected the resulting samples to pollen analysis.

Clark arranged to meet Moore on-site, about eight kilometers (5 miles) south-southeast of Scarborough and only a short distance from the North Sea. He realized at once that Star Carr was a location where Maglemose artifacts could be found in direct association with pollen-bearing peat deposits, like those in Scandinavia. Pieces of bone and antler in a poor state of preservation projected from the side of a field ditch and offered the prospect of much better preserved finds downslope, where the alluvial deposits dipped steeply toward the glacial lake. At his most charming and persuasive, Grahame got Moore to agree to a large-scale excavation under the auspices of the Cambridge department and the Prehistoric Society. Three seasons of excavation followed, during the summers of 1949, 1950, and 1951.

The Star Carr excavations were conducted on a shoestring, but with a multidisciplinary plan from the very beginning. Clark called on his expert-

Figure 8.1 **Star Carr excavations.**

ise from the Fenland Research Committee and enlisted the services of Harry Godwin, his colleague in many a Fenland enterprise. Godwin put two of his best students onto the first season's excavation to handle the pollen analysis. Both achieved success in their careers: A. G. Smith became professor of botany at the universities of Belfast and Cardiff, and Richard West later occupied the chair of botany at Cambridge. The British Museum furnished the services of F. C. Fraser and Judith King, who assumed responsibility for the conservation and identification of the animal bones. For archaeologists, Clark recruited a small team of Cambridge undergraduates. Despite unpleasant, wet working conditions, seven of the ten from the first season returned for the two later field campaigns (Figure 8.1). A team of eighteen and sixteen students respectively assisted in the 1950 and 1951 excavations. During the first year, the excavators lived in an old railway carriage next to the public house in nearby Flixton, then in a hutted camp provided by Scarborough Borough Council. By all accounts, the excavation was a happy one, if often uncomfortable because of the muddy conditions.

For its day, the Star Carr excavation was almost unique, for botanists worked alongside archaeologists from the beginning, notably pollen expert Donald Walker, who later held the chair of biogeography at the Australian

National University in Canberra. Over half the undergraduates from the Cambridge department who worked at Star Carr went on to become professionals, among them John Evans, who had also worked at Car Dyke, and Jack Golson, later to become professor of prehistory at Australian National University. Others, such as Gale Sieveking, John Hurst, and Michael Thompson, went on to distinguished careers in British archaeology. Star Carr was a real training ground for future archaeologists, a point taken by the General Board at Cambridge, which gave a nominal grant of £50 toward the cost of "providing instruction in field archaeology." The exiguous funds for the excavation came also from the Prehistoric Society and "an anonymous donor." Star Carr was excavated at a paltry level of funding unimaginable today.

Star Carr was a research excavation, but it was a wonderful teaching laboratory that gave students experience in excavating small features and delicate artifacts, as well as opportunities to develop their own powers of observation. As Grahame himself pointed out, the exceptional range of artifacts from the site also provided an invaluable teaching collection for future generations of undergraduates, his biographer among them. But the real focus of the field seasons was a complex multidisciplinary inquiry into the nature of Mesolithic culture and cultural adaptations on the western side of the North Sea. This required a careful synthesis of several independent yet interconnected lines of inquiry. The result was to influence archaeology for more than a generation and to turn Star Carr into an archaeological icon.

The 1949 Excavations

Grahame proceeded cautiously, for he was well aware of the daunting complexity of the site and of his own limited experience with waterlogged sites. Moore had located the site from an exposure of flints, also decayed antler and bone fragments in an exposed section of field drain. He had cut back the section exposed in the ditch about 0.7 meters (2.5 feet) over a front of 7 meters (23 feet). Clark's first concern was to establish whether organic remains were preserved and to explore the potential for recovering ecological data. Accordingly, between June 27 and July 21, 1949, he cut a trench 2.7 meters (9 feet) wide out at right angles from the field drain for a distance of 15.24 meters (50 feet). The cutting was kept narrow to minimize water seepage, there being only a hand baler at their disposal, with occasional use of a borrowed pump. "This single trench multiplied tenfold the material, other than flint and stone, bearing on the equipment of Maglemosian man in Britain."[5]

The trench descended through peat and organic mud, with the best preservation conditions downslope toward the lake. At first only a few scraps of antler and bone appeared, "soft as leather." As the excavators peeled off the peat and mud, they recovered perfectly preserved rolls of birch bark, and eventually a birch wood platform associated with abundant faunal remains, also worked flints and barbed antler points. The trench was deliberately kept narrow, so that the water in the saturated levels could be removed easily. Although the area exposed was necessarily small, there were numerous vertical profiles, which helped in deciphering the complex stratigraphy of the site.

Excavation was no easy task, for the timbers of the birch bark platform were waterlogged and extremely soft, and many of the artifacts of diminutive size. The students worked lying on planks laid across timber forms, searching as much for tiny botanical specimens as they were for artifacts. The first discovery of a barbed point prompted a laconic telegram to Harry Godwin: "First harpoon." Of necessity, the work proceeded extremely slowly, with careful attention being paid to the horizontal distribution of artifacts and other features. But the pace was much faster than that of subsequent excavations in the 1980s and 1990s, which relied heavily on sampling, flotation methods, and extremely fine-grained data recovery aimed notably at environmental reconstruction. For the day, however, Grahame's methods were considered adequate, although certainly not up to Mortimer Wheeler standards. They were rough-and-ready by modern hunter-gatherer excavation standards, which take a more fine-grained approach, especially to environmental data.

As Peter Rowley-Conwy has pointed out, Clark's Star Carr methods were crude compared with those used at the near contemporary Ulkestrup Mesolithic lakeside settlements in Denmark, which were excavated by Knud Andersen between 1947 and 1950. At Star Carr artifacts were recorded with reference to the square yard in which they were found. At Ulkestrup, the excavators measured all flint artifacts, bone fragments, and charcoal to the nearest centimeter in three dimensions. The generalized Star Carr measurements allowed Clark to distinguish two occupations at the British site on the basis of barbed points, a phenomenon confirmed by recent extremely high resolution pollen analysis. But the measurements were not extended to such finds as animal bones; three-dimensional recording would have allowed much more fine-grained study of the site. Of the two sites, Star Carr is the best known, partly because it was published so promptly; Ulkestrup did not appear until 1982, and then in Danish with only an English summary. More importantly, Clark's research aimed at covering as many aspects of ecology and society as possible, whereas Ulkestrup and other Mesolithic excavations of the day tended to be purely artifact descriptions. The level and scope of the investigation, not excavation methods, made Star Carr a site of global importance.[6]

By the end of the first season, Clark had already revolutionized knowledge of the British Mesolithic. He had recovered more organic artifacts and economic data than ever excavated in Britain before, and he had established the environmental tie-in for the site, as well as acquiring rich faunal data sufficient to provide valuable information on seasonal occupation, and on bone and antler technology. He had also formed a preliminary impression of the age and cultural affinities of the settlement.

Harry Godwin and his student Donald Walker soon developed a preliminary pollen sequence taken through the site, comparing it with core borings and transects taken from the surrounding area. They took samples from key stratigraphic profiles on-site and from the flank of the ridge occupied by the ancient inhabitants. By careful observation, they were able to link the birch platform to the glacial lakeshore and with a layer of mud and reeds. The platform itself lay clearly in Blytt and Sernander's Zone IV, the Pre-Boreal period of the early Postglacial defined by pollen counts. Star Carr turned out to be somewhat earlier than the classic Maglemose sites in Scandinavia, which were almost all of Boreal age.[7]

The flint industry seemed to fit with the earlier dating, for flake and blade burins were more common at Star Carr than in classic Scandinavian Maglemose sites. Furthermore, the microburin technique, so characteristic of later Mesolithic industries, was sparingly used. The resulting microliths were more irregular than the finely made geometric examples from many Danish sites. The core axes and adzes were cruder, too.

In his first preliminary report, published in the *Proceedings* for 1949, Grahame described the first season of excavations and paid close attention to the bone and antler technology, a novelty for a British site.[8] Harry Godwin contributed a preliminary pollen analysis, and Fraser and King an assessment of the faunal remains. The paper surveyed what was known about the Maglemose in Britain before Star Carr and reported on an abortive attempt to recover organic finds from a Maglemose discovery at Lackford in Suffolk. Then it paid tribute to John Moore's invaluable work, which located bone and antler in stratigraphic context, "although in his [Moore's] graphic phrase these resembled old bedroom slippers."[9] The report described the basics of the stone technology and a fine range of barbed red deer antler points made from long splinters removed from antler beams, as well as some puzzling antler frontlets that appeared to have been "treated in a highly special way." He described two elk antler axes and rolls of birch bark, perhaps used for simple containers. "In Star Carr we have one of the richest and most informative sites of the Maglemosian culture anywhere in north-western Europe," he wrote. "The archaeological evidence suggests that we have to deal with an early stage in the history of the Maglemosian culture, one in which Upper Palaeolithic traditions are still perceptible in the choice of antler rather than bone and in the methods used for working it."[10]

The 1950 Excavations

By the end of the first season, it was evident that Star Carr filled a gap not merely in the British but also in the northern European Mesolithic sequence. This was an unexpected bonus to what was already an important excavation. The dig resumed in 1950, still with a tiny budget and with a nucleus of student excavators from the previous season. This time, Clark excavated two parallel trenches (II and III) on either side of Trench I, but separated from it by one meter (3 foot) balks. He also dug two 1.4-meter (4.5 foot) pits on either side of the new trenches to test the extent of the site. The strategy was a logical one, given the important stratigraphic and organic finds of the year before. The excavators were able to confirm that the crude wooden platform consisted of birch branches thrown down into the reed bed. They found no traces of posts or other vertical structures. Occupational debris like quantities of stag antlers, glacial boulders, pebbles, and lumps of glacial clay had consolidated the wood foundations. Grahame also found wads of moss among the brushwood, identified by the botanists as *Eurynchium myosuroides* and *Camptothecium sericeum*, the former commonplace around the trunks of birch trees but present in such quantities that it could only have been brought on-site by humans.

As Cutting II advanced toward the lakeshore, most of a large birch tree and the trunk of a smaller one came to light, both of them felled at the time of occupation, "either to clear the site or to provide some kind of primitive landing stage" (Figure 8.2).[11] Both trees had been felled by a crude stone axe or adze, the larger one some thirty-six centimeters (14 inches) with bold, oblique blows that left the base in a crude pencil shape. The felled tip lay more or less at right angles to the platform. Donald Walker was able to trace the branches out into the lake muds. Barbed points were found under the trunk and between the branches, so the tree was felled during the occupation.

Although the more central cuttings yielded rich finds, the two test pits were almost devoid of finds, as if the settlement could not have been very large. Defining the limits of the site would allow plotting of the distribution of artifacts, features, and other finds over the entire occupation zone, one of Clark's fundamental approaches to Mesolithic archaeology, which he had inherited from years of examining surface flint scatters.

A second preliminary report appeared promptly in the *Proceedings* for 1950, immediately following John Moore's description of Mesolithic sites near Flixton.[12] Again, the emphasis was descriptive—the extent of the birch wood platform, the distribution of worked flints and stone beads, with amplified descriptions of the stone industry and red deer artifacts. This time Clark had more red deer frontlets to work with, some perforated on the base and shaped so as to retain the essential character of the antlers. "They may have been intended to be worn on the head, whether in mime or dance or as a kind of stalking mask," he wrote (Figure 8.3). The report on the excavations and finds was succinct, with a minimum of interpretation, even if Grahame had already developed some clear notions as to the significance of the site. The appendices were as important as the archaeological report, with Donald Walker using pollen samples and stratigraphy to confirm the site's position within the late Pre-Boreal, and the British Museum faunal experts arguing on the basis of the red deer antler that the site was visited year round.

In another paper in the same volume of the *Proceedings*, Grahame turned his attention to the earliest human settlement of the west Baltic region. His article updated the information set out in *The Mesolithic Settlement of*

Figure 8.2 **The birch wood platform at Star Carr.**

Figure 8.3   **Grahame Clark showing a stag antler headdress to John Evans (left). Gordon Childe in his trademark hat is at the right.**

Northern Europe, with new data on the fluctuations of the Litorina Sea, and focused attention on the contemporary pre-Boreal Klosterlund site in Denmark, where a full range of Maglemose artifacts, including axes, adzes, and microliths, were found. "The appearance of microlithic industries in the north of Europe, like that of axes and adzes, was ultimately another response to the spread of forests," he wrote.[13] He hypothesized that the "whole coastal culture from the West Baltic to the Arctic can best be explained in terms of a single spread," which reached back, in places, to the Upper Palaeolithic. Star Carr is not mentioned once in the article, although it was to prove germane to the issue.

The 1951 Excavations and Final Publication

The 1951 Star Carr season resumed where 1950 left off and involved more limited excavation, this time to establish the western and northern limits of

the site. A large trench on the west side of the main excavation only yielded artifacts as it approached the balk separating it from Cutting III of the
previous year, which had yielded rich finds. By the end of the season, Clark
was confident that he had defined "beyond any doubt the western and parts
of the northern and southern limits of the site."[14] Finally, John Moore
moved on-site when the excavations were completed to recover and plot
finds from the balks separating the main trenches.

No one could accuse Grahame of not publishing his excavations promptly. He was able to include the preliminary reports on the excavations in the
1949 and 1950 *Proceedings*, which might have been impossible had he not
been the editor. The papers ensured that a much wider audience of
Mesolithic scholars and colleagues were aware of the site as the excavations
were under way. In both cases, Clark limited himself to mainly factual information with the minimum of interpretation, as if he was holding his intellectual fire for the final report. In this way too, much of the analysis was
well under way by the time he sat down to write the monograph.

Preparing such a complex site for publication was an intricate process
both of analysis and writing, as well as coordinating a series of specialist
reports. Clark worked compulsively on the final monograph, which was
published by Cambridge University Press in 1954, less than three years
after the completion of the excavations. The preface is dated December
1952, so he completed his final report within eighteen months of the end
of the excavations. This astounding feat puts many modern excavators to
shame, even if the limitations of contemporary methodology made the task
somewhat easier than it would have been today.

Excavations at Star Carr

*Excavations at Star Carr: An Early Mesolithic Site at Seamer near Scarborough,
Yorkshire* is one of the classic archaeological monographs of the twentieth
century. Generations of British archaeological undergraduates learned its
pages virtually by heart. It still serves as a model of clear reporting. In his
previous works, Grahame had tested his ecological and economic perspectives on general topics. Now he used his ecological and economic approaches in the context of a single site.

Star Carr is a model of clear exposition and economical reporting, as well
as multidisciplinary research. Clark himself wrote most of the book, with a

chapter entitled "Lake Stratigraphy, Pollen-Analysis and Vegetational History," by Donald Walker and Harry Godwin, another entitled "Faunal Remains," by F. C. Fraser and J. E. King of the British Museum (Natural History), and an appendix on the Flixton excavations by John Moore. He drew the illustrations, apparently unfazed by a broken right forearm suffered when he fell from a wheelbarrow while picking apples. If ever there was a classic example of Grahame Clark's approach to prehistoric research, the Star Carr monograph is it. "The main emphasis of the present book lies on the adequate recording of the new evidence," wrote Grahame in the preface.[15] The seven chapters that follow lay out the Star Carr site in deceptively simple terms.

Chapter 1 is an overall description of the excavations and the nature of the settlement. Clark used the distribution of worked flints to outline the perimeters of the site, overlaying simple distribution maps of the density of flints and the distribution of barbed points to arrive at a settlement area of 184 to 200 square meters (220 to 240 square yards). The length and breadth of Star Carr at 15.6 by 14.5 meters (51 by 47 feet) compared well with Mesolithic settlements in Scandinavia, but it was much smaller than the dimensions of prehistoric agricultural villages from later times. On this flimsy basis, Clark argued that Star Carr was a tiny settlement and looked far afield for analogies. He quoted a companion of the eighteenth-century navigator Captain James Cook on the Tasmanians: "There were never more than three or four huts found in a place, and these capable of holding 3–4 persons each only."[16] The birch platform was "nothing more than a stabilization of the swamp surface" without piles to consolidate it. Clark believed the site was occupied more than once, by people who had a memory of the location. But the occupation was sporadic, during midwinter in January and again in April. "We have to deal at Star Carr with a community rather than with the activities of a specialized group," he wrote.[17] Both men and women were present, the latter being engaged in skin preparation, as they were among Eskimo groups. Clark commented on the small area of the platform but seems to have assumed the site was occupied by four or five families.

With the chronology and ecology he moved on to firmer ground. Godwin and Walker's comprehensive report on the stratigraphy and pollen analysis placed the site to the end of the Pre-Boreal. But Grahame had another weapon in his chronological armory. He managed to persuade

Willard Libby of the University of Chicago to run a charcoal sample from Star Carr's birch platform for radiocarbon analysis (for Clark and radio-carbon dating, see Chapter 10). During the third field season, he received a date of 9,488 ± 350 years, or 7538 ± 350 B.C., which was released by Libby in his book *Radiocarbon Dating*, published by the University of Chicago Press (1952). This, the first Mesolithic radiocarbon date from Europe, caused widespread interest because it fell within the range of dates for the Pre-Boreal obtained from Baron de Geer's long established glacial varve chronology.

Perhaps even more important, the pollen research allowed Clark to place the birch wood platform directly on the surroundings of the reed swamp bordering the lake. "The higher ground was forested with close birchwoods on the hillsides and drier parts of the valley-bottoms; pine had probably begun to establish itself and willows grew nearer the water."[18] Only the presence of weeds like goosefoot and nettles testified to any human disturbance of the natural landscape, something that Clark was attuned to after Iversen's Danish research on ancient forest clearance. He published a famous reconstruction map of the surroundings of the site, which was reproduced in generations of undergraduate textbooks—an almost unheard of detail at the time.

Grahame briefly surveyed the subsistence in which hunting played an important role, described the broad range of raw materials used by the inhabitants, and concluded that the community was "almost wholly" self-supporting, a place where artifacts were manufactured. Of the Star Carr people's aesthetic, intellectual, and religious life, there were no traces.

Clark laid out the Star Carr report in such a clear way that the casual reader could now skip to the final chapter: "Star Carr in the Context of European Prehistory." In so doing, he followed a precept that he once enu-merated to the author, who was complaining about a large volume of spe-cialist literature. "Look at the contents page, then read the introduction and conclusions. For details, use the index," he once told me with the confi-dence of a man who had followed this principle for years. In the case of Star Carr, he obliged the reader!

The monograph gives no particular priority to archaeology, appropriate with a multidisciplinary research project. Chapter 2 by Walker and Godwin describes the botanical and stratigraphic work and the ecological develop-ment of the region, a project almost as large in scope and time expenditure as the excavation itself. They tied the occupation level to the muddy lake deposits and to the Pre-Boreal with both pollen and macrofossils, as well as describing the gradual filling of the lake and spread of forest over the region. Chapter 3 moves on to the faunal remains, where Fraser and King identified a wide range of mammals from the site but concentrated most of their attention on the numerous red deer bones, which they measured and described with admirable thoroughness, concluding that Mesolithic adults were larger than modern ones. After careful study of the red deer antlers, they concluded that the site was occupied "at some time between October and April," especially in the spring, when the people were collecting fresh-ly shed antlers. Star Carr was empty during the summer, when the hard-ened antlers would have been of least use for making artifacts. At the time, the Star Carr faunal report was one of the most comprehensive of its kind, but the conclusions on seasonal occupation have generated more debate than almost any other aspect of the site.

Chapters 4–6, under Grahame's pen, described the artifacts from Star Carr in much more detail than in the preliminary reports. Most of the tool-making stone came from the local drift (glacial deposits), fashioned using a flake technology, into microliths, awls, scrapers, burins, axes, and adzes, a broad range of examples illustrated with Clark's usual skill. He dwelt at length on the red deer antler technology, on the groove-and-splinter tech-nique and the barbed points made from the long splinters of antler removed from the beams. The points were, with one exception, designed to be mounted on wooden handles instead of serving as harpoons, a pair found in the brushwood platform suggesting that at least some were mounted in pairs. He also observed a broad change from finely to coarsely barbed points through time. With admirable thoroughness, he describes and illus-trates virtually every point from the excavations. The elk antler artifacts included mattock heads, one with the carbonized tip of the handle, also bone scraping tools, duly compared with a Central Eskimo scraping tool in the normal Clark fashion (Figure 8.4).

"Miscellaneous Artifacts" included the birch bark rolls, perhaps a source of resin for mounting arrow- and spearheads. Two barbed points and a microlith bore traces of resin, which was heavily used by Maglemosians in Scandinavia. He also described a fragmentary wooden canoe paddle, one of the few wooden artifacts in the site. But Grahame lavished the most atten-tion on the stag frontlets, which he had described briefly in the preliminary reports. Twenty-one examples, all of them damaged in antiquity, came from

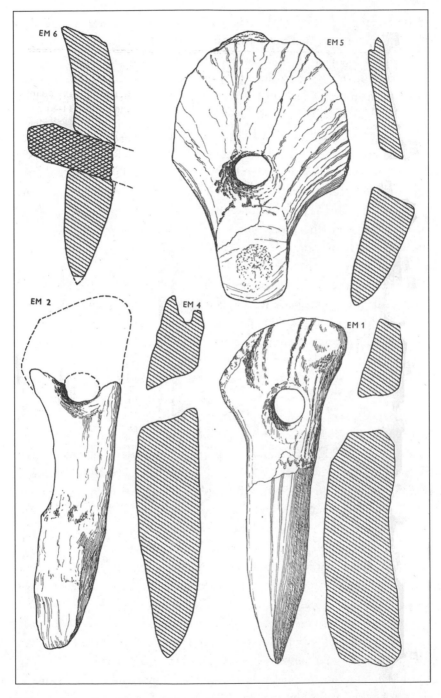

Figure 8.4 **Star Carr artifacts: Elk antler mattocks, one with a portion of the wooden handle still in place (left). Size: One-third.**

different animals, eleven of them with perforated parietal bones, and all of them modified to lighten them. The frontlets invariably came from animals with well-developed racks, but they were reduced to about a third or a quarter of their weight by thinning and hollowing the tines. At the same time, the rim and inner surface of the brain case were smoothed and trimmed, leaving a fairly even base. All this careful preparation and the mounting holes suggested they had served as some form of mask. Grahame was in his element with this interpretative conundrum and plunged eagerly into the archaeological and ethnographic literature for analogies. He quoted descriptions of Inuit caribou hunters wearing masks at mating time when they imitate the grunting of bulls, cited the few examples of dancing, masked figures in Upper Palaeolithic art, also the Tardenoisian Mesolithic burials under heaps of red deer antlers on the islands of Hoëdic and Téviec off the Brittany coast. From the Mesolithic, he moved on to a Bronze Age barrow burial with red deer antlers at Mildenhall in Suffolk and illustrated a Tungu shaman from Siberia wearing a reindeer antler headdress. After this classic archaeological and ethnographic tour de force, he drew no conclusions, beyond a statement that the frontlets were used either for stalking or "magical purposes" (Figure 8.5).

Chapter 7 was Clark at his best, attempting an interpretation of the Star Carr in a much broader context. He explained how the dig was undertaken in the hope of discovering a British counterpart to the well-known Maglemose sites in Denmark at a time when there was considerable cultural homogeneity across Scandinavia, the partially dry North Sea, and eastern England. In the event, Star Carr turned out to be of late Pre-Boreal age, with a markedly different material culture, close to that of the Maglemose people but with notable differences. These included the use of flakes and burins, with only sparing use of the microburin technique, important differences in microlith forms, and cruder, smaller axes and adzes. But the most important contrast lay in the antler and bone industries, with the Star Carr people making far more use of the former, a practice characteristic of Upper Palaeolithic rather than Mesolithic technology. The groove-and-splinter technique seemed to be of particular significance, being used widely by Late Glacial groups, such as those who inhabited Alfred Rust's Meiendorf and Stellmoor sites in northern Germany. He traced the roots of the technology into Magdalenian cultures in France and Spain, with red deer being used widely in areas south of reindeer territory.

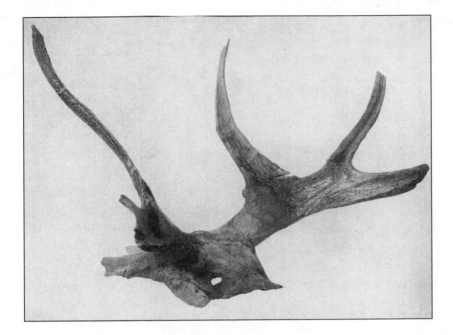

Figure 8.5 **A stag antler frontlet from Star Carr.**

Groove-and-splinter technology occupied more of Clark's time than almost any aspect of the Star Carr research. He described it in not only one of the preliminary reports and the monograph but also a separate paper published in the *Proceedings* for 1953 coauthored with "one of his pupils," Michael Thompson, who went on to a distinguished career in archaeology.[19] The paper described how the Star Carr people removed multiple antler splinters from the beams of red deer antlers. First, they cut off the crown and tines and then used sharp flint burins to score the natural grooves in the antler. Cambridge colleague Charles McBurney and Michael Thompson experimented with modern red deer antler. They found that a length of string or leather thong inserted through a hole under the isolated splinter enabled them to lever up the fragment and break it loose at either end. The 1953 paper finds Clark at his best, identifying and describing a simple artifact-manufacturing technique, then confirming his analysis with controlled experiments (usually performed by others), and searching for analogous finds elsewhere, in this case from Maglemose collections in the American Museum of Natural History, New York, and in the

National Museum of Denmark in Copenhagen. Thompson found additional material on the Continent while working on his doctoral dissertation. The two authors concluded that the technique "formed an integral part of the Upper Palaeolithic blade and burin tradition . . . Shaped into the heads of many of the principal weapons used in the higher forms of hunting by which Upper Palaeolithic Europeans lived."[20] One is at a loss to explain why this paper was not incorporated into the Star Carr monograph, for it duplicated much of the material published in it and appeared only shortly before the final report.

The Star Carr people used a technology with strong Upper Palaeolithic and Late Glacial foundations, even if it was distinctively Mesolithic. Clark pointed to important differences from the later Danish sites, especially the preponderance of fine-toothed barbed points in the English site. He lamented the lack of Pre-Boreal exemplars on the eastern side of the North Sea, except for Klosterlund, where no organic materials had been preserved. The flake and blade scrapers found there closely resembled those from Star Carr. So did the microliths; and microburins were rare. There was, he wrote, a broad continuity of Mesolithic culture across the North Sea, but the archaeological record was too incomplete for more detailed comparisons. Meanwhile "Star Carr helps fill a crucial gap in the prehistory of north-western Europe," between the Late Glacial cultures of northern Germany and the classic Maglemose sites of Scandinavia. He urged further study of human settlement and its ecological context during the intervening Pre-Boreal period, when forests began to transform the landscape of northern and northwestern Europe. But despite Star Carr being a "real link" between the Upper Palaeolithic and Mesolithic, "much remains to be done. The Star Carr excavations have opened up rather than closed a field of prehistoric research."[21]

Grahame's last sentence was prophetic, for he saw clearly the potential of ecological research in archaeology at a time when most prehistorians were little more than vaguely aware of pollen analysis and wet sites. Star Carr rapidly became an icon of a new generation of multidisciplinary archaeological research for generations of Cambridge undergraduates, many of whom took archaeological posts far from the comfortable world of British archaeology. Above all, Clark's classic diagram showing how the Mesolithic group had exploited local animal, vegetable, and mineral resources for clothing, food, ornamentation, and shelter stuck in the mind,

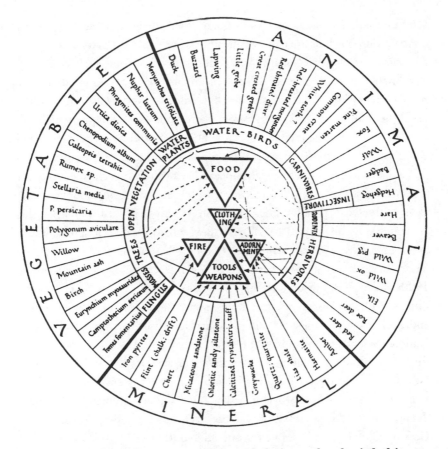

Figure 8.6   **Selected raw materials and their use by the inhabitants of Star Carr. A famous Clark diagram.**

for it made the fundamental point that no Stone Age site could be excavated without careful reference to Quaternary geology (Figure 8.6). By any standards, Star Carr was a triumph of multidisciplinary research, especially in its careful melding of ecological data, its faunal analysis, and its single radiocarbon date. It was all the remarkable for being completed on a budget of a few hundred pounds.

Star Carr was well received on both sides of the Atlantic, but the reviews display little sense that the monograph was a real turning point in the archaeology of the day. The reviewers were generally kind. In *Antiquity*,

Grahame's old friend Therkel Mathiassen called the book a "very important contribution," high praise from a colleague whose opinion Clark valued. The American prehistorian Hallam Movius described the monograph as "an outstandingly fine piece of work." He wrote that it was "the closest thing to a model excavation report which this reviewer has ever seen." But he criticized the undue emphasis on the groove-and-splinter technique, which had been described by the French excavator Denis Peyrony as early as 1905 and was already well-known at several Upper Palaeolithic sites.[22]

Grahame's ecological research appeared at a time when change was afoot in American archaeology. A few American scholars were beginning to think along somewhat parallel lines. Gordon Willey had just published his remarkable fieldwork in Peru's Virú Valley, which used aerial photographs and foot survey to trace changing settlement patterns against a river valley landscape, an approach foreshadowed by Cyril Fox in Cambridgeshire in the 1920s. Robert Braidwood of the University of Chicago was starting his multidisciplinary researches in southwestern Asia, which brought geologists and zoologists into the field alongside archaeologists—thanks to the first National Science Foundation grant for archaeological research.[23] But before the 1950s, only a handful of American archaeologists were aware of Grahame's writings on human adaptation and subsistence, among them Hugh Hencken of Harvard University, whom Clark credited with introducing him to the potential of wet site archaeology before World War II. Gordon Childe's syntheses of Europe and southwestern Asia were widely read to the point that his Neolithic and Urban revolutions were virtual archaeological and historical canon, but none of Clark's earlier works had enjoyed anything like such a wider readership. *Prehistoric Europe* and *Star Carr* established Grahame Clark firmly in the American archaeological mind. The multidisciplinary perspectives and anthropological approach in these volumes placed anthropology, ecology, and subsistence at the heart of archaeological research at least in general terms about a decade before they became a mainstream concern in American archaeology.

Few American archaeologists, then or now, have been interested in the European Mesolithic, but *Star Carr* transcended this narrow specialty, with its brilliant reconstructions and cogently argued descriptions, not only of an artifact scatter but of a 10,000-year-old site, one of the first ever radiocarbon dated, set in a wider environmental setting. The methodologies applied at Star Carr exercised a significant influence on such important North

American excavations as the Ozette village on Washington State's Olympic Peninsula and soon became routine on many sites, albeit in more sophisticated forms. Richard Daugherty's excavations into an ancient Makah Indian village at Ozette buried by a catastrophic landslide were especially remarkable, both on account of their extraordinary organic finds, the innovative methods used to dig and conserve collapsed wooden huts and their contents, and for their sensitive relationships with the local Indian groups.[24]

The Star Carr monograph appeared about a decade before the furor over the so-called New Archaeology erupted in American archaeology in the hands of Lewis Binford and others. The New Archaeology drew on long familiar theoretical constructs in other disciplines and on some in anthropology, among them systems theory, cultural ecology, and multilinear evolution.[25] However, Binford and other disciples of the "new" thinking never gave full credit to Grahame Clark, who had been using such approaches, albeit in very simple forms, in his research since the late 1930s.

Star Carr was highly visible in the archaeological literature because people tended to think of the northern European Mesolithic, and hunter-gatherer sites generally, in terms of this single, well-preserved site and little else. One can hardly blame them, for the organically rich Scandinavian sites were largely inaccessible to scholars not fluent in the northern languages. One is reminded of modern hunter-gatherer studies, when Richard Lee and Irven DeVore's celebrated 1966 Man the Hunter conference influenced an entire generation of thinking about hunter-gatherer society and the behavior of early hominids, which popularized such notions as "man the hunter" and "woman the gatherer."[26]

Later Researches at Star Carr

Few archaeological sites are so thoroughly published by their original excavators that later investigators can return there and resume where they left off. Grahame was anxious that his Star Carr research be revisited and reappraised, not only by himself but by others. Unfortunately, his excavation records leave much to be desired. They are not comprehensive enough for detailed use in the field or for fine-grained studies of potential activity areas, but the finds were well curated in Cambridge and easily accessible to potential researchers. Later researchers have used the collections and the monograph as their jumping-off point. Clark himself regarded such efforts with complete detachment, for his research on the site was long completed.

Grahame returned to Star Carr himself in a widely quoted 1972 paper, compiled as a module for undergraduate teaching, published as *Star Carr: A Case Study in Bioarchaeology*.[27] In it, he attempted to update his thinking on the site and made some revisions—the identification of bones from a small domesticated dog at the site, a summary of new Mesolithic finds elsewhere in Britain, and some new examples of the groove-and-splinter technique and Mesolithic stag frontlets from the Continent. He also surveyed the bioarchaeological evidence anew, adding a simple site catchment analysis and distribution maps in an attempt to map the territory and seasonal range of the Star Carr group. This was based on an assumption of winter occupation and a population of no more than four families. He argued that Mesolithic Britons lived in two scattered populations, one in the north and another concentrated in the Thames Valley, a conclusion that amplified his original doctoral work of forty years earlier, which spoke of Maglemosian and Tardenoisian culture areas in England.

A Case Study in Bioarchaeology was Clark's last word on Star Carr and represented little advance on his earlier thinking, which is hardly surprising, for he had maximized the site's potential, given the exiguous funds at his disposal and the infant nature of both palynology and zooarchaeology. Without further fieldwork there was little more to add. After some initial reappraisals, which focused mainly on the issues of the function of the site and seasonal occupation, the site was subjected to twelve years of highly selective paleoecological and archaeological investigations from 1985 to 1997 and became a testing ground for a new generation of extremely detailed ecological research.[28]

The new multidisciplinary excavations, headed by Paul Mellars and Tim Schadla-Hall, focused on an important cutting deliberately laid out twenty meters (66 feet) east of the main Clark excavation. The major burden of the laboratory work was shouldered by Petra Dark.[29] This trench yielded important new environmental and cultural evidence, including another wooden structure—a concentration of large timbers, some split like planks, all laid in the same direction. The timbers were willow and aspen, both species that grew by the lake at the time of occupation. Only a small portion of the structure was uncovered, for the excavators lacked the large-scale conservation facilities to uncover more of it. But they theorized it may have been some form of trackway leading down to water's edge. In 1989, the research team recovered a large block sample in the lower, organic levels of the trench for detailed laboratory analysis on a fine-grained scale unimagined in Clark's day. They also investigated dryland areas north and east of the original site, where new field surveys and test pits established that the site extended far beyond the confines of the small platform in the reeds. Grahame's small Star Carr settlement was a myth and something quite different.

The extensive paleoecological investigations were far more detailed than Harry Godwin and Donald Walker's original pollen analysis based on a mere eight samples. The new researches used AMS radiocarbon dating and high resolution analysis in millimeters rather than the original centimeters, as well as specialist expertise on identifications unavailable a half century ago. Twelve closely spaced AMS radiocarbon dates on charcoal and minute plant remains calibrated and correlated with tree-ring readings from central European pines dated the newly excavated occupation to between 8700 and 8400 B.C., a good thousand years earlier than Clark's original date.[30] But two AMS dates from organic artifacts recovered in the Clark excavations dated to between 7400 and 7100 B.C., as if the site were occupied later as well. The new chronology gives the site a life of at least three hundred years, confirming Clark's suspicions of a repeated occupation.

Godwin and Walker had concluded that the Star Carr people had no impact on the surrounding environment. The new researches proved them wrong. Petra Dark used the distribution of tiny charcoal flecks to show that there was an initial period of intense charcoal deposition that lasted for about eighty years, then a century with little activity, followed by fairly continuous deposition for a further 130 years. Botanist Jon Hather identified the charcoals as those of reeds, burned off when they were dry between autumn and spring, when the new growth began. Mellars and Dark believe the reeds were fired repeatedly by humans, largely because the samples of high charcoal frequency are localized at the site, as if burning was tightly controlled. Such conflagrations, commonplace among historic foragers, could have provided people with a better view of the lake and a convenient landing place for canoes and also could have fostered new plant growth which would attract feeding animals.

The Clark report described Star Carr as a winter settlement, but later investigators such as Anthony Legge and Peter Rowley-Conwy restudied the bones and argued for late spring and early summer occupation.[31] Now X-ray analysis of unerupted teeth in deer jawbones and comparisons with modern samples have identified many ten- to eleven-month-old animals, which would have been killed in March or April. This new seasonality data agrees with minute finds of tightly rolled leaf stems of reeds burned in early growth between March and April, and also with aspen bud scalers that date to the same time of year. Not a winter settlement, Star Carr may have been occupied from March until at least June or early July.

Grahame Clark excavated Star Carr in a search for a Mesolithic wet site where he could anchor Maglemose culture to Postglacial climatic change. He excavated with minimal funds and focused his entire attention on the site, which superficial investigation suggested was no more than a few meters across. His students never surveyed the surrounding landscape for more sites, except very superficially. One can hardly blame him, for Star Carr was, after all, the first site of its kind in Britain, and Grahame was single-minded in his pursuit of an excavation once he started it. Half a century later, and with infinitely more funds and much more sophisticated research, we now know that Star Carr was larger and more complex than Clark ever imagined and part of a much wider settlement pattern that is still little understood.

As Grahame showed, the site was occupied at a time when dense birch forests pressed on the lake, confining human activity to lakeshore areas. But he was wrong in stating that the people did not alter their environment, for we now know they modified it repeatedly with burning and stone axes. This is why the appearance of stone axes at Star Carr is so important. As Clark once again pointed out, they may represent the first efforts of Europeans to cope with dense forest and to develop basic woodworking skills for laying trackways and other large-scale projects. Grahame would be very pleased with the new generation of Star Carr research, for, as the excavators said, they built on a firm foundation of pioneer research carried out under very difficult conditions and minimal funding. The remarkable discoveries on the shores of the long-forgotten glacial lake were another reason why John Grahame Douglas Clark was elected to the Disney Chair two years before the final report appeared. There were no other prehistorians in Britain, let alone Europe, who saw the way ahead for Stone Age archaeology with such clarity.

9

⬥

Disney Professor

*Let us hold fast to the idea that in essence culture symbolizes a
relationship, or rather an intricate web of interrelations, between society
and environment, and that culture change involves a more or less complex
series of adjustments between them.*

The Study of Prehistory[1]

Nineteen fifty-two was the annus mirabilis of Grahame Clark's career,
the moment when years of hard work came to fruition and he
assumed the Disney Chair. He inherited a department that had undergone
considerable change since the war. In 1948, archaeology and anthropology
became a two-part tripos, which allowed undergraduates considerably
more choice than hitherto. Dorothy Garrod had been a quiet, self-effacing
chair, who was happy when engaged in her own research. She had been
elected to the Disney in her fiftieth year, but the war intervened before she
could make much of a mark. She had served, like Grahame, in the RAF
Photographic Interpretation Unit at Medmenham. Despite her prestigious
Cambridge chair, her heart was in Europe. Directly after VE Day, she
crossed the Channel and visited the cave paintings at Lascaux before the
cave was opened to the public. She itched to excavate overseas again, but
currency exchange controls made traveling abroad, and certainly fieldwork, almost impossible. Instead, she threw her energies into reforming
the tripos.

Garrod was distant, shy, and hard to get to know, but she worked very hard on university committees, often with scant respect from the general board of the University, which controlled funding. She was unaccustomed to the hierarchy and negotiation style of her senior academic colleagues. As a woman, she was not made a full member of the university until 1948 and did not participate in social functions at which many bureaucratic problems were resolved informally. Garrod was also a dull public lecturer who preferred to write rather than present her findings orally. But her academic reforms within the department were of importance. As we have seen, for many years the teaching of prehistory had been heavily skewed toward France and the classic Stone Age sequence in the Dordogne and north Spanish caves. Garrod extended the range of Stone Age archaeology teaching to encompass both southwestern Asia and tropical Africa, while the writings of Gordon Childe brought a wider perspective to later prehistory. She herself introduced a course for undergraduates entitled "World Prehistory" in 1946, the first time such a course had been offered anywhere. But Dorothy Garrod was never comfortable in her professorial role and longed to return to her fieldwork. In 1952, she retired early and departed to live and excavate in France.[2]

Clark was a logical choice for the Disney. He was fresh from his triumphant and well-publicized Star Carr excavations, had just published *Prehistoric Europe*, and was associated with the cutting-edge perspective of economic prehistory (Figure 9.1). His long years of service at the university held him in good stead, even if his single-minded devotion to archaeology was somewhat forbidding. Furthermore, he had long experience with the department and the tripos and a global perspective from years of editing the *Proceedings of the Prehistoric Society*. As befitted a Disney Professor, he took the Sc.D. degree from Cambridge on the basis of his published work. At first, he had wavered between the Litt.D. or Sc.D. but was persuaded to take the latter when he was offered the free scarlet gown of the Sc.D. from the estate of a deceased geologist.[3]

On paper, Clark was an ideal candidate and a Cambridge man into the bargain. But he was not a popular teacher in the postwar department after the war. As a university lecturer, he had acquired a reputation for poorly prepared lectures. On one famous occasion, he actually delivered a Part II lecture to an audience of beginning and uncomprehending undergraduates. His mind was almost invariably elsewhere, preoccupied with new discover-

Figure 9.1 **Grahame Clark holding a Star Carr elk antler adze. Oil painting by Ruskin Spear, 1953.**

ies, fresh ideas, his own writing. But herein lay an unexpected strength of his teaching, which was often submerged by a monotonous delivery—his enthusiasm for discoveries that changed established thinking. For minutes on end, he would wax eloquent and with an engaging enthusiasm on a new find of a wooden spearhead or, at a lecture attended by the author, on a newly unearthed Neolithic dugout canoe from Holland. That was another side to a scholar whose teaching, while sometimes magisterial and always up-to-date, was at best pedestrian. The enthusiasm with which he spoke of the new find was infectious. The canoe stuck in one's memory. The rest of the lecture did not.

Like his predecessor, Grahame never took willingly to the byzantine committees and machinations of university politics that were the inevitable accompaniment of requests for additional faculty and physical plant. He never learned how to work the system and press for new staff, so the department remained small and clannish. On the advice of Harry Godwin, he acquired funds for an assistant in research. The first incumbent was Eric Higgs, who went on to make extraordinary contributions to the department's research programs (see Chapter 10). Clark was, however, aggressive in pursuing good undergraduates, especially if he could locate them in other university departments and persuade them to transfer to archaeology and anthropology.

Clark was one of those department heads who never held formal meetings and made decisions by himself. Sometimes he did not bother to inform those affected at all. His three years as chairman of the faculty were famous for their rapid-fire consumption of lengthy agendas. Whenever a debate showed signs of beginning, he would abruptly override his fellow department heads with a decision and plow ahead with the next item. On occasion, he is said to have corrected manuscripts while sitting at the table. The discussion would proceed. Some minutes later, he abruptly announced that a decision had been made. As far as the department was concerned, his priorities were crystal clear and well ordered: every member of the faculty was encouraged to make time for study and research, then for graduate students, and finally for undergraduates in that order. Fortunately, the department was small and research students thin on the ground, so undergraduates rarely felt shortchanged, even if Clark's abrupt manner and formidable personality made him a remote figure.

John Coles, Charles McBurney, and other colleagues got on well with Grahame. They appreciated his strong encouragement of personal research and saw his self-centered interests as part of his passion for original work. Others were less enthusiastic. Glyn Daniel, who admittedly disliked Grahame, described Clark's Disney years as not entirely happy ones for the department. "We were all of us aware of an alarming and chilling self-cen-

Figure 9.2 Grahame Clark (left) and Stuart Piggott (right), apparently at cross-purposes, with an undergraduate Cambridge field class at Stonehenge in the 1950s. Courtesy John Mulvaney.

teredness. It was so difficult to conduct any reasonable conversation or get the business one had come to see him about properly discussed."[4] Clark would immediately turn the conversation to whatever research he was doing. He always found people difficult, even if they shared his enthusiasms. To talk about his latest thinking or research was his way of dealing with colleagues and visitors. But he did care passionately about the department's role in training the archaeologists of the future, especially for rapidly expanding opportunities far from Cambridge and the comfortable world of British archaeology (Figure 9.2).

The Reckitt Lecture

The year 1953 also marked the culmination of Grahame's thinking on economic prehistory, which he conveniently summarized in the British Academy's Reckitt Archaeological Lecture for 1953. (He had been elected a fellow in 1951.) The first in this biennial lecture series had been delivered by Stuart Piggott, who had spoken eloquently on William Camden and *Britannia*. Clark used the occasion to talk about prehistory as a "historical discipline," concerned with "development and change in the sphere of human affairs."[5] He criticized those who found archaeological data too fascinating and "squandered on empty analyses of form energies which might more profitably have been devoted to the study of prehistory." Here he expressed familiar thoughts that often surfaced in his writings—the danger of narrow artifact typologies, the perils of treating archaeology as a natural science, of not embracing multidisciplinary perspectives. He pointed out that "the economic activities of man . . . illustrate so vividly the interrelations of culture and physical environment that their study is so rewarding."

The Reckitt lecture brought together the diverse strands of Clark's thinking on economic prehistory, honed by his Star Carr research and his wide readings for the *Economic Basis*. He quoted little-known ecological descriptions of physical environments by Australian Aborigines and Navajos in the American Southwest, "as much part of . . . life as the tools they made from natural products." He discussed the limitations inherent in the subsistence activities of Magdalenians at Petersfels in Germany, Ahrensburgian faunas from Rust's Late Glacial sites at Meiendorf and Stellmoor, and the Mesolithic people of Star Carr. His listeners were reminded that Mesolithic hunter-gatherers discovered animal domestication and that "the great turning point in prehistory" was food production. "The introduction of farming to temperate Europe was nothing less than majestic, not only in its historical consequences, but also as an achievement in creative evolution." None of the artifactual changes associated traditionally with food production, such as pottery or polished axes, were significant in and of themselves. The most decisive criteria for determining the origin, spread, and progress of farming were biological—changes in animals and plants and "evidence of ecological disturbance resulting from the practice of farming and from ever increasing transformation of the habitat which this entailed." The research of Iversen and other botanists, also controlled experiments, had shown beyond doubt that the first European farmers practiced slash-and-burn agriculture, which was used in medieval Europe and "till yesterday in the forests of Finland and Carelia" as well as in many other parts of the non-Western world.

The ecological approach to archaeology cast an entirely new light on the changes in land utilization that marked so much of later European prehistory. Population growth, a new cycle in environmental exploitation, population movements, and the increasing use of marginal soils led in the long run to more settled, more intense forms of agriculture.[6] These intriguing new questions were more interesting than the older historical problems concerned with such issues as the diffusion of crops. New functional approaches such as the study of grain impressions and hand imprints on pots, detailed work on morphological changes in domesticated animals, and so on, offered far more promise. A new generation of research lay ahead, based on new sources of information and a perspective that approached human culture as an ecological issue.

At this point, Grahame produced his now famous circular drawing of the raw materials used by the inhabitants of Star Carr (see Figure 8.6). "If prehistoric man lived by eating animals and plants, he depended equally on natural substances, whether organic or otherwise, for the fabric of his material culture, seeking out what he needed and shaping it to meet the requirements of his social life," he told his audience.[7] There was a dynamic relationship between culture and ecosystem in both the technological and subsistence spheres. What determined the different choices of raw materials for artifacts made at Star Carr and later Maglemose sites? Were the choices due to technological advances or to the intended use of the artifacts for different purposes? This kind of research raised previously unasked questions. He quoted the example of prehistoric sheep breeding and wool manufacture, which could not take hold over wide areas of Europe until permanent deforestation had resulted in sufficient open pasturage.

He concluded his lecture with another famous drawing, this time a nine-sided systems diagram entitled "Interactions Between Different Aspects of the Socio-Cultural Component of Ecosystems Comprehending Agriculture" (Figure 9.3). Most of the arrows were double-ended to stress that ecological changes were a reliable index of economic transformation. No aspect of human culture could be considered in isolation from the habitat and biome or from other elements of the culture itself. "Even at this basal level, at which economy so to speak interacts with ecology, the decisive factor has been social choice, and second that every advance in the control of the natural environment has enlarged the scope within which this choice could operate." The thesis was a simple one: economic progress marks

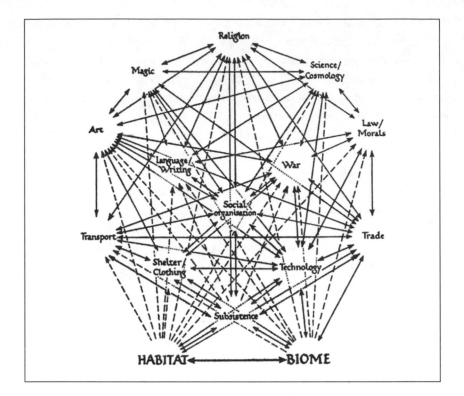

Figure 9.3   **Interactions Between Different Aspects of the Socio-cultural Component of Ecosystems Comprehending Agriculture. The refined systems diagram, as used in the Reckitt Lecture, 1953.**

stages in the liberation of the human spirit and accelerates processes of culture change and diversification. "Advances in the means of production have indeed determined history, but only in the sense that they have widened the range of choice open to human societies."[8]

The Reckitt lecture was Grahame Clark's most explicit statement on economic prehistory, and it governed much of his teaching and research for the rest of his career. He returned to the same general topic in his inaugural lecture, "The Study of Prehistory," at Cambridge on November 26, 1954, with a plea for a broad perspective and close relationships with anthropology and history, as well as the natural sciences. "The proper field is surely prehistory," not prehistoric archaeology as a discipline.[9] He considered what he called "primary prehistory"—prehistory before written records—of universal relevance to humanity, and therefore of fundamental importance. Prehistory was "essentially a social study," he remarked, by the nature of the evidence a study of ancient societies, not individuals. He criticized overly simplistic evolutionary perspectives on early humanity as being divorced from the realities of culture change and environmental adaptation.

In reality, culture, the mechanisms of cultural transmission, and the natural environment were closely connected. Given the limitations of archaeological evidence, one could profitably start by studying the economic bases of ancient societies. Such societies were elements in ever changing ecosystems. One could achieve little beyond "decorating museums" without collaboration with natural scientists. "The scope of prehistoric societies is thus as all-embracing as social life itself and includes the whole range of human activities from subsistence to worship."[10] The scope of archaeology at Cambridge was global. The track record of earlier Cambridge scholars reflected such eclectic interests, and it would continue to do so. Such a global perspective was important to all of us. "Is it altogether too fanciful to suggest that the study of world prehistory may even help to nourish the solidarity of mankind on which our well-being, if not our very existence depends?"[11]

The Reckitt and inaugural lectures were the last time for many years that Clark's ecological and economic interests came to the fore, for his interests shifted into the international arena.

Colleagues, Blades, and Trapezes

When Clark was Disney, archaeology was still a tiny discipline in which all the major players knew one another well. Richard Atkinson in Cardiff, Grahame Clark in Cambridge, Christopher Hawkes in Oxford, and Stuart Piggott in Edinburgh formed a powerful quartet and dominated British archaeology in the 1950s and early 1960s. Clark enjoyed a lifetime friendship with Piggott, whom he had met in Trundle days. Piggott, an easygoing and relaxed man, is said to have had difficulty with Clark's austere manner, even in the field, but the two cooperated closely for a lifetime. Christopher Hawkes worked on the Iron Age and was an ardent and extremely skilled typologist, a specialty Clark had largely abandoned in the 1930s. He was a complex character and a scholar in the Germanic tradition, whose work on the Iron Age was much concerned with diffusion. His brand of culture history was anathema to Grahame, who wrote a memorable paper criticizing the almost neurotic preoccupation with prehistoric invasions into the United Kingdom. His "Invasion Hypothesis in British Archaeology," which was published by *Antiquity* in 1966, advocated explanations based on indigenous evolution. Hawkes's reply in the next issue accused Clark of being "a lifetime member of the younger school." There was little love lost between the two of them.

The other major intellectual influence of the day was, of course, Gordon Childe, whose syntheses of European prehistory and of the origins of food production and civilization in southwestern Asia were required reading for all archaeologists. Simple, well-written narratives, his books became archaeological canon between the 1930s and early 1960s. The reasons are easy to discern. Childe was an excellent writer who had a sense of history distilled from artifacts and an encyclopedic knowledge of sites and artifacts, both well-known and obscure. Furthermore, he was a masterly linguist who could converse readily with obscure colleagues far from the mainstream of archaeology. His Neolithic and Urban Revolution did not come under attack until the advent of multidisciplinary research into the origins of food production by Robert Braidwood in the 1950s. New radiocarbon chronologies also undermined much of his thinking about European prehistory based on artifact typologies.

Childe was an important influence on Grahame throughout his earlier career. He encouraged the young scholar, especially when president of the Prehistoric Society, and contributed regularly to the *Proceedings*. The two became good friends, even going on a short walking tour in Scotland in 1942. When Childe retired from the Institute of Archaeology in 1956, Clark devoted the 1955 *Proceedings* to a festschrift in his honor entitled *Contributions to Prehistory Offered to Vere Gordon Childe*. He paid graceful homage to his mentor and longtime colleague, praising the "range and depth of his interests and sympathies." A galaxy of European prehistorians paid tribute with short contributions, among them Robert Braidwood, Henri Breuil, Dorothy Garrod, Kenneth Oakley of the British Museum, who wrote an essay of continuing value on ancient fire, and many continental colleagues. Stuart Piggott made the point that Childe had inspired much research with his bold ideas, among them his suggestion that Windmill Hill pottery came from a western European tradition. A bibliography of Childe's works rounded out the tribute, which appeared early in 1956, only a year before the depressed and now retired scholar committed suicide in Australia.

Grahame Clark kept few of his letters, which complicates the life of his biographer, but he did save two haunting notes from Childe, written a few days before his suicide in Australia's Blue Mountains. "The Bandstone cliffs of the Blue Mts—700–1000' vertical and actually undercut—still seem the safest to fall over accidently," he wrote as if planning his demise, which came when he jumped over a convenient precipice. We do not have Grahame's reply to this extraordinary communication. A second letter sent a few days later enclosed the manuscript of his article (later entitled "Retrospect" by *Antiquity*) with the comment: "I have sketched what I can recall of the development of my own thinking . . . that may in time come in useful if only for obituary purposes." Clark forwarded the "Retrospect" on to Glyn Daniel, who published it in *Antiquity* in 1958.[12]

Clark's own paper to the Childe festschrift was a reconsideration of the Peacock's Farm site, using new pollen data from Harry Godwin and additional comparative information about Mesolithic cultures in Britain and France.[13] Godwin now assigned the critical Mesolithic scatter to the Late Boreal, Zone VIc, while Grahame placed the flint assemblage in the earlier, and now better known, Mesolithic Sauveterrian cultural tradition of France on the basis of its few burins and scrapers and use of the microburin technique, rather than in the later, better-known Tardenoisian culture with its well-made microliths, which had been his basis for comparison twenty years earlier. He also raised the question of indigenous origins, suggesting that Peacock's Farm and the few other Sauveterrian occurrences in Britain may have had local "epi-Palaeolithic roots." This represented somewhat of an intellectual shift from his more diffusionist thinking of *Mesolithic Age* days. The following year, Godwin and Clark collaborated again on a paper describing recent Maglemose spear point finds at Brandesburton, south of Star Carr, and also a point from nearby Hornsea, which bore a close resemblance to the famous Leman and Ower harpoon of the 1930s.[14]

Two years later, the 1958 *Proceedings* carried Grahame's last original contribution to Mesolithic research. His article "Blade and Trapeze Industries of the European Stone Age" surveyed numerous flint assemblages, from North Africa and Spain to Thessaly, which contained a high percentage of snapped blades turned into trapeze-shaped microliths, leaving their sharp edges intact.[15] This is a classic Clark paper in the older mode, which used the familiar typological and distribution map approach of his earlier career on a continent-wide scale. Blade and trapeze industries did not occur in Britain. They were a continental phenomenon, perhaps associated with incipient domestication of sheep as well as with hunting and gathering. As he had with the British Sauveterrian three years earlier, Clark weighed two hypotheses—a diffusionist model or indigenous origin. He stressed that blade and trapeze industries were not a "unitary phenomenon." In all probability, they did not originate from a single source and might have deep roots in ancient Late Glacial stoneworking traditions. He even wondered if they were a forerunner of some form of European Pre-Pottery Neolithic, the work of pottery-less farmers, such as those recently unearthed by Kathleen Kenyon at Jericho. With the exception of a paper on the prehistory of archery published in 1963, prompted by two radiocarbon dates for wooden bow staves in the Somerset Levels, "Blade and Trapeze Industries" was Clark's last effort at original, detailed synthesis along the lines of *Prehistoric Europe*, one of his trademarks for a quarter century of his long career.[16]

Micklemoor Hill

Fieldwork was very much on Grahame's mind after the triumphant publication of Star Carr, something he considered an essential part of any young archaeologist's training. He had been much impressed by the excavations by the German archaeologist Gerhard Bersu at the Early Iron Age village at Little Woodbury in the chalk country near Salisbury in southern England just before World War II. Bersu had removed large areas of topsoil, then scraped the underlying chalk, finding plans of farm houses, storage pits, even crop drying frames. The excavation transformed knowledge of Iron Age communities outside places of refuge like hill forts and was supported by the Prehistoric Society.[17] (Bersu was interned on the Isle of Man during World War II and carried out excavations there.) Clark decided to test an Iron Age site within easy reach of Cambridge using the same approach.

An amateur archaeologist had recently recovered considerable amounts of Early Iron Age pottery dating to the fifth century B.C. from Micklemoor Hill, near West Harling in Norfolk. This seemed a likely site, so Grahame began operations in 1948. Star Carr intervened, and it was not until

1952–1953 that excavations resumed. Most of the work was shouldered by Clare Fell, assistant curator of the Museum of Archaeology, who assumed responsibility for much of the excavation report, and, above all, the pottery. The acid gravel subsoil at West Harling was very different from the chalk at Little Woodbury, but the excavators still were able to recover the plans of two houses that resembled those from Bersu's site in size and plan. The larger dwellings had two concentric rings of posts, boasted of porches, and were about fifteen meters (49 feet) in diameter. The West Harling people kept cattle and sheep, and also cultivated cereal. A visiting Danish botanist had identified the impression of a grain of spelt on a potsherd.[18]

Micklemoor Hill merely whetted Grahame's appetite for earlier Neolithic dwellings, which were still almost unknown, even in the classic chalk regions of southern Britain, where floor plans could be identified with ease. He was constantly on the lookout for another site with organic remains or, failing that, a settlement in a sandy location where he could trace postholes and structures from discolorations in the subsoil, like his colleagues in the Low Countries and on the chalk.

Hurst Fen

In 1954, Grace, Lady Briscoe, a local landowner with archaeological interests, published the results of some excavations on her property at Hurst Fen, near Mildenhall in Suffolk, in the *Proceedings of the Cambridge Antiquarian Society*.[19] Her excavations revealed a scatter of Neolithic pottery and flint artifacts on sandy soil over an area about 165 meters by 82 meters (180 by 90 yards). Grahame felt the site had considerable potential for unearthing Neolithic dwellings, especially since Lady Briscoe found dark patches containing potsherds and flints in the subsoil. He descended on Hurst Fen in 1957–1958 with teams of undergraduates but left much of the excavation, and especially the laborious scraping of the surface of the topsoil, to the department's assistant in research, Eric Higgs, who had been appointed in 1956. Higgs also undertook the metric analysis of the flint artifacts, especially the scrapers, while research student Ian Longworth, later to become a keeper in the British Museum, studied the pottery.

Hurst Fen could have been an ideal place to find Neolithic long houses, storage pits, and other structures, but the site never fulfilled its promise. The compacted brown culture layer with its artifacts lay close to the sur-

Figure 9.4   **A sectioned pit at Hurst Fen, 1957.**

face. Once removed, soil discolorations came to light, but it was necessary to remove about forty-three centimeters (17 inches) of sandy soil before the dark marks could be defined adequately for photography. In the end, the excavators scraped some 1,860 square meters (20,000 square feet) of subsoil in a vain quest for house plans. The few postholes that appeared had no coherent relationship to one another.

Two hundred "hollows" lay across the site, none of them deep or narrow enough to be postholes, but up to 1.2 meters (4 feet) across. Most were barely 0.3 meter (1 foot) deep, the deepest only 0.45 meter (18 inches) (Figure 9.4). Some contained charcoal and flint potboilers; others lay in clusters, just like those found at other Neolithic sites in southern England and Europe.[20] The Dutch archaeologist Professor H. T. Waterbolk, an experienced excavator of Neolithic settlements in the Netherlands, visited Hurst Fen during the excavations and agreed that the most economic explanation for the "hollows" was that they represented the lower parts of storage pits used for housing grain. Impressions of grain

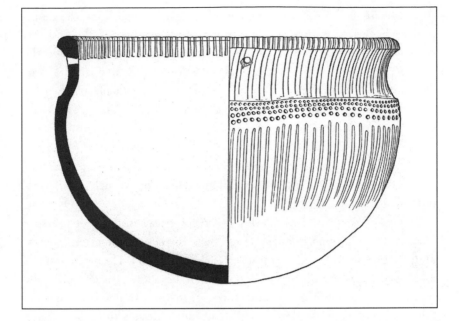

Figure 9.5 **Mildenhall ware from Hurst Fen. Courtesy the Prehistoric Society.**

and even an apple pip on Hurst Fen potsherds strengthened the case. Unfortunately, however, the pits formed no discernable pattern as a whole, beyond evidence for clustering.

Hurst Fen was a disappointment after Star Carr, for severe erosion of the local soils had removed all traces of structures. But both the stone industry and the ceramics were of importance.[21] The flint industry, with its leaf-shaped arrowheads and large convex scrapers, was typical of primary Neolithic sites in southern Britain. Longworth's study of the potsherds, making up about three hundred vessels, compared the bag-shaped Hurst Fen pots with their heavy rims, burnished surfaces, and incised decoration with those from other contemporary Neolithic sites. He confirmed the site's distinctive Mildenhall ware as a regional style—archaeologist Isobel Smith's Neolithic A group (Figure 9.5).[22]

In his brief discussion, Clark attributed Hurst Fen to the closing stages of the local Middle Neolithic "as represented by the causewayed enclosures of Abingdon, Windmill Hill, and Whiteleaf."[23] Clearly, he was disappointed in the excavation, which had the potential to reveal the first settlement plan for a Neolithic site in eastern England. Nevertheless, the excavation yielded important typological information, defined the eastern English Neolithic more clearly, and provided invaluable training for the department's undergraduates, the present writer included. This biographer learned how to scrape subsoil at Hurst Fen—and also not to stand too close to posthole profiles as they were being prepared for photography. A pristine example collapsed under my inexperienced weight in front of an exasperated Grahame. I was exiled to a remote trench for the rest of the excavation.

Hurst Fen was Grahame Clark's last major excavation. Sheer pressure of work and changing intellectual interests turned his attention increasingly to the much broader issues of world prehistory. He did one more excavation: at Peacock's Farm, the site where he started, in 1960. The dig was a small one and had a specific purpose. It was a time when radiocarbon dates were upsetting established chronologies for the British Neolithic and pushing the widely accepted date of about 2000 B.C. back at least a millennium, with the period lasting three times longer than previously believed. (For Clark and radiocarbon dating, see Chapter 10.) There was widespread skepticism at the new chronology among Neolithic archaeologists, so Grahame and Harry Godwin decided to obtain samples from the Peacock's Farm sequence. They cut a deep section close to their original stratigraphic cutting and found no potsherds, but had no trouble picking up the Neolithic level, a flint flake, a sheep toe bone, and a scatter of charcoals for twelve dates in a level that was full of pollen grains and easily assignable to the original sequence. Two samples yielded dates of 2910 ± 120 and 2990 ± 120 B.C., and the pattern of the dates as a whole was a powerful vindication of the earlier timescale. The dates from the fenland closely matched a reading obtained from a pollen sequence at nearby Holme Fen and two Neolithic sites in northern England, but were later than samples from Hembury in southwestern England and from seven Irish early farming sites.[24]

Thereafter, Grahame confined himself to analysis, visiting sites and synthesis, at which he was a master. He also gained deep satisfaction from the many important excavations conducted by the department at home and overseas during his later years as Disney Chair.

"I Had Little Alternative but to Accept Invitations"

The Disney brought new responsibilities and exciting opportunities. He became heavily involved in committees inside and outside the university. "With professors of archaeology still rare in Britain, I had little alternative but to accept invitations," he complained.[25] He served on the Ancient Monuments Board, the Royal Commission on the Historical Monuments of England, the Management Committee of the London Institute of Archaeology, and the councils of learned societies. But his lifelong concern was with the Prehistoric Society. His record of attendance at meetings was virtually continuous, his editing of the *Proceedings* by this stage an integral part of his professional life. John Coles, then assistant editor, recalls editing and completely rewriting papers with Clark as they traveled to and from London in the train.[26]

The publication of *Prehistoric Europe* brought increased visibility and an opportunity to travel to the United States for the first time. In 1952, Grahame was asked to the inaugural meeting of the newly formed Wenner Gren Foundation for Anthropological Research in New York. The endowment behind the foundation had begun life as the Viking Fund, established by the Swedish industrialist and entrepreneur Carl Axel Wenner-Gren in 1941. Wenner-Gren had made a fortune in Electrolux refrigerators, but his endowment came under suspicion from anthropologists because of doubts about his role in World War II. The new foundation was headed by Paul Fejos, a Hungarian who had established himself in Hollywood before the war.[27] By chance, he met Wenner-Gren in Indonesia and was recruited to set up the fund. Fejos worked hard to dispel suspicions about his sponsor and succeeded in persuading Alfred Kroeber, the doyen of American anthropologists, to chair the inaugural meeting. He also made it clear from the beginning that the foundation would support all four fields of anthropology, including prehistoric archaeology and human paleontology, as well as fostering an aggressively international perspective. Most of the delegates at the initial meeting were from the United States. Clark was one of four representatives from Britain. It was here that he first met Professor Gordon Willey, the Maya archaeologist from Harvard who was a pioneer of settlement archaeology. The two became good friends and exchanged visiting appointments at Cambridge and Harvard in later years.

The standard of teaching was adequate but not exceptional. Charles McBurney enthralled a tiny audience of "Palaeoliths" with Stone Age lectures delivered at lightning speed and an intense enthusiasm that brought several now well-known archaeologists into the professional ranks. At the time, he was working on the huge Middle and Upper Palaeolithic cave at Haua Fteah in Libya, which he had first investigated during his war service. As a result, his lectures were a refreshing counterpoint to Burkitt's much narrower perspective and got his students thinking about wider horizons. Grahame taught the Mesolithic with an eclectic perspective, making frequent use of ethnographic analogies from European folk history and other parts of the world, which, again, opened students' minds. Not even injuries could stop him. When he was found to have a degenerated disk in his back, he lectured lying on a firm plank. Every year, a steady stream of archaeologists visited and gave lectures, including such luminaries as Desmond Clark and Louis Leakey, who were themselves Cambridge graduates. They and others, notably Australian archaeologist John Mulvaney, now looked to Cambridge for young archaeologists trained in the latest ecological and environmental approaches, men and women with field and laboratory experience and a wide intellectual perspective.

The Cambridge training included at least a modicum of fieldwork, invariably carried out on a shoestring, and usually under the aegis of a department faculty member. The university itself made little or no provision for research, even in fields like archaeology, which, at the time, was still very undeveloped. Researchers depended on grants from their colleges and from limited private money held by the department, or from the very limited funds of the Prehistoric Society, but the grants were invariably tiny. This meant that student labor was all-important. It was remarkable how much was achieved, often far from Cambridge, witness the stupendous Haua Fteah excavations of the late 1940s and early 1950s, which involved a whole generation of student archaeologists. The artifacts and faunal remains from the cave provided laboratory experience for undergraduates for a decade afterward.

President of the Prehistoric Society

After more than thirty-five years of teaching, research, and editorship, Grahame was elected president of his beloved Prehistoric Society in 1959.

He used the occasion of his presidential address both to celebrate the centenary of the establishment of the Antiquity of Humankind by Boucher de Perthes, John Evans, Joseph Prestwich, and others, and to mark the fiftieth anniversary of the founding of the Prehistoric Society of East Anglia. He paid tribute to the many volunteers who kept the society alive through thick and thin and made his usual plea for closer associations with natural scientists and scholars from every relevant academic discipline.

His mind set was moving once again beyond multidisciplinary research to a new vision of prehistory as a vehicle for studying human diversity. "Prehistoric archaeology is only one of many means of studying prehistory," he said. "But further than this, it is by no means certain that prehistoric archaeologists are the only people qualified to interpret prehistory; and, again, there is surely room for more than one kind of prehistory, as there is for more than one kind of history."[28] This curiously prophetic statement resonates with today's archaeologists, who realize they do not necessarily have a monopoly on the interpretation and writing of the past.

Different prehistories implied a much wider focus of prehistoric research. Grahame pointed out that a sixth of the papers published in the *Proceedings* in the immediate postwar years were from outside Europe and southwestern Asia. This number was a reflection of the overseas military service of many members. But regrettably the focus was again narrowing to Europe, despite a growing overseas membership of about a fifth. "We have paid our part in breaking down the insularity of British Archaeology," he remarked. Now the Society "must move forward onto an altogether ampler stage and play our part in advancing the conception of prehistory as an essential heritage of the human race." He quoted O. G. S. Crawford's first *Antiquity* editorial: "Our field is the earth, our stage in time a million years or so, our subject the human race." Grahame threw down the intellectual gauntlet: "Our studies will gain immeasurably if we see them only in the widest perspective. . . . Think of your efforts as part of an effort to understand the common past of humanity."[29]

His presidential address may have caused few ripples in the archaeological pond, but it was a sign of a new direction in his career as a teacher and synthesizer of prehistory on a grand scale.

10

❦

World Prehistory

From the student's point of view one of the main attractions of prehistoric archaeology is the way it brings them even at an undergraduate level to the very brink of the unknown.

Prehistory at Cambridge and Beyond[1]

Grahame Clark was by nature and inclination an intensely private man whose public aloofness hid an extremely kind nature. His personality never allowed him to be comfortable in casual social situations with students or in the public eye. He had the inclination neither to appear on television nor to write lower-level books for the widest audience. Nor could he compete with the charming and suave Glyn Daniel, who was never at a loss for words on the lecture platform or in front of a camera. So Grahame remained in the background, contenting himself with occasional swipes at "what might charitably be termed post-TV books."[2] For all his reluctance to become a public figure, Grahame was a tenacious missionary for prehistoric archaeology and wrote constantly for a wider audience, especially later in his career. His concern with such works deepened in his later years as Disney, when he became seriously engaged with world prehistory as a fundamental intellectual issue.

By the time Grahame came to write the first global prehistory of the modern era, he already had several books of broader appeal to his credit.

The first was *Archaeology and Society*, which appeared in 1939 and went through three editions, largely on the basis of its student sales. At the time, there were no other basic textbooks on archaeological method and theory. A year later, his *Prehistoric England* was published by Batsford and was in a fourth edition by 1948. In 1946, he wrote *From Savagery to Civilization*, which might be thought of as a companion volume to *Society*, a general statement on what happened in prehistory. We should step back in time and examine this short book, for it contains ideas that resurfaced in his later synthetic works and in his *World Prehistory*.

From Savagery to Civilization

From Savagery to Civilization, published by Cobbett Press just after the war, was a short student text "written under wartime difficulties over a longish period, much of it in trains." This was a small book, he noted, "concerned with tracing the main steps by which man has emerged from the brutes and attained to civilization."[3] Clark used a tripartite subdivision of prehistory pioneered by anthropologist Edward Tylor in the 1880s but employed long before him: savagery (hunter-gatherers), barbarism (food producers), and civilization. Grahame modified this simple, unilinear scheme to allow for lower and higher savagery, the former subsuming the prehistory of archaic humans, higher savages appearing with the Upper Palaeolithic. He was to espouse this general scheme for the rest of his life.

With the exception of the *Homo erectus* finds at Zhoukoudian in China, the narrative never ventures away from Europe and the Mediterranean region. There are no startling revelations. Barbarism with its agriculture and animal domestication was, we are told, "the origins of life as we know it, for barbarism is essentially the foundation of civilization."[4] By today's standards, the book is an anachronism, especially in its perceptions of hunter-gatherers as living precariously and its simplistic evolutionary tone. It is an interesting reflection of the staggering advances in prehistory over the past half century that there is no mention of Olduvai Gorge, while the Desert Fayum is cited as the earliest farming community in the world, with Egypt being thought of as the cradle of the first agriculture. There is no mention of Childe's Neolithic and Urban Revolutions, and the discussion of the origins of civilization dwells almost exclusively on technological innovations. To Clark, technology was always an important catalyst of cultural change and progress.

From Savagery to Civilization is not one of Clark's best books, perhaps because of its peripatetic birth on the rails between Cambridge and London. The approach was old-fashioned even for the 1940s, with its insistence on a form of unilinear evolution and its broad subdivisions of prehistoric human societies into barbarians and savages. Even the two reprints of later years, the last in 1953, add little to the original text. Its magisterial tone sets it apart from Childe's brilliant, contemporary syntheses, by which it pales in comparison. Nevertheless, *Savagery* enjoyed some success. It was published in the United States and was translated into German and Hungarian.

Grahame was involved in some other book projects aimed at a wider audience, among them a widely distributed small volume, *The Stone Age Hunters*, published as part of a series spun off an ambitious coffee table book on prehistoric societies and early civilizations published by Thames and Hudson in 1967. He also collaborated with Stuart Piggott on *Prehistoric Societies,* a broad survey, mainly of European prehistory, which appeared under the Hutchinson imprint in 1965. But his serious efforts at global synthesis began in the 1960s, as the Cambridge department became the center of a major diaspora of young archaeologists to remote corners of the world.

The Great Diaspora

At the time of his retirement, one of Grahame Clark's proudest possessions was a map of the world stuck with colored pins showing the locations of Cambridge graduates as far afield as Australia, Canada, New Zealand, South Africa, and the United States.[5] His own experience went back to the days when Cambridge was virtually the only university training professional archaeologists. When he obtained his Ph.D., about the only academic jobs in British archaeology were found at Cambridge itself. But the department turned out a steady stream of talented graduates who went abroad to practice archaeology, notably a succession of African prehistorians (already mentioned in Chapter 3).

The expansion in archaeology began in the late 1950s and continues unabated to this day. When it came, the expansion was as much overseas as at home, and Cambridge, with its Haddon Museum, well-grounded anthropological curriculum, and growing international perspective, was well placed to cater to a growing demand. Miles Burkitt and Dorothy Garrod had inspired an earlier generation of archaeologists to seek careers abroad. These graduates now came to Cambridge for a new dynasty of recruits, who became involved not only in research but in training local archaeologists in Africa and elsewhere. Merrick Posnansky, who took a Cambridge diploma in archaeology in 1967, was appointed professor of archaeology at Legon University in Ghana, where he introduced formal degree courses to train Ghanaian archaeologists. In 1956, Ray Inskeep, who had worked at Haua Fteah cave in Libya, was encouraged by Grahame to work on rock art in Tanzania, and then he went out to become keeper of prehistory at the Rhodes-Livingstone Museum in Northern Rhodesia under Desmond Clark. He was specifically charged with working on much later Iron Age societies, at the time unknown north of the Zambezi River, not on Stone Age cultures. In 1958, he returned to Cambridge as the retired Miles Burkitt's successor, where he brought an up-to-date African perspective to a department that was already looking outward in ways unimaginable twenty years earlier. (Inskeep subsequently took an appointment at the University of Cape Town in 1960.)

Another seminal figure joined the Cambridge department in 1956. Eric Higgs was a retired sheep farmer and London University graduate who took the diploma in archaeology at Cambridge as a mature student in 1953. He remained in Cambridge and was appointed to Clark's newly established assistantship in research three years later. Higgs had worked at Haua Fteah during the final 1955 season, when he assumed responsibility for the enormous faunal collections from the cave. By 1957, he was firmly entrenched in a makeshift faunal laboratory in the department, where an entire generation of undergraduates labored over the Haua Fteah bones, each assigned specific body parts. Never was zooarchaeology so effectively taught. He also excavated a Mesolithic settlement at Downton in Wiltshire, which served as a training ground for many of the same students.[6]

Friendly, yet possessed of a ruthless intellect, Higgs challenged the undergraduates of the day in a way that served them well in later years. To work with Higgs was to be presented with a constant kaleidoscope of new ideas, with a feeling that your work mattered, that you were challenging a frontier. The long hours and constant intellectual interchange were intoxicating stuff for young students who labored in the "Higgery." Clark and

Higgs worked well together, although neither had any illusions about the other. They were both professionals, the one publically austere and Olympian, the other more approachable but also a formidable, machiavellian personality. Stone Age students in particular benefited from the association, which added a new dimension to the rapid-fire lectures and engaging enthusiasm of Charles McBurney.

The later 1950s and early 1960s produced a generation of young archaeologists who were brought up on economic prehistory and a sense of the importance of sound artifact typologies, and with a burgeoning international perspective. Some of them elected to remain in Britain, among them the current holder of the Disney Chair, Colin Renfrew, Barry Cunliffe, professor at Oxford, and Martin Biddle, famous for his excavations at medieval Winchester. Grahame himself strongly encouraged everyone to go abroad, where, in his judgment, the best opportunities lay. Both Louis Leakey and Desmond Clark came searching for graduates. Richard Wright went out as warden of the Olorgesaillie site museum in Kenya's Rift Valley, and then on to the University of Sydney, Australia. He was followed by Glynn Isaac, a graduate of the University of Capetown and Cambridge, who soon became deputy director of the Center for Prehistory and Paleontology in the National Museum of Kenya, then a professor at the University of California–Berkeley, and one of the world's leading paleoanthropologists at Harvard before his premature death in 1985. The present writer went out as Ray Inskeep's successor in Livingstone and built on his predecessor's trail-blazing Iron Age research.

Many of the new jobs opened up on the far side of the world. Charles Higham, for many years professor of anthropology at New Zealand's University of Otago, recalls asking Grahame whether he should apply for a minor archaeological post in the United Kingdom. Clark had just returned from a term's teaching at Otago. "Higham, do you want to be a porter or a station master?" said Grahame in his sweeping way.[7] Higham chose the station master route, and he went on to a highly successful research career in southeast Asia and a Chair at Otago. Clark's point was simple and entirely consistent with his long history of painting archaeology with a big brush. Most opportunities were overseas, far from the comfortable backwaters of British and European archaeology. That was where the future of archaeology lay.

After his retirement in 1973, Grahame wrote *Prehistory at Cambridge and Beyond* (1989), a manifesto that commemorated the remarkable diaspora of Cambridge archaeologists since the 1930s. The book is part biography, part archaeological history, and part self-justification. He regarded the diaspora as one of his major achievements—and it was, insofar as he could take credit for it. To some extent, the expansion of archaeology was a product of rapidly changing higher education and of a world in which archaeology had found a legitimate role in writing unwritten history and in the areas of conservation, heritage, and tourism. But the fostering of world prehistory as a legitimate intellectual concept was a strategy of Clark's from his earliest days as editor of the *Proceedings*. When the currents of history presented Cambridge with the opportunity to train archaeologists to write this prehistory, he encouraged them to do so with a single-minded intensity and a breadth of vision that still dazzles.

He offered encouragement at every turn. The author vividly remembers sending Grahame a copy of a monograph on Zambian Iron Age archaeology based on his doctoral dissertation, which Clark had supervised with brisk, if distant, efficiency. His criticisms had been shrewd and right to the point. Back came an airmail letter acknowledging the book and offering some sage comments. "Your report brings back memories of Star Carr," he wrote. "We fended for ourselves and so did you. You have added a chapter to prehistory."[8] The unexpected letter was welcome encouragement for a former pupil living far from Cambridge.

Grahame's influence on an entire generation of archaeologists was immense. He felt undergraduates benefited from exposure to the latest ideas. The Cambridge training was, even at its very best, necessarily superficial and very much what one individually made of it. Clark was a believer in doing archaeology—in casting young archaeologists out into the field on their own to develop their practical aptitudes and acquire a wide range of experience. He came from an era when one learned by doing, a far cry from the years of courses and theoretical training that form part of the lengthy and formalized graduate programs of today, with all their sometimes ludicrous checks, balances, and formalities. His attitude of making people "station masters" at an early age paid rich dividends for a discipline in desperate need of working archaeologists with a broad perspective. In large part, the world prehistory we know today began with the Cambridge diaspora of the 1950s and 1960s.

Radiocarbon Dating and the Origins of Farming

The work of the Danish botanist Johannes Iversen on forest clearance, long friendships with historian Michael Postan and Stuart Piggott, and the Hurst Fen excavations had given Grahame a lasting interest in the origins of agriculture. He considered the beginnings of farming and animal domestication the most significant turning point in human prehistory, the source of all later cultural developments. However, he did not take an active role in the broader issues of the origins of food production until the development of radiocarbon dating by University of Chicago scientists Willard Libby and J. R. Arnold in 1949.

The news of the revolutionary dating method reached Cambridge within a few months. O. G. S. Crawford heard about it while dining in St. John's College and promptly announced it in *Antiquity*. Libby's new method came as Clark was spending considerable time "trying to envisage world prehistory."[9] He was frustrated by his seeming inability to develop accurate chronologies for widely separated parts of the globe, which could be linked one with another. Did, for example, agriculture begin in one place or in several, and separately in the Americas? He soon heard of the new dating method from Crawford, also from Harry Godwin and his contacts in the natural sciences. Cambridge was to boast of one of the first radiocarbon laboratories in the subdepartment of quaternary research. So important did Godwin consider radiocarbon dating that he made it the topic of his prestigious Croonian Lecture to the Royal Society in 1960, pointing out that many of the first dates were for pollen dated levels and postglacial events.[10] Grahame was able to attend a series of important conferences on radiocarbon dating at which he urged the processing of samples from stratigraphically reliable archaeological sites with well-researched ecological settings. His persistence at conferences and his sedulous fostering of scientific contacts paid off. The radiocarbon date from the Star Carr excavations was one of the first prehistoric samples to be processed. Clark watched as the traditional European chronologies based on artifact typology, cross-dating from Mediterranean sites, and informed guesswork fell before the onslaught of an entirely new independent chronology that allowed the dating of important prehistoric developments at widely separated locations. The chronological framework for a truly global prehistory had finally arrived. But he was well aware of the pitfalls—the importance of blocks of dates and the need to work with general patterns of individual readings and the need for many theoretical shifts as chronologies became more refined.

World Prehistory: An Outline

With the end of active fieldwork, Grahame began to write more intensively. He had never been far from a typewriter, But now the pace intensified. Toward the end of his life, he became obsessed with writing, beginning a new book as soon as he finished its predecessor. His daily routine, even when he was Disney, revolved around writing. It was inevitable that he would eventually sit down and write a prehistory of humankind. In 1960, he was probably the only living archaeologist who had the intellectual breadth and knowledge to undertake such a seemingly overwhelming task. Years of editing the *Proceedings*, his contacts with archaeologists in many lands, and wide travels in Europe gave him unique qualifications for the work at hand—and his interest in international archaeology dated back to the Future of Archaeology Conference during the war years, if not earlier. All these intellectual strands came together in the first world prehistory ever written with the aid of radiocarbon chronologies. Clark saw the opportunity and acted on it.

No one knows when the idea of a one-volume prehistory of humankind came to him. Glyn Daniel claims in his biography that the idea began with a proposal from Sir Sidney Roberts of Cambridge University Press for a *Cambridge Prehistory of the World*. Daniel outlined a three-volume work. He was asked to edit it but proposed instead a three-person team—Grahame, Geoffrey Bushnell, the Cambridge Americanist, and himself. Eventually, a meeting was held at which Clark informed his fellow team members that the press now wanted a single volume written by the three of them. Bushnell and Daniel promised to think about it. Daniel alleges Clark quietly wrote his *World Prehistory* in the meantime and then sent inscribed copies to his colleagues. No one had told them of the change of plan.[11]

Whatever the truth of this unsubstantiated claim (which seems unlikely, given that Glyn's wife, Ruth, drew the maps for Clark's book), Cambridge University Press published *World Prehistory: An Outline* in 1961, a book designed "to present a brief outline of man's prehistoric past." The preface apologized for the incomplete coverage and for the arbitrary way in which conclusions were sometimes drawn. "As a teacher, the author is aware that even an imperfect text may have its uses, more especially to those prepared to adventure more widely in the literature of the subject."[12]

World Prehistory appeared at a turning point in prehistoric archaeology. Radiocarbon dating was still a relative novelty, ecological approaches were still not widely used, and the major theoretical furors of the 1960s had barely begun. To even attempt the book was an act of some temerity, simply because enormous areas of the world were still complete archaeological blanks, far more so than they are today. Europe and the Mediterranean basin were relatively well known, even if their prehistory as being revolutionized by spectacular finds like early Jericho and the first dates for the beginnings of European agriculture. The Leakeys had just found *Zinjanthropus* and *Homo habilis* at Olduvai Gorge, and human origins had been pushed back to over 2 million years. Chinese and Southeast Asian archaeology were virtually unknown; Australia, the Pacific Islands, and New Zealand were a near blank. Archaeology in the Americas was confined, in the main, to North America, Mesoamerica, and Peru, while theoretical debate had moved little further than the revolution theories of Gordon Childe and Robert Braidwood's new thinking about early agriculture, animal domestication, and the hilly flanks of southwestern Asia.[13] Any synthesis of world prehistory was at best a jigsaw puzzle, and a very incomplete one at that. There were simply not the archaeologists in the world to fill in the gaps. "The aim is not to produce a chronicle," we are told, "a kind of Bayeux tapestry worked flatly on a roll of fabric, but something more like a history painted in depth on a canvas of fixed dimensions."[14] On the whole, the author succeeded.

Grahame's *Outline* came in at a mere 284 pages and encompassed human prehistory in nine chapters. The balance of coverage is interesting, for no less than 57 percent of the book covered central and western Europe, where most archaeological work was carried out. The figure dropped to 52 percent in the second edition and only 33 percent in the third, a reflection of Clark's constant travels and a tidal wave of new research far from Europe. To keep up with new finds, he maintained a file cabinet with drawers for each chapter that were filled with reprints from former students and archaeologists from around the world.

Chapter 1, "Man's Place in Nature," described environmental change and biological evolution—human origins. He recited the familiar litany of glacials and interglacials, pluvials and interpluvials, which was the simplistic environmental backdrop for the Ice Age of the 1950s, but he mentioned in passing deep-sea cores from the Caribbean that showed as many as fifteen Pleistocene glaciations. We learn about loess and low sea levels, subdivide the Würm glaciation and its equivalent tropical pluvials, and discuss the familiar Holocene climatic stages, which Clark labeled the Neothermal.[15] The environmental background was too general to have more than the most superficial significance, but it was an accurate reflection of knowledge of Ice Age environmental shifts at the time.

"Biological Evolution" skated over human origins at breakneck speed, starting with our primate ancestry and the importance of upright posture, then proceeded to three genera of Australopithecines, one of them *Homo*. Clark was suitably vague about the evolutionary position of the Australopithecines (no one could be anything else at the time) and, surprisingly, makes no mention of the controversies surrounding the first toolmakers, or *Homo habilis*, hot issues at the time.[16] From the Australopithecines, Clark moved quickly through *Homo erectus*, then known mainly from the Java and Beijing specimens and a scatter of fossils from Europe. He pointed to the variability among the Neanderthals and considered them an intermediate form between such archaic humans as the Swanscombe individual from England's Thames Valley and the Steinheim skull with its well-developed brow ridges from Germany. He made no mention of important and well-known African fossils such as the Broken Hill skull from Northern Rhodesia and the Florisbad cranium from South Africa, which were (and still are) evidence for just as much human variability south of the Sahara at the time.

The diversity of Neanderthal anatomy was a powerful argument for thinking that "*Homo sapiens* almost certainly emerged somewhere in Eurasia and most probably somewhere in western Asia."[17] Many scholars of the day would have agreed with him, since the Skhul burials from Mount Carmel, excavated by Dorothy Garrod, were considered prime evidence of Neanderthal variability. It was modern humans who spread into cooler latitudes and outlying parts of the world such as the Americas during the Late Ice Age and Postglacial periods. This diaspora "was made possible by the relatively unspecialized character of *Homo sapiens*, but above all by the possession of culture, by means of which man had been able to adapt himself to the widest range of environments."[18]

From biology and environment, chapter 2 turned to culture, specifically that of the Lower Palaeolithic. "To qualify as human, a hominid has, so to
say, to justify himself by his works: the criteria are no longer biological as
much as cultural."[19] Clark admitted the importance of coming down from
the trees, speech, and bipedal posture, but he considered toolmaking, not
tool using, an overriding criterion of humanness. He dismissed the eoliths
of a previous generation in a few sentences and attributed the earliest stone
tools to Australopithecines at Olduvai. Apparently, he was unaware of, or
chose to ignore, the detailed studies of Oldowan choppers and flakes by
Mary Leakey and their well-publicized claims of ancient living floors at
Olduvai. The Olduvai habitation sites have now been reclassified as meat
caches, but it is surprising to find the earliest camps being attributed to
Middle Pleistocene hand axe makers in Africa and Europe.[20] He drew attention to the Clacton and Lehringen wooden spear fragments, which were
evidence for skilled hunting by these archaic humans. The Neanderthals
made more specialized tools, settled cooler latitudes, and had a concern for
burial and life after death.

Elsewhere, human existence was backward. Take tropical Africa, where
"Lower Palaeolithic cultural traditions persisted, albeit with modifications,
down to comparatively recent times. From the point of view of world history, most of Africa, India, and south-east Asia were henceforward by-
passed by the main currents of creative change throughout the remainder of
prehistoric times." Of course, their cultures changed, "but it is worthy of
note that such evolution . . . often followed patterns set by Advanced
Palaeolithic peoples or their Mesolithic successors [in Europe and the
Mediterranean regions]."[21] This extraordinary statement haunted world
prehistory for a generation, and in some circles it still does. It is a classic
case of arguing from the familiar to the unfamiliar, in this instance without
a good excuse. Clark was arguing from ignorance, not firsthand experience.
He had never visited India, Southeast Asia, or tropical Africa. Had he done
so, he might have argued very differently.

"It was somewhere between Atlantic Europe and Inner Asia that man
seems first to have given signs of freeing himself from the narrow conceptual limits within which Lower Palaeolithic peoples had been confined,"
began chapter 3.[22] Clark commenced his survey with the familiar western
French Upper Palaeolithic sequence, paying special attention to the
Aurignacian and Gravettian cultures. He followed the general hypothesis for

the origins of the Upper Palaeolithic laid out by Dorothy Garrod in her memorable paper on the subject in the *Proceedings* in 1938, in which she traced the origins of the Aurignacian, and the blade-based Upper Palaeolithic technology to southwestern Asia, on the basis of stratigraphy in her Mount Carmel caves. Clark argued that the Aurignacian and Gravettian came from the same "Pre-Aurignacian" base widely distributed over western Asia by 35,000 radiocarbon years B.C. The Gravettian, stratified above the Aurignacian in central and western Europe, dated to about 28,000 B.C. His Upper Palaeolithic discussion covered familiar ground and dealt cursorily with cave art. "The basic drive behind the cave art, as seen for instance at Lascaux, was a sense of the hunter's dependence on the continued abundance of game and on his ability to secure victims."[23] Sympathetic hunting magic was the dominant explanation for Stone Age art at the time. He described the obscure Szeletian culture of central Europe with its bifacial points, the Solutrean, Magdalenian, and other specialized European cultures, as well as what little was known of the archaeology of Siberia, notably the Ma'lta site near Lake Baikal. Siberia was the "obvious source for those earliest intruders into North America, who laid a basis for the prehistory of the new World as a whole."[24]

From the Upper Palaeolithic, Clark moved onto familiar ground with his beloved "Mesolithic Communities." He stressed the transitional nature of Mesolithic cultures and their important role in the origins of food production in southwestern Asia, and in diversifying the farming cultures that spread to many parts of the Old World. "It was Mesolithic people who carried on the old way of life," he wrote, in an indirect reference to his work with surviving folk culture in Scandinavia in *Prehistoric Europe*. They were the cultures who domesticated plants and animals in southwestern Asia "under stress of arid conditions that followed immediately on the end of the last Pluvial period in parts of western Asia." Here Clark adhered to the oasis theory, which was part and parcel of Gordon Childe's Neolithic Revolution hypothesis. His evidence for desiccation after the Ice Age was the soon-to-be discredited increase in gazelle bones in the upper, post–Ice Age levels of the Mount Carmel caves. He placed the actual process of domestication at the feet of the Natufian culture, well defined at Mount Carmel's Mugharet el-Wad cave, but he stressed just how pointless the "who invented agriculture" question was, an argument also made eloquently by a new generation of processual archaeologists in the 1960s. Clark was quite prepared to ask the question eventually, but only when "a much closer net-work" of radio carbon dates was forthcoming. Most of the Mesolithic discussion is confined to Europe, with no less than eight pages devoted to the Maglemose and other familiar societies. He noted, however, an expansion of settlement in Eurasia and the survival of "Advanced Palaeolithic cultures" in Siberia "until the appearance of pottery."[25]

Sixty-eight fast-moving pages take us from human origins to the advent of food production in a survey of the Palaeolithic heavily weighted toward familiar European sites and societies. Chapter 4, "The Invention of Farming and the Rise of Mesopotamian Civilization," moves at similarly breathtaking speed. The "innovators" among the Mesolithic peoples of southwestern Asia were "in a sense responsible for the whole future of civilization in the Old World."[26] Clark wrote these words when the entire portrait of the earliest food production was changing dramatically, as a result of Kathleen Kenyon's excavations into the lowest levels of Jericho in the Jordan Valley and Robert Braidwood's multidisciplinary researches at Jarmo and other sites in Kurdistan. He described the earliest occupation at Jericho, which he considered the work of Mesolithic Natufian hunter-gatherers, dating to about 7800 B.C., followed by massive Pre-Pottery Neolithic levels, including the already famous walled town, which caused a sensation when announced by Kenyon some years before.[27] The inhabitants lived in "greatly enlarged social groups" and had developed agriculture before 6000 B.C., much earlier than the simple farming settlements in Egypt's Fayum Depression, thought to date to about 4,000 B.C. Braidwood's Jarmo site with dates of the first half of the first millennium was an "outlier rather than . . . an ancestor."

Food production began, then, in southwestern Asia, probably at several locations, as a result of increasing desiccation after the Ice Age. Clark made no mention of Gordon Childe's Neolithic Revolution, which seems surprising, given the dominance of his friend's theory at the time. But *World Prehistory* is a cautious, descriptive book, concerned, as Clark always was, more with data than with social theories. Thus the omission, also in *From Savagery to Civilization* of sixteen years earlier, is perhaps hardly surprising.

From food production, we are in the grip of human progress. We proceed to "a new stage in the advance towards civilization," when settled farming communities "took to potting, probably some time towards the end of the sixth millennium B.C."[28] We visit three main centers of such farming activity: Cilicia and western Syria as far south as Jericho, the Hassuna and

Halaf sites in northern Iraq, and the Iranian Plateau. Here again we are on familiar and well-explored ground, although at the time Clark himself had not traveled in these lands. The colonization of southern Mesopotamia came from the "buff-ware province of the Iranian uplands, so as to speak a reservoir from which human floods broke out from time to time." The first colonists were the 'Ubaid people, well-known from Leonard Woolley's heavily publicized Ur excavations of the 1930s. They settled a "land of opportunity" that provided fertile soils, rivers for long-distance trade and communications, and a challenge "that evoked in response nothing less than the development of a new form of city life and within less than a thousand years the emergence of a specific Sumerian civilization."[29] The ensuing summary of Sumerian civilization and of Mesopotamia down to Alexander is purely descriptive and based on Childe's sequence outlined in his *Most Ancient East*.

Chapter 5, "The Later Prehistory of Africa," included ancient Egypt. The Egyptian Neolithic and Predynastic received seven pages of coverage and dynastic Egypt a mere four and a half. Clearly, Clark considered the prehistory more important than the ensuing civilization, arguing that farming diffused into the Nile Valley from the Levant and that unification was a gradual process. He did draw attention to the Mesopotamian influences in late Predynastic art, such as the long-necked mythic beasts on the Narmer palette, and raised a question as to the extent of foreign influence on the formation of early Egyptian civilization.[30] Egyptian civilization owed much, he wrote, to "being near enough to share in the basic advances made in the creative zone of south-west Asia."

Egypt was also "a buffer rather than a connecting link between the progressive territories of western Asia and a continent that had already during Late Pleistocene times slipped far behind in the race of progress."[31] He described the Capsian hunter-gatherer culture of North Africa, which he once thought to be the ancestor of Europe's Mesolithic Tardenoisian culture, East African pastoralists, "polished axe cultures of the equatorial forests" based on the flimsiest of evidence, and the diffusion of ironworking from Carthage and Meroe, as well as the Bantu expansion into sub-Saharan Africa.[32] Meroe and Nubia receive virtually no coverage, Axum in the Ethiopian highlands is ignored, and the coastal "stone towns" of East Africa are summarized in two sentences. He attributed indigenous stone buildings in Africa south of the Zambezi River to Arab influence. As for

Great Zimbabwe, it was an "impressive kraal . . . built on such a scale as to attract the misleading designation of temple." Many of the other Zimbabwean ruins were "best interpreted as forts, and many of these were doubtless erected against the Portuguese colonists."[33] Such interpretations were inexcusable five years after the publication of a definitive monograph on Zimbabwe that included architectural studies, pottery typologies, and radiocarbon dates.

Clark's disastrous account of later African prehistory ends with an Olympian statement to the effect that "it is well to remember that at a time when North Americans and Europeans were already riding in railway trains and reading newspapers the Bushmen of South Africa were still practicing a culture in many respects comparable with those existing during Neothermal times in the northern temperate zones." And a few sentences later: "of even greater relevance to our times is the circumstance that many of the Africans working in mines operated by Europeans return to families whose general way of life recalls that prevailing in Britain during the earlier part of the pre-Roman Iron Age."[34] Clark's vision of world prehistory as a chronicle of human progress comes across clearly in chapter 5, as well as a clear disdain for the achievements of black Africa, surprising in one who had sent more than a few of his students to work there. One must remember, however, that the intellectual climate of the day was one in which Hugh Trevor-Roper, professor of history at Oxford, could blithely describe pre-European African history as the "mere gyrations of native tribes" and get away with it.

The sixty pages of chapters 6 and 7 survey the "Foundations of European Civilization" in two narratives, first the Neolithic and then developments since the rise of Mycenae. Here, once again, we cover familiar ground, with nothing new for regular readers of Clark's works or Childe's popular syntheses of European prehistory. The summaries adhere fairly closely to the commonly accepted diffusionist view of the day, with both food production and metallurgy spreading from southeastern Europe into more temperate regions. This scenario was to endure for another decade or so until calibrated radiocarbon dates forced a reevaluation of European prehistoric chronologies.[35] Like others, Clark believed Mycenae had played a central role in fostering the development of Bronze Age cultures in Europe. His survey of later developments carries through the expansion of the Roman Empire and the spread of Christianity, even to the Age of Exploration.

India, China, and Japan were unfamiliar archaeological territory to most archaeologists of the day, except for Mortimer Wheeler's much publicized Harappa and Mohenjodaro excavations, which had revealed much about the ancient Harappan civilization of the Indus Valley.[36] Clark traces what little was known about early agriculture in the Indus region and attributes the origins of what was then called the Indus civilization to both local roots and "colonists from the hills." He could do little more than speculate, for research into Indus origins was effectively nonexistent. The civilization itself collapsed, perhaps as a result of climatic change and widespread Aryan population movements caused by drought. The Aryans, beloved by Clark's late guru Ellis Minns, were "hard-drinking cattle raiders" whose chariots used "for war and sport" resembled those of the Mycenaeans and Hittites. Inevitably, Clark's account of Indian prehistory was somewhat disjointed, especially in its ability to make meaningful connections between the Harappan and later societies, the predecessors of the Mauryan civilization of the Ganges Valley.

The account of the origins of Chinese civilization also brought many readers in touch with unfamiliar archaeological evidence. Clark focused on the Huang-Ho (Yellow River) valley and early loess agriculture, notably on the village of Pan-po, one of the few early farming settlements known in northern China at the time. He rightly placed the origins of Chinese civilization within the then little-known Lung-shan cultures and carried the story through the Shang civilization to Chou and Han dynasties.

Southeast Asia was a virtual blank on the archaeological map in 1960, but Clark traced the origins of rice cultivation back to at least the second millennium B.C. and drew attention to the bronze-using Dongson culture of North Vietnam. He could say nothing about the archaeology of New Guinea and Melanesia and confined his discussion of Japanese prehistory to Jomon hunter-gatherers and Yayoi farmers, with a brief survey of later developments.

Twenty-eight pages cover the Americas, from first settlement to living hunter-gatherers. "One may reasonably assume the earliest immigrants to have taken the same route as a number of the larger mammals," he writes.[37] He theorized that first settlement took place before Ice Age sea levels severed the Bering land bridge and when thawing of ice sheets permitted movement southward. Initial colonization was in the hands of Clovis people, whose ultimate roots, including bifacial projectile points, were in

Siberia. "Siberian industries in fact have a strong 'Mousterian' element, one which by analogy with the Szeletian of central Europe might almost have been expected to give rise to bifacial points." He follows the familiar scenario of the day: a migration of Stone Age big-game hunters southward onto the Great Plains, who expanded southward into Central and South America. Paleo-Indians adapted to other environments including the Desert culture, which endured for millennia. "A depressing feature of their way of life is that the food quest can have left them but little leisure."[38] But Desert culture was no backwater, such adaptations leading in the Southwest and Valley of Mexico to maize agriculture. Here he was influenced strongly by a newly released (and now discredited) radiocarbon date of 3000 B.C. for maize found in Bat Cave, New Mexico, and was writing before Richard MacNeish's remarkable finds of early maize in Mexico's Tehuacán Valley. He dates maize domestication to at least the third millennium B.C.

There followed a very brief description of the development of Mesoamerican and Andean civilization, which suggested that Peruvian complex societies owed much to influences from the north in the early first millennium B.C., Mexico "being the main imaginative focus at this stage." The Maya were "a relatively pacific confederation of cities, dominated to a large degree by a priestly caste." Clark had read his Eric Thompson, a British Mayanist, who believed their lords were priestly astronomers, obsessed with calendars and the movements of the heavenly bodies. He did not have a high opinion of Inca civilization, which was "much too weak to withstand the impact of a small but resolute body of Spanish adventurers," their technology being "miserably defective."[39] The six remaining pages of the chapter passed briefly over the Basketmakers and Ancestral Pueblo of the Southwest, Archaic, Woodland, and Mississippian cultures in the eastern United States, and coastal and arctic cultures in the north, where he admired a way of life "which marks one of the most effective adaptations to an environment of exceptional severity."[40]

Chapter 10 returned to the other side of the world, to Australasia and the Pacific. Why Clark put this chapter after the New World is hard to discern, for logic would put it after "India and the Far East." The clue lies in the statement that it "was the last continent settled by man." At the time he wrote the first edition, Grahame had no firsthand experience of Australian archaeology, despite having trained John Mulvaney, now the doyen of Australian archaeology, who invited him to Australia after publication of the book. First settlement, we are told, could only have been by boat and at the hands of *Homo sapiens*. The least advanced inhabitants at the time of European contact were the Tasmanians, whom Clark describes from ethnographic sources at some length. Their archaic technology and lifeway he attributed to their isolation resulting from rising sea levels after the Ice Age. As for the Australian Aborigines, they "preserve a stage in the evolution of *Homo sapiens* probably anterior to the emergence of Negroids, Mongoloids, Whites, and American Indians."[41] They were settlers from southeast Asia, some of the same migrants colonizing Melanesia. The archaeological evidence for early settlement was almost non existent, except for the Keilor skull from a site northwest of Melbourne. One radiocarbon date from the terrace where the skull was found dated to the seventh millennium B.C.

Clark theorized that the first Aborigines arrived in Postglacial ("Neothermal") times. Today, first settlement is dated to at least 35,000 years ago, perhaps much earlier. Later Australian cultures included both microlithic industries and also composite scrapers and adzes, again still hardly known at the time. Clark emphasized the importance of living Aboriginal culture in interpreting the archaeological record.

Human settlement of the Pacific received less than two pages, and it was little more than a generalization about the efficacy of ancient canoe navigation and the innovations needed for voyagers to cross open oceans, colonize small islands, and return. The cursory account is hardly surprising, given that almost nothing was known of Pacific prehistory at the time. New Zealand and its flightless *moa* birds received but a sentence.

World Prehistory ended in a "Retrospect," in which Clark stated that "the story of mankind in prehistory may be viewed most simply as one of biological progress, of life lived more abundantly, and, however one defines this, more fully." Growing biological effectiveness led to increasing human dominance over animals, plants, and the environment, as well as to an extension in the area of settlement and a rise in human populations. Most of the retrospect repeated Clark's familiar statements on the nature of human culture and social evolution, already laid out in his Reckitt and inaugural lectures. "To the individuals who comprise human societies the effect of social evolution has been to enrich the quality of their lives. Culture is transmitted from one generation to the next, often using mythological stories, or by written histories in literate societies. Awareness of a common past is critical to the continued existence of nations and human societies."

This was why "prehistory, the only kind of history capable of being shared by men of all levels of cultural attainment, whether of ancient literate traditions or only recently preliterate, is so peculiarly relevant to a world which from the standpoint of science and technology is already one."[42]

World Prehistory was not a sophisticated book. Clark gave his essay no theoretical embellishments and wrote a descriptive narrative of what happened in prehistory drawn from the literature available to him and from personal contacts in many lands. A colleague once described the book to the writer as a "collation of culture histories," an apt description of the first major work of archaeological synthesis to make use of radiocarbon dating as a global dating tool. In many respects, *World Prehistory* was the last of the old-fashioned prehistories, written before the full impact of radiocarbon dating and ecological archaeology had come to bear on the past, and before the explosion of archaeology, archaeologists, and archaeological theory in the 1960s and 1970s, which rapidly put much of the book out of date. The book was also a salutary reminder of just how provincial prehistoric archaeology was in 1960 and how thin on the ground were prehistorians outside the narrow confines of Europe, the Mediterranean, and North America.

Grahame also knew that some of his senior colleagues would feel that to attempt such a book was an act of folly, on the grounds that so little was known of so much of the world and syntheses of this type had to be based on solid data, well-excavated sites, and local surveys. He violently disagreed with this perspective, which smacked to him of the ardent provincialism of archaeology in the 1930s that he remembered so well. Grahame believed that the time had come to look at the human past on a truly global scale in time and space, to both develop a theory of world prehistory and provide the stimulus for research outside well-trodden areas. History has proved that he was right. *World Prehistory* rapidly became a widely used textbook and an important stimulus for the very kinds of research Clark wanted to encourage. Well aware of the book's limitations and imperfections, he at once started collecting material for future editions.

The book received a mixed, if generally favorable, reception. It was widely praised for its usefulness as a textbook and for its global perspective. In the *Proceedings*, African archaeologist Desmond Clark, a former pupil, called *World Prehistory* an "amazing clear and readable synthesis . . . of the causes and effects behind the different evolving cultural stages."[43] But he criticized the overemphasis on Europe at the expense of other less well known areas. Nevertheless, he praised the work as a "milestone in prehistoric studies" that was "indispensable." Robert Braidwood at the University of Chicago was more sanguine in an *Antiquity* review. There was "no other book on prehistory which offers the world and then proceeds to deliver it even in outline form." Clark had attempted the impossible "with intrepidity . . . and come off rather well—all things considered." But he criticized the lack of cohesion and neatness, the overemphasis on description, where Clark neither "asks nor worries over very many *how* or *why* questions (although he does, by implication, now and then answer a few—not always correctly to Braidwood's taste)."[44] The tone was encyclopedic and "also necessarily a bit soporific." Braidwood, with his strong anthropological perspective and major concern with the processes of cultural change at the beginnings of agriculture, had a different agenda to that of his European colleague, who was primarily concerned to lay out what we knew and did not know about human prehistory. Clark's background had always been the data and lack of data, environmental change and the broad evolutionary sweep of human prehistory, an approach that was reflected in his teaching and all his later books.

Nearly half a century later, we can appreciate the importance of *World Prehistory,* despite its defects and glaring gaps. Quite simply, this groundbreaking book put the subject on the map as a serious intellectual issue. Grahame Clark did not invent world prehistory, but, through his teaching, students, and writings, made anthropologist, archaeologist, and historian take it seriously as an intellectual concept. He was well aware there were omissions and some errors in the book, stemming from the sheer scale of the work, and he devoted many of the closing years of his career to traveling to explore the nuances of this vast subject further.

11

⪦⪧

Travels of a Prehistorian

Let us view all histories and all prehistory in a world perspective; in honouring the achievements of our own and of all other peoples, we are after all acknowledging our own humanity.

Aspects of Prehistory[1]

During the 1950s and 1960s, Grahame and Mollie Clark traveled extensively throughout Europe, sometimes with their children and sometimes without, continuing in a tradition, especially of Scandinavian travel, that went back to the beginning of his career. Holidays abroad combined archaeology and pleasure. Ever the compulsive writer, Grahame kept detailed "field notes" of their travels, just like an excavation diary. In 1953, for example, the family enjoyed a magnificent vacation in Norway and Sweden. They rented a log cabin at Grovelsjon on Lake Femmen, close to the Norwegian border, where they were able to watch herds of both domesticated and wild reindeer. The domesticated beasts were eating shed antlers from the previous season as they appeared on the ground amidst the melting snow.

The travels accelerated and became more exotic as Grahame's international reputation grew. Clark was also a faithful conference goer who attended both large gatherings such as the International Union of Pre- and

Protohistoric Sciences and smaller meetings, like those of the Prehistoric Society and more specialized meetings like those on radiocarbon dating in the late 1950s. He attended fewer conferences after 1960 but traveled more extensively and widely than ever before, in large part as a consequence of *World Prehistory*.

Unlike Gordon Childe, who had little time for America, Grahame thoroughly enjoyed his visits across the Atlantic. He had crossed to New York by ocean liner for the Wenner Gren meeting in 1952, soon after assuming the Disney Chair. He and his family returned five years later, this time to Harvard University, where he taught for a semester as the Grant McCurdy Lecturer. They crossed to Quebec and spent a holiday at Boothbay, Maine, before coming to Cambridge. Grahame taught a graduate seminar entitled "The Stone Age in Northern and North-Western Europe During the Post-Glacial Period," which ran parallel to one on the Palaeolithic given by Harvard's Hallam Movius and attracted most of the same students. They included several now eminent prehistorians, among them Dena Dincauze, a northeastern North American specialist, Olaf Prufer, who became an expert on the Hopewell tradition of the Midwest, and Robert Rodden, later to enjoy a close association with the Cambridge department. The reading list for the seminar featured two books by Childe and three by Clark, including *Archaeology and Society, Prehistoric Europe,* and *Star Carr*, as well as the Reckitt lecture. The other readings were Scandinavian. Grahame's somewhat formal manner made communication with the students somewhat difficult, but the Clarks were more sociable than they had been in Cambridge. Gordon Willey was very friendly, but Grahame and Movius never hit it off, Grahame being critical of the latter's large-scale Abri Pataud excavations in France, which struck him as overly expensive for what they would produce in terms of knowledge.[2] The Clarks had trouble adjusting to the severe Massachusetts winter, but the semester was a valuable learning experience.

Their travels continued—to the Dordogne in 1959, where they visited Hallam Movius's Abri Pataud excavations and saw the Lascaux cave paintings for the first time.[3] Then they traveled southward to Barcelona, where they met the Spanish prehistorian Luis Pericot and toured the Costa Brava. In 1960 Grahame was in Prague, where he toured the Archaeological Institute. Two years later, he was at the Pre- and Protohistoric Conference in Rome.

Nea Nikomedia and
European Farming

Grahame had long been interested in the origins of European agriculture. His interest quickened with the release of many new radiocarbon dates from across the Continent. In the early 1960s, his eyes turned to Greece, where the provincial archaeologist *(ephor)* in Macedonia, Dr. Petsas, had drawn attention to the destruction of many prehistoric occupation mounds, or tells, by the resettlement of refugees from Turkey. Robert Rodden, a Harvard student studying at Cambridge under Clark's supervision, went out to survey the area alongside Petsas. The two archaeologists recommended excavations at a mound named Nea Nikomedia near the village of Veroia in western Macedonia. Grahame was "particularly keen on this project because of my concern at the time with the early spread of Neolithic farming economy."[4] He was issued one of the excavation permits allocated to the British School of Archaeology at Athens, but Rodden carried out the excavations in his name, accompanied by several Cambridge students, among them David Clarke, Charles Higham, and Colin Renfrew. He was assisted by R. W. "Squire" Hutchinson, former curator of the Minoan palace of Knossos on Crete, who had much experience of Greek laborers and "knew that interesting chap who helped capture the German general during the last war." The 1961 excavations produced a radiocarbon date of 6220 ± 150 B.C., which suggested to Clark "that Macedonia might have played a key role in the transmission of Neolithic farming culture from Anatolia to Central Europe" (Figure 11.1).[5]

This was Grahame's first visit to Greece, whose prehistory he had only encountered through the literature. He arrived with Mollie in his Mercedes on July 4. Delayed by a broken axle in Larissa, they took shelter under a brightly colored umbrella and put a moistened towel around his head to prevent the heat "addling his brain." They celebrated their silver anniversary by taking the students out to dinner in Naoussa, a community famous for its wines. Charles Higham remembers that the meal included "cakes, ice cream, and brandy." After an enjoyable stay on the dig, Grahame continued on from Nea Nikomedia to Turkey, where David French of the British School in Turkey took him to visit James Mellaart's excavations at the ancient farming village of Çatalhöyük in central Anatolia, with their remarkable wall paintings.[6]

Figure 11.1   **Excavations at Nea Nikomedia, Macedonia, Greece.**

In 1962, Eric Higgs visited the Nea Nikomedea site while on a site survey in Epirus. As he was traveling homeward from Igoumenitsa across Epirus to Macedonia by Land Rover, it occurred to him that the surrounding mountains might contain Stone Age caves and rockshelters. Rhys Jones, one of the students with him, found Middle Palaeolithic artifacts in the Louros Gorge in Epirus. "A most significant day as we have found a prolific Mousterian industry. We must have got hundreds of Mousterian flakes and some very pleasant tools," wrote Charles Higham in his diary for July 31. "I have filled myself with ripe plums this evening." Higgs returned the following year and excavated the nearby Asprochalico cave, where he unearthed Upper Palaeolithic occupation overlying the Middle Palaeolithic, the first such record from Greece. To Grahame's pleasure, the Asprochalico excavations led to a sustained campaign of Stone Age research in northern Greece by both Higgs and a young Cambridge-trained prehistorian, Geoff Bailey.[7]

The Early History of Agriculture Project

Nea Nikomedia and a flood of radiocarbon dates had caused Grahame to become increasingly preoccupied with the beginnings of European farming. His article "Radiocarbon Dating and the Spread of Farming Economy" appeared in the *Proceedings* for 1965, a survey of known dates that Clark believed to confirm the spread of agriculture from the southeastern Balkans and Greece. "The pursuit of radiocarbon dating is one of those elegant exercises in pure science that is fully justified as an end in itself," he wrote. "Physics tends to give higher and sometimes much higher dates," he remarked, as he (and others) expanded the "bellows" of European Neolithic chronology from its previously compressed position, espoused by Gordon Childe, Stuart Piggott, and others.[8]

In the same year in which this paper appeared, Lord Robbins gave his presidential address to the British Academy, in which he suggested that it was time for the academy to initiate its own major research projects. The notion was not to subtract from existing individual research but to obtain funds for longer-term projects on major topics of importance. Grahame had been active in Section 10 (Archaeology and Anthropology) of the academy since his election as a fellow in 1951 and was chair from 1974 to 1978. He perceived a unique opportunity for research into the origins of agriculture and helped Section 10 develop a proposal for research on the early history of agriculture, which was one of the first projects to be approved by the academy's council.[9]

From the start, the project was conceived in multidisciplinary terms, with close collaboration between the human and natural sciences. The academy duly appointed the Standing Committee on the Early History of Agriculture with two distinguished members from the Royal Society, the botanist Sir Joseph Hutchinson, and Grahame's old ally Harry Godwin. The archaeologists were Christopher Hawkes, Grahame Clark, Martin Jope, the chair at the University of Belfast, and Stuart Piggott. The first meeting of the committee was held on April 23, 1966, at Peterhouse, in the same room once used by the Fenland Research Committee. Hutchinson was elected chair and Eric Higgs appointed project director.[10]

Grahame had prepared long and hard for this moment. His archives contain some of the prosaic but necessary to-and-fro correspondence with Hutchinson and Lord Robbins that helped steer the project toward Cambridge, with its long history of multidisciplinary inquiry, its strong archaeology programs, and its internationally known agricultural research. The agricultural connection was of particular importance, with Hutchinson himself having a long experience of working with small-scale farming societies, as well as being a crop geneticist. The informal approach of the Fenland Research Committee thirty years earlier was reborn as another interdisciplinary group, this time with a much broader canvas. No less than four members of the early agriculture committee had been founding members of the Fenland group. The new project would never have come into being without the experience of the Fenland Research Group before World War II.

Both the committee and the university moved quickly, and the project began on a small scale under Eric Higgs in late 1967. From the beginning, the research focused on developing new opportunities for studying prehistoric agriculture in Europe, with selective excavations in southern and southeastern Europe and in southwestern Asia, some resulting from Cambridge research, others from projects set up by British Schools of Archaeology abroad or by liaison with archaeological authorities in countries such as Bulgaria and Israel. Much effort went into studying animal bone collections from such key sites as Nea Nikomedia in Greece and Knossos in Crete. Although most of the research involved southeastern Europe and the eastern Mediterranean, Higgs and his colleagues pursued related topics within the context of prehistoric economies in general, such as experimental domestication, exploitation patterns of a modern reindeer economy in western Greenland, and the esoterica of cave climates. As Grahame pointed out in his foreword to the first volume published by the project, the scope of archaeology, like natural science, was global.

Grahame maintained a close interest in the project over its nine years of active research. The first three were occupied with what the researchers called "ground clearance": proposing objectives and approaches that were theoretically valid yet practicable. *Papers in Economic Prehistory*, published in 1972 under Higgs's editorship, was an eclectic collection of papers that represented this first stage. Eric Higgs and Michael Jarman contributed the theoretical perspective, which held that animal and plant domestication were "natural developments of processes common in human and non-human exploitation patterns."[11] A tentative development of this theme with a European perspective appeared in a disparate collection of papers entitled *Palaeoeconomy* three years later.[12] In this collection it was argued that little had been done to further research into prehistoric economies as a coherent study since the appearance of Grahame's *Prehistoric Europe* twenty years earlier. The papers in the book covered a wide spectrum of topics, from musk ox exploitation and reindeer economies to territories and prehistoric economies in ancient Italy and Bulgaria. An appendix described the site catchment analysis method developed by Higgs and Claudio Vita-Finzi, which proved to be one of the lasting legacies of the project. This approach involved inventorying economic resources within successive concentric circles around a site (defined by walking distance) to establish what was available for the inhabitants to exploit in the "catchment area" of a site.[13] In their chapter in the second volume, Higgs and Michael Jarman stressed their belief that "while archaeology needs scientific aids, it is not enough for either participant that science should have the subsidiary role of providing only the technological devices with which to answer archaeological questions."[14] They also argued for testing theoretical explanations in the field before publishing them, a process that eliminated the ones that proved impracticable, "a fate which seems to await many current hypotheses."[15]

Unfortunately, Eric Higgs died in 1976, when the final volume, *Early European Agriculture: Its Foundations and Development,* existed in rough outline only. Michael Jarman completed the third publication, which was dedicated to Higgs and appeared in 1982. This was a remarkable collection of essays that covered basic principles, territories, and mobility and the palaeoeconomic perspective of the project. The authors described three ecological zones: coasts, lakes, and littorals; lowlands; and uplands, with a separate chapter on megaliths. A short coda at the end summarized the main conclusions of nine years' work: that human economic behavior could only be understood with reference to the behavior of other animals, and that three important variables interacted with one another, namely, population, available resources, and technology for their exploitation. The project spent much time trying to devise methods for examining these factors in archaeological terms and applying them to different ecological zones.

Under this theoretical argument, "the 'Neolithic invasion' may be viewed as the rapid colonization by a species of a rapidly changing economic niche (as opposed to new territory) pretty much as soon as circumstances permitted."[16] The early agriculture project had shown there was a "secure, even vital, place" for bioarchaeological research, but that such research would involve closely integrated inquiry, not a simple level of teamwork, in which specialists, each with their own interests, worked alongside one another on a site such as Star Carr or Peacock's Farm.

The early agriculture project, with its strong biological leanings, was widely criticized, especially by those who did not want to think of developments in prehistory in terms of animal as well as human behavior. Its enduring legacies were, however, of the highest importance. New methodologies like froth flotation, which produced much larger plant samples, site catchment analysis, and sophisticated analytical approaches to both animal and plant remains were lasting contributions.[17] So was the project's insistence on closely integrated multidisciplinary research. The results were diffuse and sometimes frustrating and confusing, but they represented a major advance on simpler multidisciplinary thinking and a new threshold in the kind of archaeology that Clark had long fostered. The project also validated his long-held view that there was no "jump" between hunting and gathering and farming, with sedentism encouraging the same kinds of social developments in both kinds of societies. He wrote an important paper on coastal settlement in Scandinavia on this very subject in 1983, which followed on an earlier paper on megalithic graves in Sweden. He argued that fisherfolk were capable of building elaborate monuments. On another occasion, at a 1982 conference in Ireland, he remarked, "one certainly does not enter a new state of consciousness when one first milks a cow!"[18]

Travels to the Antipodes

As the early agriculture project unfolded, Grahame continued to travel, this time far afield from Europe. His first visit to the Antipodes came in 1964, when he was invited to lecture as William Evans Professor at Otago University in New Zealand's South Island. Otago was the first university in Australia and New Zealand to offer anthropology. The subject had long been taught at Otago by H. D. Skinner, a Gallipoli veteran who had learned the subject from Baron von Hügel and A. C. Haddon at Cambridge in

1917–1918 and returned to New Zealand in 1919. He was succeeded in 1958 by Peter Gathercole, a Peterhouse graduate who fought hard to expand the department, an exhausting and uphill battle. In mid-1962, he was having a drink with the dean of arts at the university, who was "ruminating into his glass" on possible nominations for the William Evans for 1964. Gathercole recalls, "Off the cuff I said: 'Grahame Clark, if he'd come. He's interested in prehistory worldwide, you know. His book on the subject was published last year.'" The dean acted at once and Grahame was appointed for the first term of 1964. By all accounts, Clark seized the chance to experience Maori culture and learn something of its history firsthand and to visit some of his former students on the other side of the world.

The Clarks first traveled to Auckland from Australia, having sailed out from England on the SS *Orcades*. Grahame won a prize for his fancy dress in a parade held while crossing the Indian Ocean—a menacing Viking chief, complete with helmet, shield, and sword! In Auckland, Grahame was able to gain an initial impression of Maori culture and to visit several fortified earthworks, the celebrated *pa*. Roger Duff at the Dominion Museum in Wellington showed him his *moa* hunter collections from the Wairau Bar site and also took him to visit a Maori settlement on the northwest coast of South Island, as well as the Grey River greenstone deposits, which were widely prized in prehistoric times. The family traveled from Christchurch by bus, waxing lyrical about the scenery on the way.

Grahame's time at the University of Otago in Dunedin with its fine nineteenth-century architecture permitted him to travel widely and to appreciate the contrast between the rich culture of the North Island and the hunter-gatherer societies of the regions south of Canterbury, as well as the high volume of trade between north and south. His public lectures were somewhat disappointing, but archaeologist Helen Leach recalls how his informal meetings with second-year students about to enter a more specialized third year led to discussions on "seasonality, meat weights, Maori middens and other topics that were relatively new issues in the long history of archaeology in New Zealand." They must have been akin to good Cambridge supervisions.[19] Grahame's international reputation did the fledgling Otago department a power of good. He was careful to talk enthusiastically to the right people, including the vice chancellor of the university, for he approved of the evenhanded approach to anthropology and archaeology fostered by Gathercole and his colleagues.

Clark's visit resulted in expanded coverage of New Zealand in later editions of *World Prehistory* and gave critical momentum to a struggling department. Charles Higham, he of station master fame, arrived as a lecturer in 1967. Peter Gathercole lobbied constantly for a chair of anthropology, which was not approved until 1968, to be filled in 1969. Grahame had returned to Dunedin in 1968. His son William was studying zoology and getting married, while Phillip was working on a farm at nearby Edievale Moa Flat. The vice chancellor of the university sought Grahame's views on the candidates for the new chair. He was very pleased when his former student (and favored candidate) Charles Higham was appointed Foundation Professor of Anthropology, the first professor of prehistory in Australasia at the age of twenty-eight in 1969. Higham promptly began a research program in Thailand, which continues to this day and has brought international recognition to the university.

A Commonwealth Visiting Scholar's appointment also took Grahame to Australia in May 1964, just as archaeology in that country was beginning to expand rapidly.[20] Cambridge graduate John Mulvaney was teaching ancient history and archaeology at Melbourne University and was squeezing in part-time fieldwork during university vacations, while Jack Golson, a Cambridge archaeologist who had been influenced by Michael Postan and first worked in Auckland, was the newly appointed professor at the Australian National University in Canberra. The Clarks were whisked off the plane in Sydney and taken by Cambridge graduate and university lecturer Richard Wright to see a rockshelter at Marramarra, some thirty-two kilometers (20 miles) south of the city. The site with its deep overhang could only be reached by boat through dense mangrove swamps, but its rich midden fill had been removed for use as manure on a long vanished orchard. Stone implements, traces of hearths, and stencils of boomerangs and human feet, once buried under the midden, could be seen.

At the University of Sydney and the Australian Museum, they met colleagues, inspected archaeological and ethnographic collections, and then visited Vincent Megaw's excavations at Curracurrang rockshelter, which overlooked a stream flowing down to a narrow inlet into the sea. In Armidale, where he lectured at the university, Grahame spent time with Isabel MacBryde, a Cambridge graduate teaching at the University of New South Wales, and visited three of her rockshelter excavations in the Grafton and Clarence areas. Their journey took them to Brisbane, where again he lectured. They saw more excavations and a fine collection of shields in the Queensland Museum. In Melbourne to the south, Grahame visited the much eroded Keilor site, where the famous skull had been found, viewing the charcoal lenses from which the radiocarbon samples came. John Mulvaney took the Clarks to his rockshelter at Fromm's Landing, over-looking the lower Murray River, 113 kilometers (70 miles) from Adelaide. There he had recovered a 5,000-year prehistoric sequence, complete with radiocarbon dates, extending down five meters (16 feet) to bedrock.[21] Grahame stepped down into the excavation, notebook in hand, and exam-ined the thin strata (Figure 11.2). He was impressed by the "traces of soot left by aboriginal fire-places." A third expedition took the Clarks to the Mount William stone axe quarries, which were used by Aborigines into modern times. John Mulvaney was much cheered by such a distinguished visitor to validate his work, for he worked largely in isolation. His closest colleagues were hundreds of kilometers away.

Norman Tindale, Australia's leading anthropologist, arranged for Grahame to meet some Aborigines. They left Mollie in Alice Springs to visit Ayres Rock and flew west in a single-engine Cessna, a first for Grahame, who enjoyed extensive views of Mount Leibig and the Macdonnell ranges. The airplane landed on a sand strip at the Papunya Aboriginal Station, where some eight hundred Aborigines were camped, some of them being resettled away from the huge rocket ranges to the west. "The latest arrivals still occupied their traditional wurlies [shelters] together with the dogs which they used as blankets or hot-water bottles at night," Grahame wrote. He observed that the dense concentration of people had turned the sur-rounding country within easy walking distance into "a virtual desert." The practice of sinking wells for cattle had the same effect, for the drinking herds decimated the land. The solution, he wrote, was "sparsely situated holiday inns serviced by air and not accessible by road," which would attract tourists and provide employment for Aborigines. The Aboriginal station was a depressing place, where basic medical care and education were provided. "It gave one an insight into the cultural dichotomy to pick up the tip of a boomerang beautifully finished and every now and then scraps of paper inscribed with elementary exercises in English."

The women "found occupation breeding children," but the men still went on walkabouts. Grahame was able to spend a couple of days on trips with three members of the Nglia group, including Tjurdi, an old man who

Figure 11.2 Grahame Clark examining the stratification at Fromm's Landing, Australia, May 1961. The notebook clutched in his hand was subsequently lost in the outback. Photograph by W. S. Tindale. Courtesy South Australian Museum.

remembered Tindale from his researches in the area in 1932, and a singer named Jack Njiru. The first day they traveled by Land Rover to a kangaroo totem place and to a small chloric schist quarry, where Grahame found "a number of discarded blanks and a wooden digging stick of the kind used to recover the raw material and trim it into shape." As Njiru sang, the party used iron crowbars to produce a half dozen *tjuringa* blanks. The next day, the group set out for another stone source but were frustrated by breakdowns.

Both days, the men shot kangaroos from the Land Rover, which they cut up deftly with chert flakes "recovered nearby, some of which still had the remains of resin derived from the sticky leaf sheafs of common Porcupine Grass . . . used for mounting them on their original handles." This was the living Stone Age, people "whose economy and technology were still comparable with those prevailing in Europe during the Old Stone Age."[22] A quarter century after meeting Donald Thomson, Clark was able to witness hunter-gatherers using a form of stone technology that was a legacy from the Stone Age—although the *tjuringa* blanks from the quarry were destined for the tourist trade in Alice Springs. The experience was an important validation of his reconstructions of ancient hunter-gatherer life, as well as a chance to observe the ways in which they used space in their seasonal round.

The Australian sections of *World Prehistory* were rewritten as a consequence of the 1964 journey. The stone quarry visit resulted in a paper on traffic in adze and axe blades, published in the *Economic History Review*.[23]

More Travels

Grahame and Mollie continued to travel at a hectic pace. In November 1965, for example, Grahame lectured at Pennsylvania State University, then lectured again at the American Philosophical Society, where he gave a talk entitled "Prehistory and Human Behavior." The next afternoon, he spoke at Temple University, before visiting Boston, flying on to the University of Michigan at Ann Arbor, where he discussed the Australian Stone Age with graduate students and met James Griffin, the leading expert on the archaeology of eastern North America. He gave a public lecture on the origins of farming and then flew on to the University of Chicago, where he spent time with Robert Braidwood of Jarmo fame. From there, it was on to Denver and talks at the University of Colorado and Colorado Women's College, before a short flight to Albuquerque, where he lectured and visited a

Basketmaker rockshelter at Armijo with archaeologist Cynthia Irwin-Williams. After a presentation at Berkeley on the origins of farming, they flew across the Pacific to Auckland and Dunedin to visit their sons before flying home via Bangkok, where they spent a day sightseeing.

In 1968 the Clarks traveled to Japan via Moscow to attend the International Conference of Anthropological and Ethnological Sciences. En route they visited Taiwan, the Philippines, and New Zealand, the latter for a second time. This gave Grahame a unique chance to indulge his passion for Chinese porcelain, which he had long enjoyed in the Department of Oriental Antiquities at the British Museum. He examined Jomon pottery in Japan, some of the earliest in the world, as well as a magnificent collection of Chinese Shang bronzes at Kyoto. In Taipei, he visited the Academia Sinica, where he lectured on "Late Glacial and Post Glacial Hunters." His hosts showed him collections of Chinese antiquities at the National Palace Museum brought from the mainland by Chiang Kai-shek, including the definitive Shang artifacts from the Chinese archaeologist Li Chi's Anyang excavations. He was also presented with a pirated copy of *Archaeology and Society* from a bookstore in Taipei!

The highlight of the trip came in the Philippines, where they received VIP treatment, complete with Buick and driver at their disposal, thanks to "wealthy friends of archaeology whose collections of Chinese porcelain were an accepted status symbol." They were able to visit the fabulous Locsin collection of Sung, Yuan, and early Ming porcelain. The highlight of the Philippines trip came when they visited the Locsin estate, a two-hour drive south of Manila, where a cemetery excavation was in process. Grahame himself was asked to continue the excavation of a grave that had already been cleared by the estate laborers down to burial level. He soon exposed some fine Yuan porcelain (A.D. 1279–1368), but lunch under the palm trees intervened—suckling pig served on china plates. As they departed, Grahame was presented with a box containing the porcelain he had excavated![24]

From Manila, they flew on to Australia and New Zealand but were too tired to return via Mexico City as they had originally intended.

In 1971, Grahame had another chance to visit the American West for a small seminar on early agriculture at the School of American Research in Santa Fe, New Mexico. Here he met Richard MacNeish, who had completed his remarkable excavations in search of early maize in Mexico's Tehuacán Valley.[25] This trip gave him the opportunity to visit Mexico City and the nearby ancient city of Teotihuacán. Robert Heizer of the University of California–Berkeley introduced him to the arid Great Basin environment of the west. He also visited Paleo-Indian expert Marie Wormington at the Denver Museum of Natural History and viewed her remarkable collections of early stone projectile points from the plains. He traveled from coast to coast in Canada in 1976 and attended a symposium entitled New Perspectives in Canadian Archaeology. "Indian and Inuit points of view strongly put forward," he noted.

World Prehistory: A New Outline

World Prehistory was an immediate success and was, on Grahame's own admission, the publication that opened new doors for him. His far-flung travels in the 1960s resulted in considerable part from the visibility given him by the first edition, which was reprinted four times. All of his travels added substance to the second edition, entitled *A New Outline*, which appeared in 1968. Clark also took account of a flood of new radiocarbon dates and introduced a new, mode-based classification of lithic technologies. Mode 1 was Oldowan technology from the Lower Palaeolithic, Mode 2 hand axes. Modes 3, 4, and 5 encompassed Middle and Upper Palaeolithic and microlithic technology respectively. "It is possible to observe a clear progression during the Palaeolithic Age in the technology of flint and stone," he wrote in a somewhat old-fashioned tone. The modes have never caught on widely, except among paleoanthropologists, largely because the terms are so general as to be almost meaningless. A new chapter surveyed the major advances in knowledge of the beginnings of farming in the Old World, including the unexpectedly early radiocarbon dates for agricultural settlements at Jericho and Jarmo. Africa received more positive treatment in this edition, but it was still "a kind of cultural museum in which archaic cultural traditions of modes 2 and 3 continued to adapt to ecological change . . . without contributing to the main course of human progress." But there were positive achievements, such as equatorial forest agriculture. "The later prehistory of Africa reminds us that there are indeed more ways of contributing to the heritage of mankind than by guiding the main lines of technological advance."[26]

The new edition brought strong reaction from Africanists. Clark's former student Thurstan Shaw wrote a long review article in the *Journal of*

African History, in which he praised the mode scheme for the Stone Age as "important" but wrote that, as an African archaeologist, he found the book disappointing. "There are a number of inaccuracies here, and much of the large body of work on African prehistory published in recent years seems not to have been consulted." Why had Clark not consulted his African colleagues, who would have pointed out glaring errors ahead of time?[27] Tropical Africa seems to have been an intellectual blind spot for someone more interested in the ancient origins of food production and the beginnings of literate civilization.

Aspects of Prehistory

A year after the new edition appeared, Grahame enjoyed a stint as a visiting Hitchcock Professor at the University of California–Berkeley, when he spent time with his former students Desmond Clark and Glynn Isaac, talked paleoanthropology, and attended a conference of Africanist archaeologists. Louis Leakey paid a hasty visit and "gave an over simple talk in the seminar room and frankly caused some embarrassment. He was full of all the rich people who were supporting his research and the size of his audiences." Grahame also complained about Peruvianist John Rowe's approach to fieldwork. Rowe "put on a considerable act about the irrelevance of excavation in Peru, for he felt that sherd sampling from surface exposures could do the trick. His orders were displayed in the Anthropological Museum." His lectures stressed the importance of basic archaeological evidence and were published as *Aspects of Prehistory* by the University of California Press in the following year.

Aspects is a short book that discusses the relevance of world prehistory in terms of its ability to open up broad perspectives that humanity needed to survive in a changing world. Grahame asked: "Do we have to fit ourselves for the one world of science and technology by wholesale abandonment of our traditional histories or lore?" The answer was a firm no. "The answer can only be for us to each study our own history, the history of our own group in the context of our own civilization, our own civilization in the context of other civilizations, and all civilizations in the context of world prehistory." In a classic Grahame Clark-ism, he added: "We do not have to become bored to death in order to live together; we merely have to be tolerant."[28]

From the perspective of prehistoric times, we were all on much the same level. "Our survival depends on, among other things, our ability to view one another in a historical context appropriate to a world that shrinks in size and grows in potential danger with every passing year."[29] The two other chapters surveyed humanity's material progress and the "dawn of self-awareness." He discussed his newly formulated modes of technology. Artifacts, he stressed, were the signposts of prehistory, for they were the means by which humans adapted to their environments. Economic progress empowered the human spirit by allowing people to assign importance to the everyday activities of ancient life and develop explanations of supernatural forces that were beyond their grasp. World prehistory was based on data and unglamorous field research—something that his American colleagues sometimes forgot.

Material progress enabled humanity to multiply, to occupy almost all natural environments, to dominate other animals, and to evolve a new form of social life distinct from that of other animals. Human behavioral patterns were shaped not by instinct but by diverse culture. The distinctively human abilities and qualities—artistic expression, speech, conceptual thought, comprehension of the passage of time, social obligations, and religion were, in a broad sense, adaptive. Archaeology's chronicle of *Homo sapiens sapiens* testified to the emergence of increasingly human patterns of behavior.

Aspects of Prehistory is Grahame Clark's most articulate essay on the broad issues of world prehistory. The essay brings out his unchanging view that technology and material progress were of overwhelming importance to human cultural evolution. Reviewing *Aspects* in *Antiquity*, Hugh Hencken described it as a "pleasant and thoughtful little book."[30]

World Prehistory in New Perspective

The second edition of *World Prehistory* was only 331 pages long, very much an ongoing project. Nine years later, after Grahame's retirement, a third edition, *World Prehistory in New Perspective,* appeared, encompassing 554 pages, with many more illustrations. It is worth jumping ahead in time and examining this final version briefly here. A decade of new discoveries and theoretical advances made for a much more comprehensive treatment and a conscious effort to avoid any suggestion of ethnocentrism. Clark still focuses on later periods. Earlier prehistory receives a mere thirty-eight pages, the main emphasis being on cultural developments since the emergence of modern humans. Thereafter, the organization is geographical: Southwest Asia followed by Europe, then "the African achievement," fleshed out in more detail this time but with sub-Saharan Africa still being described as "peripheral." India and East Asia are followed by the Americas, then North and Middle America, and finally Australia and Oceania. The book was a generally accurate portrait of human prehistory as we knew it in the mid–1970s, with a marked emphasis on Europe. This resulted partly from our state of knowledge at the time, but also from Clark's belief that "Europe created the one world that called for a world prehistory as well as developing the very concept and working methods of prehistory." European technology, capitalism, and imperialism developed the world economy and its modern communications. "To say so much is not to lessen the contributions made by other civilizations or the peoples who have only lately emerged from traditional societies to share in the economy, experience and the imagination of the world at large." To Grahame Clark, world prehistory was a chronicle of human progress and human adaptation. "Prehistory, like history itself, is about what happened," he remarks, which is why *World Prehistory* in all its editions is overwhelmingly a descriptive synthesis.[31] As Robert Braidwood perceptively remarked in his review of the first edition, Grahame was more concerned with *what* happened rather than *how* or *why,* which have become the preoccupations of today's prehistorians. In that sense, he belonged to an earlier generation of prehistorians.

Retirement

Austere, dedicated, even remote, Clark was hardly an ideal department leader, yet his enthusiasm for archaeology, his passion for environmental approaches, and his insistence on a global perspective galvanized the department into much broader curricula and more ambitious research in the 1960s and 1970s. A steady stream of graduates went from Cambridge to museums and universities as far afield as Australia, New Zealand, and South Africa.

He had inherited a small department having no more than fifteen students in 1935 and no more than thirty in the early 1950s. By 1974, a year after his retirement, forty-six undergraduates were enrolled in Part I and forty-five more in Part II. There were forty archaeology research students. His tenure of the Disney Chair was a successful one, in large part because of his single-minded insistence on the importance of prehistory in the wider order of things. He believed that there was a bright future for young archaeologists far from the United Kingdom. By the time he retired from the Disney in 1973, world prehistory had become an intellectual reality, and many Cambridge students were engaged in adding new chapters to his synthesis.

As retirement approached, further honors came to him. In 1967, he received the Hodgkins Medal of the Smithsonian Institution. Four years later, the Wenner-Gren Foundation awarded him its prestigious Viking Fund Medal. By this time, he was a Corresponding or Foreign member of a large number of American and European Academies. He was appointed a Commander of the Order of the British Empire (C.B.E.) in 1971 for his services to archaeology. In the years immediately after his retirement, he was honored with the Lucy Wharton Gold Medal of the University of Pennsylvania (1974), the Gold Medal of the Society of Antiquaries in 1978 (for "he had made the learning and practice of British prehistory known and admired in all the continents"), and the Chandra Medal of the Asiatic Society a year later.[32]

But the honor that gave him the most pleasure was the two festschrifts dedicated to him. In 1970, Grahame retired as editor of the *Proceedings of the Prehistoric Society*, having held the honorary position for thirty-five years. John Coles, now editor, devoted the second part of the 1971 volume of the *Proceedings* to "Contributions to Prehistory offered to Grahame Clark," in recognition of "his outstanding services to Prehistory in general and to the Prehistoric Society in particular."[33] Eighteen papers from luminaries around the world, many former students, ranged over such diverse topics as horse riding in temperate Europe (Terence Powell), evidence for agricultural origins in the Nile Valley (Desmond Clark), and the Cambridge excavations at La Cotte de St. Brelade in Jersey (McBurney and Callow). John Mulvaney wrote about Australian prehistory, Hallam Movius and Alison Brooks about Aurignacian scrapers, Jacques Nenquin on the archaeology of islands in Lake Victoria, Uganda. The special volume was recognition of his extraordinary influence on the course of prehistoric research over more than a generation.

The second tribute was a volume of essays by his former students, edited by Gale Sieveking, Ian Longworth, and K. C. Wilson. *Problems in Economic and Social Archaeology* appeared in 1976, with a gracious foreword by Charles McBurney, "your oldest pupil."[34] The papers in the 626-page book came from all over the world, wherever his students now worked. Five contributors wrote on African topics, both Stone Age and Iron Age. America and Asia accounted for five contributions on everything from early agriculture to a Maya vase depicting a ball game. No less than eight articles covered Australia and New Zealand, a measure of Clark's influence on Antipodean prehistory. The topics were eclectic—Maori shell trumpets, plant domestication, and ethnoarchaeology among them. Seventeen papers covered Britain and Europe, papers reflecting Clark's broad interests in his home stamping grounds. Remarkably, nearly all the contributors paid tribute to the seminal importance of both *Star Carr* and *Prehistoric Europe* to their thinking. This had become the foundation upon which a new generation of Clark-trained scholars were building their own research.

The first signs of their innovations are apparent in this volume, especially in David Clarke's essay, "Mesolithic Europe: The Economic Basis," in which he criticized the overemphasis on hunting at the expense of vegetable foods in studies of Mesolithic subsistence, as well as the consistent underestimation of the sophistication of hunter-gatherer societies of this period.[35] *Problems* is a monument to a single archaeologist's influence on an entire generation, a volume that presented a mass of new data from many parts of the world without much theoretical elaboration, the kind of archaeology that was Grahame's meat and drink. His students were becoming his legacy, as he had hoped, doing good archaeology in many parts of the world far from the hustle and bustle of theoretical ferment which was engulfing so many archeologists in what he perceived of as fruitless debates. He wrote to Kent Flannery after enjoying his analysis of the origins of civilization: "As one untroubled by pondering whether I ought to be a processual or cognitive processual archaeologist, I enjoyed reading your article, and am still not convinced I am suffering from senile decay. . . . Each little cock seems to crow in its own territory without realizing how restricted it is."[36]

12

⤬

Last Years

*Science has expanded our knowledge of the universe but at the same time
it has extended and intensified the existential concerns of mankind
without doing anything to help the individual faced with the certain
prospect of death to find a meaning in life.*

"A Path to Prehistory" [1]

Grahame Clark retired from the Disney Chair in 1973 and plunged
immediately into another academic world. He left behind him a small
department that was alive with new ideas, especially through the work of
David Clarke, a brilliant young theoretician who was a tutor in Peterhouse,
and Eric Higgs, with his cadre of (mainly) graduates known as his "storm
troopers." Clark himself had had little personal contact with many of the
students passing through the department, largely because of his seemingly
remote personality, which led to his (unjustified) reputation as being
humorless. After Grahame's retirement and the premature death of both
Clarke and Higgs, many students dispersed and the department became less
adventurous and less exciting. The retiring Disney's tenure of office had its
most enduring impact in distant lands far from Cambridge.

With retirement came a congenial move. Grahame returned home one
evening and informed Mollie out of the blue that they were moving to
Peterhouse. He had just been elected master of the college, having been a fel-

low since 1950.[2] The seven years of his mastership (1973–1980) were among the happiest of his life. The Clarks took up residence in the lovely Queen Anne–style master's lodge overlooking the chapel and the old court, where they entertained visitors from every walk of life and all parts of the world. Grahame had a passionate devotion to his college and a strong sense of the importance of the college community, which had been such a seminal part of his own intellectual development. The master's lodge was a wonderfully serene place to work and a lovely setting for Grahame's growing collection of Asian jade and porcelain, which he delighted in showing visitors, including undergraduates. He became deeply absorbed in the rhythms of college life, to the point that even prehistory sometimes took a backseat. Visitors found themselves whisked off to support Peterhouse crews from the River Cam towpath at the May bumping races.[3] "These things are important," he would say. "We can't spend all of our time thinking about archaeology." With his strong sense of history and deep intellectual indebtedness to Peterhouse, the conservative but increasingly mellow Grahame was a distinguished and much admired master. At the end of his seven-year stint, the college elected him to an honorary fellowship. He continued to participate in college affairs whenever possible, until the end of his life.

Even while master, Grahame was writing busily, deeply immersed in the broad issues of world prehistory, more than any other scholar in archaeology. Apart from the third edition of *World Prehistory*, he also revisited his beloved Mesolithic with a new book published in 1975. Archaeology was a welcome escape from the rough-and-tumble of college and university politics. So was the Clarks' country cottage at Aldeburgh on the North Sea coast, purchased in 1957 to replace a dilapidated houseboat owned in earlier years, which he found "life-enhancing" for more than four decades. Here Grahame toiled away at his typewriter but also indulged a passion for dinghy sailing. His antics under sail were said to be as lethal as his driving, but he never drowned anyone (Figure 12.1). Mollie also encouraged him to paint in oils as a way of turning his mind away from constant writing.

The Earlier Stone Age
Settlement of Scandinavia

The Earlier Stone Age Settlement of Scandinavia was an attempt to bring together the new evidence that had accumulated since the appearance of *The*

Figure 12.1 **Sailing at Aldeborough.**

Mesolithic Settlement thirty-eight years earlier. Instead of revising his original book, he decided to write a new one to reflect a "generational tide in ideas." He originally planned two volumes, one on early settlement and then another on later prehistory. He abandoned the latter volume, as it required too much of an intellectual reach and the reception of the first volume was not as favorable as he would have liked.

Earlier Stone Age Settlement took advantage of additional travels after the war, including his 1947 Leverhulme journey to northern Scandinavia, a 1955 family holiday in central Sweden, and regular attendance at radiocarbon conferences and other meetings. In 1971, Grahame and Mollie had traveled to southern Norway and northern Jutland, where they visited sites of the Norwegian "dwelling-place culture" and discussed palynology with an old friend, Norwegian botanist Knut Faegri, a pioneer in palynology. The return journey took them from Oslo to Frederikshavn, where they saw Lyngby sites and collections, to the Litorina Sea shorelands of the Limfjord and the landscape of Therkel Mathiasen's Gudenaa culture.[4]

The following year, a visiting professorship at Uppsala University at the Institute for Nordic and Comparative Archaeology, housed in the former archbishop's palace, allowed ample time to examine the landscapes around Lake Mälar and both sites and rock engravings in western Uppland. He gave lectures, was honored with a Filosofie Doktor *(honoris causa)* from the university, and traveled widely. (The National University of Ireland awarded him a doctor of letters in the same year.) Grahame also journeyed to Finland, where he again studied traditional peasant culture and saw firsthand the dramatic effects of the isostatic recovery of the land in Ångermanland, in a landscape with a vertical displacement of over 280 meters (918 feet). He visited Bronze Age cairns located along the former coastline between thirty and fifty meters (100 to 164 feet) above modern sea level. By the time he returned to Cambridge, he had a broad knowledge of the archaeological record and collections throughout much of Scandinavia that was unique among non-Scandinavian archaeologists of the day. He lamented not having visited much of Finnmark, Öland, and the island of Bornholm in the Baltic.

The new book followed the general pattern of the old. Chapter 1 discussed some basic concepts, among them the now familiar notion that human cultures were part of living systems and the importance of bioarchaeology. Clark stressed the importance of new microscopic approaches to material culture such as edge-wear analysis and the vital role played by ecosystems in human lives. In *Prehistoric Europe* he had discussed European prehistory in the context of the broad floristic zones of the continent. Working now in a more restricted territory, he could consider environment in relation to individual communities and the ways in which they minimized risk by exploiting several ecological zones, taking into account the advances in settlement archaeology and archaeological survey of recent years. Here he was strongly influenced by the new technique of site catchment analysis, which had been applied with success by Claudio Vita-Finzi and Eric Higgs in the Mount Carmel region of southwestern Asia during the Early History of Agriculture Project.[5]

With its talk of social territories, home bases, social hierarchies, and redistribution networks, the chapter reflects the influence of other researchers on Clark's thinking, especially Peterhouse archaeologist David Clarke (see Chapter 13). The new emphasis on settlement and landscape of the 1960s and 1970s was a logical follow-on from his earlier research. The basic theme of the book was shifting settlement patterns and changes in resource exploitation, as well as the processes of culture change, which Clark considered to be closely connected to the adaptive value of different cultural patterns and to the workings of ecosystems. In this, he was quite close to the thinking of American cultural ecologists of the day.

Thereafter, the book followed a familiar path, with a discussion of Postglacial climatic change and the ways of identifying it. From there, Clark described the Late Glacial settlement of Denmark and Scania, working his way northward through four chapters from south to north. He identified three different Late Glacial cultural groupings on the northern European plain on the basis of tanged flint points, but there were distinctive bone and antler tool types that cut across these areas. He considered three levels of grouping—the local group, social territories, and what one could call tech-noterritory distinguished by artifact forms. This was one of the earliest attempts to interpret the archaeological record of Late Glacial sites in terms of human behavior.

The book updated the classic descriptions of Maglemose and Ertebølle culture in *Mesolithic Settlement* and chronicled the northward spread of human settlement as glaciers retreated over Finland and central and northern Sweden. As always, Clark illustrated the text with his own maps and drawings, more of them than in *The Mesolithic Settlement*. He was at his best when discussing seasonality and subsistence, but there was little shift in the overall paradigm. The book covered little new ground except for a general updating.

The *Earlier Stone Age Settlement* was not as well received as its predecessor. Carl-Axel Moberg expressed the feelings of many of Clark's northern colleagues in *Antiquity* when he noted that an explosion of new knowledge was transforming Scandinavian archaeology and implied the book was already out of date.[6] The pace of research, of new discoveries, was simply too intense for an outsider to keep up with, especially with a plethora of new hydroelectric schemes and other projects yielding highly significant new archaeological finds, including Mesolithic cemeteries. Furthermore, a new generation of Scandinavian scholars had moved far beyond Clark's earlier ideas and were using approaches based on formal systems theory and other American ideas that Grahame could not fully accept and ignored in his book. He often reacted with distaste to the theoretical debates that now surrounded him on every side. "I have avoided the kind of polemical writing occasionally suitable in the periodicals," he remarked rather pointedly in the preface to *The Early Settlement*. "What I have aimed to do . . . is to present hypotheses in the light of explicit theory and in terms of systematically acquired data."[7]

Clark's sense of what this meant differed from that of his younger colleagues, who were arguing for more scientific rigor. A lifetime of pursuing environmental archaeology and pushing the notion of multidisciplinary research had directed Grahame onto a directional track that he now found hard to leave, and *The Earlier Settlement* showed it.

"Books of Essay Proportions"

"Above all she [Mollie] has learned to accept that the launching of one book serves only to clear my study for another," wrote Grahame at the end of the *Earlier Settlement* preface.[8] He devoted the remainder of his life almost compulsively to a steady stream of books that reflected his thinking on the most general issues of archaeology. All of them drew heavily on a lifetime of traveling and general writing. The third edition of *World Prehistory* was close behind *Earliest Settlement* in 1977. "There followed, in a way as anticlimax, other books, of essay proportions and thematic approaches," writes John Coles aptly.[9] Clark had had some success with two popular books in the early 1960s, *Prehistoric Societies*, written with Stuart Piggott, and *The Stone Age Hunters*, a lavishly illustrated short paperback for textbook use. He now turned to writing four books for a more general audience. They were intended to advance the archaeological themes and causes he held dear.

Many days, however, he was still busy with a multitude of commitments, among them the perennial problem of underfunding for archaeological science and the need for an equality of research funding relative to the natural sciences. Pressure put on the Science Research Council led that important funding body to identify science-based archaeology as a research area worth supporting. A working group under government science adviser Sir Sam Edwards recommended founding a committee—the Science-based Archaeology Committee. Grahame took the chair at the first meeting on July 1, 1976. Over the next nineteen years, four of them under Grahame's leadership, the committee funded about 235 science-based archaeological projects, including the Radiocarbon Accelerator Unit at Oxford University, in which Clark had a important founding role.[10] In 1980, he delivered the J. C. Jacobsen Memorial Lecture to the Danish Academy of Science, in which he pointed with satisfaction to the promising results already flowing from the unit. The blocks of dates coming from AMS laboratories were essential if we were to understand the nature and rate of culture change in the prehistoric past.[11] Despite many distractions, writing was still his highest priority. His evenings ran on a well-greased routine. He would work upstairs until about 9 P.M. and then come down to play cards with Mollie until it was time to go to bed.[12]

In 1978, the Clarks traveled far afield again, this time to New Delhi, where he gave the first Wheeler Memorial Lecture at the invitation of B. K. Thapar, director-general of the Archaeological Survey. Thapar had spent some time at Cambridge and had provided material for the revision of *World Prehistory*. The two lectures allowed Clark to survey and praise Wheeler's disciplined approach to Indian archaeology and his notable excavations at Harappa and Mohenjodaro. In his second lecture, he urged Indian archaeologists to break out of the rigid shackles of chronology and formal excavation procedures to examine new questions. The anthropological approach offered potential for studying such exciting issues as culture change and human diversity. Both were familiar topics at home, but they were important messages for archaeologists locked in the practices of an earlier generation.[13] The Clarks visited many monuments and sites, including the Taj

Figure 12.2 "We were photographed with the Taj in the background by the photographer who took Mr. [James] Callaghan on the same seat the day before—[he] claimed to rate a prof of arch. above a PM [Prime Minister]." Clark travel notes, 1978.

Mahal, as well as the residence in New Delhi once occupied by the British commander in chief. Clark was fascinated, as one of them, Field Marshall Birdwood, later served as master of Peterhouse (Figure 12.2). He was also struck by the contrast between wealth and poverty and enjoyed "threading a Land Rover through crowds of peasants intermingled with sacred cows as we negotiated villages."[14]

Mesolithic Prelude appeared in 1980, a short volume based on a Munro lecture, given at Edinburgh University in the previous year. Grahame returned to the theme of ecological approaches to the Mesolithic, which he had discussed in his previous Munro lectures thirty years earlier. He reviewed the history of the term "Mesolithic," the old notion of a hiatus, which was discredited by excavations at Mas d'Azil in France as early as 1889. The ecological approach allowed one to look at the Mesolithic in terms of continuity from the Palaeolithic to the Neolithic. He took note also of Russian attitudes to the Mesolithic, specifically the thesis advanced by G. I. Mathyushin that considered it the "most important epoch in history. "The time is now ripe to expound and justify the proposition that the Mesolithic, so far from being a dead end, was in fact an essential prelude to fundamental advances in the development of culture."[15] In fact, this proposition was already widely accepted. Clark gave a succinct review of what was then known of Mesolithic cultures in southwestern Asia and Europe, as well as of the "Neolithization of Mediterranean and Temperate Europe." He drew attention to the reaction against diffusionist views of the spread of agriculture into Europe resulting from new calibrated radiocarbon chronologies, stressing that Mesolithic groups continued to flourish alongside farming societies, even sometimes adopting domesticated animals.[16]

The three descriptive chapters cover familiar ground for readers of *World Prehistory*, but they helped make Clark's point: that the main turning points in the remoter human past were primarily biological and social—the appearance of anatomically modern humans and the development of stratified societies "which made possible the growth of advanced civilization." Human self-awareness and the ability to express feelings symbolically were the all-important catalysts for more recent prehistory. "The long process culminating in the domestication of animals, plants and not least of men themselves can hardly have been carried out in any other way than through the intensification and ultimately the transformation of earlier [cultural] systems."[17] He doubted whether Mathyushin was right in rating the

Mesolithic so highly, but no one could deny that more Mesolithic research was urgently needed in all parts of the world.

Three years later, Methuen published *The Identity of Man as Seen by an Archaeologist*. The catalyst for this short book was an essay, "Archaeology and Human Diversity," published in the *Annual Review of Anthropology* for 1979, in which Clark had argued that cultural diversity based on the development of different cultural traditions underlay the entire process of humanization.[18] *Identity* expanded on this theme, drawing attention to the features that distinguished humans from other primates—culture and cultural behavior. What does it mean to be a human being? The identity of humans was best sought in their history, not through science. He wrote of the evolution of humanity as "a kind of hierarchy in time." Archaeologists may have been thought to have a preoccupation with technology, but such an impression was misleading. They were studying the works of human hands, "the most eloquent memorials of their evolution as social beings." Cultural diversity was one of humanity's most precious assets in an increasingly homogenized modern world. The loss of this diversity "challenges our very identity as men."

Clark began his journey in search of human identity with the essential differences between humans and nonhuman primates, the medium of culture providing humanity with an incomparable facility to change and be changed. Of critical importance too was the ability of individuals to question social norms and press for change, which may have accounted for humanity's greater success at adjusting to environmental change than animals. Unique too was the human quality of self-awareness, of being able to perceive messages relayed by the senses from the outside world. Belief systems and "a procession of rituals" bound societies together and nurtured their identities. Thus architecture, iconography, and religious paraphernalia from the past provided a rich window for examining ancient human diversity.

From differences, we turn to methods for studying human diversity—familiar ground to readers of Clark's earlier books. "Approaches to Archaeology," Chapter 4, touched on antiquarian investigations, evolution, natural history, social evolution, and Marxism and the methods of culture history. "The Genesis of Cultural Diversity" discussed how archaeology studies culture change over very long periods of time. Here Clark returned to issues of continuity and the tempo of change, to the propensi-

ty of human cultures to diversify. Stability required "harmonious relationships between social systems and the habitats and biomes in which they
operated." Dynamic ecosystems were "veritable theaters of change"—we
are treated once again to the famous ecosystem diagram, featured in the
Reckitt lecture of 1953 and in other publications, among them his Childe
Memorial lecture, "Prehistory Since Childe," delivered in 1976.[19]
Diversification of human culture resulted from adjustments to a changing
ecosystem, the degree of social acceptance of change, and the power of
articulate speech to communicate new ideas, as well as humanity's "self-
conscious sense of identity."[20]

Societies had individual identities that had existed in the past and were
transmitted to future generations. Cohesion, self-assurance, and identity
were infinitely variable and served to separate a group from its neighbors.
The same distinctive identity came into play when one society interacted
with another, exchanging artifacts, commodities, and ideas. Cultural diversity increased and accelerated through time, especially with the spread of
modern humans during, and immediately after, the Late Ice Age. The transition from hunting and gathering to food production took place in many
parts of the world and was one of the most important, if not the most
important, development in the human past. More secure food supplies,
higher population densities, and more sedentary settlement enhanced the
trend toward diversity, more sophisticated economies, and far more elaborate material culture.

Chapter 5, "The Findings of Ethnography," takes us into familiar anthropological waters. Clark was often at his best writing about ethnography in
relation to prehistory. The influences of a career spent thinking about
ethnographic analogy, his trips to Australia and New Zealand, and his sedulous reading of Captain Cook and other historical sources came together in
a smooth and undemanding synthesis, which yet again bears testimony to
the seminal importance of Australian anthropologist Donald Thomson on
Clark's thinking before World War II. There is nothing new here, merely a
restatement of a well-aired methodological approach that Clark now wore
like a comfortable jacket.

Chapters 6 and 7 dealt with issues of hierarchy, homogenization, and
dehumanization. During the past 5,000 years, social inequality and hierarchical societies developed rapidly throughout the world. Civilizations
developed in response to a need for administrative expertise and law and

order, as well as for hierarchical societies headed by rulers legitimized by divine associations. Powerful ideologies lay behind these civilizations. Clark ended his discussion of hierarchical societies with a description of preindustrial European civilizations, such as seventeenth- and eighteenth-century France, in which the Sun King, Louis XIV, "diffused" rays of civilization from his palace at Versailles. A modest, largely subsistence agriculture supported lavish consumption in the higher levels of society, including the production of highly sophisticated furniture and silverware. "The finest material embodiments of the human spirit were the products of societies in which spending power was concentrated in the fewest hands. Even more significantly in some respects, it is precisely such objects, the finest in their respective classes, that attract the admiration and wonder of the citizens of modern egalitarian societies reduced to staring in museums and show houses at relics of the great civilization in which their forebears however vicariously once shared."[21]

Next he returned to a theme that loomed large in his paper for the *Annual Review of Anthropology*, reproducing much of the text for the second time. Archaeology and anthropology had displayed some of the remarkable cultural diversity of humankind, the "variousness" of humanity, as anthropologist Clifford Geertz once put it. Modern industrial society, with its better communications, global economies, and standardized products, was homogenizing human society. Societies everywhere were becoming egalitarian once again. Conspicuous consumption was no longer a measure of social prestige, as it had been in earlier times. Yet people everywhere valued their cultural identity—their heritage—and would defend their identity against the forces of anonymity and homogenization. Traditional customs and values, even national frontiers, have profound value to those whose lives they help to shape. Homogenization, when carried to its conclusion, "destroys not merely the diversity of cultural patterns but the dignity of man himself." How, then, could one arrest the destruction of cultural diversity? "The first need is to acquire a full, caring and loving understanding of indigenous cultures and their unique sets of values" and to involve indigenous peoples themselves in conserving them.[22]

At the same time, there was a real danger that the inequality removed by the Industrial Revolution would be carried to ludicrous extremes. Clark pointed to the recently discovered magnificent jade burial suits of the Han Prince Liu Sheng and his wife Tou Wan as examples of the benefits of social hierarchies. "Without a hierarchic structure, without a marked degree of inequality in consumption, the astonishing diversity of Chinese, Egyptian, or Anglo-Saxon culture would never have developed." This was not a matter of speculation, for archaeology had revealed what human societies in these areas were like before hierarchical societies arose. They were more or less egalitarian, their material culture impoverished. He ended by quoting the sociologist Rolf Dahrendorf: "The very existence of social inequality . . . is an impetus towards liberty because it guarantees a society's on-going dynamic, historical quality. The idea of a perfect egalitarian society is not only unrealistic. It is terrible."[23]

Identity made Grahame's usual passionate case for the importance of archaeology as a way of studying and fostering human diversity, as a vital tool for writing and teaching human history, a plea repeated again and again throughout his career. To his chagrin, the book was largely ignored by reviewers, except for a devastating review by the Cambridge anthropologist Sir Edmund Leach in the august pages of *Nature*.[24] Leach described the book as having a more personal perspective than *World Prehistory*. *Identity* was a work that reminded all kinds of anthropologists of their mutual interests. Clearly Clark had in mind a reintegration of social anthropology and prehistoric archaeology. It was "clearly the functionalist, 'everything fits together like the gear wheels of a watch', kind of social anthropology advocated by Malinowski." But contemporary anthropology had moved beyond functionalism. Anthropologists had long enjoyed a dialog with historians and sociologists about the significance of cultural diversity rather than discussions with prehistorians whose "commitment to stratified sedimentary deposits gave them an *a priori* bias toward a stage-by-stage, evolutionary interpretation of their data. Only in Marxist countries is such an evolutionary perspective still commonplace. Although Clark rejects simplistic stage-by-stage, unlinear social evolution postulated by Morgan and Marx, he insists that the archaeological record documents a cumulative advance in technology."

Leach pointed out that Western archaeologists still transported the facts of present-day ethnography into the remote past to flesh out the bare archaeological record. He added wickedly: "In the present context this is an odd conjunction since Grahame Clark's personal political convictions lie well to the right of those of Margaret Thatcher." Clark "seems to want his readers to believe that the chaps with the better gadgets are 'better' chaps

Figure 12.3   **Grahame Clark's painting of Henry Moore's reclining figure at Snape, Suffolk (c. 1990).**

in some overall human sense, either because technological sophistication implies better adaptation to the environment or because the making of objects for conspicuous display is a marker of social hierarchy, and the development of social hierarchy is what humanization is all about." He pointed out that Clark stopped well short of being an admirer of high technology, for he considered Western society contaminated with "egalitarian notions." In the author's eyes: "Humanity reached its peak under the Ancien Regime; the rot set in with the French Revolution (Clark, p. 151) and things have been getting worse ever since. Montesquieu who first taught his eighteenth-century contemporaries to admire cultural diversity would have certainly felt the same." Leach's message was clear: Clark was toying with long outmoded approaches to cultural diversity.

Grahame seemed obsessed with writing books. Mollie encouraged him to paint in oils instead, with some success (Figures 12.3, 12.4). Undeterred

Figure 12.4 **Grahame Clark's painting of Barbara Hepworth's** *Family of Man* **sculpture at Snape, Suffolk. Hepworth had an affinity with Stonehenge, whence her use of rectangular uprights in her sculptures.**

by Leach's severe criticism, Grahame wrote yet another essay on the same general topic. *Symbols of Excellence: Precious Meterials as Expressions of Status* appeared in 1986, under the Cambridge University Press imprimatur. This short book was a sequel to *The Identity of Man*, which argued that we owe our identity as humans to our belonging to societies that share common values. Now Grahame turned his attention to symbols in the archaeological record—material objects that represented something abstract. This, he wrote, was a step beyond subsistence and ecology, which had now become commonplace approaches to the prehistoric past. "Fruitful though this has been in promoting and giving direction to research, its uncritical pursuit only serves to advance a reductionist and therefore inadequate view of man."[25] Human survival depended not only on successful adaptation but on maintaining "standards of excellence."

Technology did not necessarily serve material ends, witness the Shang bronzes with their connections to ancestor worship and Andean metalwork before the Spanish conquest. Humans had enhanced their success as primates by exercising "discrimination in their choice of symbols of excellence."[26] Archaeology had shown how human societies have placed the highest values on useless substances in daily life. He quoted the almost forgotten American economic writer Thorstein Veblen, who argued in 1899 that the propensity for emulation is a powerful economic motive.[27] Archaeology had produced rich documentation of the history of precious substances, the history of which can only have resulted from "societies enriched by aesthetic sensibilities and sufficiently aware of persons to wish to symbolize relations between them as individuals and as enactors of social roles." The very process of humanization was a product of aesthetic feelings as well as mind.

Clark identified three stages in the history of precious substances. The first stage, during the Upper Palaeolithic and Mesolithic, saw valuable commodities such as seashells and jewelry used mainly to identify ethnic identity and to grade individuals by age and sex. Neolithic communities extended the realm of the precious to include substances of mineral origin. Chinese societies used polished jade, for example. The rise of hierarchical polities headed by powerful rulers and the emergence of classes of specialized artisans called for the use of "graded insignia to legitimize the exercise of power."[28] The third stage was one when economic and political power passed from "hierarchs" to the general body of the population. The consumption of the most sought-after goods is now democratized away from a minority to the general populace, unimpeded by sumptuary laws or other restrictions. Perhaps standards have fallen in an era when no new court jewelry is commissioned and anyone with the money can buy precious stones. Today, the wheel had turned full circle. The most skilled professional jewelers and artisans were once again focusing attention on the qualities of the finest stones and other substances and displaying them with the minimum encroachment.

The next four chapters surveyed different raw materials, starting with the organic— ivory, rhinoceros horn, cowrie shells, coral, amber, and jet. In each, Clark followed his classic pattern of a broad-ranging survey, starting with Palaeolithic occurrences and then bringing the story into historic times. He surveyed jade from China, New Zealand, Europe, and the

Americas. From jade, he moved to gold and other valuable metals and then to precious stones, where he noted the tendency for attitudes toward precious substances to remain the same over long periods of time, confirming "the force of inertia in history."[29] Their rankings of esteem might change with fashion, discovery of new precious materials, or additional sources, but they always remained of value. Clark classified precious stones in two groups—opaque to translucent and transparent. Lapis lazuli with its brilliant colors, turquoise, chalcedony, and opals fell in the first category. Garnets, emeralds, corundum, diamonds, enamel, and pearls came under the transparent category, the latter having an important role as symbols of regeneration in Christianity.

Chapter 6 summarized the symbolic role of precious substances in human affairs (for display of authority and social ranking) to mark religious rites and, above all, as currency. Today, in a more homogenized global order, precious metals were used for Olympic medals and other sports trophies, to commemorate excellence in every field of endeavor. "The more democratic communities become, it would seem, the keener the anxiety of individuals to excel their neighbors."[30] The conclusion seemed obvious. Regardless of social circumstances, a concern for excellence and a desire to recognize it through symbols embodying precious substances was widespread among our species, especially over the past 5,000 years, when humans "have dragged themselves from the morass of primitive communism and set their feet on ground firm enough to support civilized ways of life."

Illustrated with color plates, *Symbols of Excellence* is a slight book, but it allowed Grahame a chance to share his admiration for Stone Age art and to combine it with his lifelong interest in art generally. He wrote that he deemed it a privilege to "explore the values of the civilizations coming within his purview and not least the symbols which have served to define status and acknowledge outstanding achievement." As was apparent through much of his writing, Grahame was an elitist who had a strong belief in the importance of individual achievement and human progress. This book reflected these beliefs. Like his good friend Gordon Childe, who was at the other end of the political spectrum, Grahame believed that the future of humankind lay in the ability of people from different cultures and political perspectives to cooperate in solving common problems. We were self-aware human beings; we had a responsibility to cooperate for the future good of humanity.

Symbols received few reviews, which is a pity, as it is an unusual and at times captivating book with its broad range of examples and fascinating excursions into the byways of modern history. Colin Renfrew wrote in *Antiquity* that Clark's interests had shifted to what makes humans unique and described the book as "an elitist work," which did not delve much further into the subject than Thorstein Veblen had in the 1880s. He noted that the author seemed to express a mild regret at the passing of the kinds of aristocratic social systems that produced magnificent symbols of excellence.[31]

In 1992, Cambridge University Press published the last of his books, *Space, Time, and Man: A Prehistorian's View.* "Only a long emeritus author would venture on such a book, which inevitably goes far beyond anything he is qualified to write about," he wrote to Charles Higham.[32] Another brief volume, it was an attempt to show how people achieved their humanity in part by attaining a fuller comprehension of their own place in time and space. Clark recognized from the start that animals of any species could only survive and reproduce because of their skills in exploiting natural environments. Animals, unlike plants, moved around and had a sense of space. Only humans had a conscious awareness that they existed in time, from the past to the present and into the future. Throughout prehistory, humans anticipated needs by collecting toolmaking stone and later by trade, exchange. The more advanced material culture and technology became, the larger the investment needed to sustain it, the greater the need to anticipate the future. The more profound the impact of modern technology, the more humans thought about the short- and long-term future.

The notions of time and space entertained by preliterate people were limited primarily to the nature of their economies and the structure of their own societies. Literate societies provided a better appreciation of the dimensions of time and space in ancient times. During the past five thousand years, notions of time and space had expanded dramatically to encompass not only the entire world but space as well. "From an early stage in his prehistory man has asked himself not only how the natural world operates, but why he himself is there." People had found it necessary to search for explanations in terms of "ancestors remote in time yet still embodied in myths and rituals."[33]

Chapters 2 and 3 explored what was known about the dimensions of time and space in preliterate societies, their use of culture to adapt to diverse environments, and their ability to navigate across large oceans and to trade raw materials such as axe blade stone over long distances. Awareness of time came first from an awareness of individual mortality, which led, ultimately, to burial rituals and to myths about ancestral beings to account for the passing of time. Archaeology showed us that cultural traditions were transmitted over generations, centuries, even millennia. Genealogies played a vital role in this process. With farming, perhaps earlier, came the need to measure and observe the passing of the seasons by using the movements of the heavenly bodies. Clark discussed briefly the controversial researches of the American astronomer Gerald Hawkins at Stonehenge, Alexander Thom's work on the astronomical alignments of megaliths, and Alexander Marshack's painstaking efforts to document Upper Palaeolithic records of the passage of time. "At the very least it may be that in the planning of Stonehenge care was taken to use the movements of the heavenly bodies as pointers to the scheduling of social activities."[34]

When civilizations developed, awareness of space expanded rapidly. Chapter 4 documented the inventions that helped in this process—Egyptian ships, Mediterranean seagoing, Greek colonization of remote lands, and so on. He discussed the road network of the Roman Empire, the development of maps by the Romans and Chinese, and the Age of Exploration that led, ultimately, to the global economy. The deepening of historical time began with the Egyptian king lists and later with Mesopotamian equivalents and Chinese histories. Clark then went on to the history of time measurement, from water clocks, sundials, and hourglasses to mechanical time measurement devices.

In chapter 6, "Evolution and World Prehistory," Clark covered ground familiar to archaeologists and pointed out that "in our own generation we have been able to visualize our past as human beings in the context of geological time and the prehistoric basis of our recorded history." He followed this familiar essay with an examination of extraterrestrial space and time and the history of scientific astronomy from the Greeks to space exploration, for "modern cosmology embodies our most extended awareness of the dimensions in which we have our being."[35]

Space, Time, and Man made two opposing suppositions. First, the emergence of intelligence capable of envisaging the evolution of the universe was the purpose of the whole phenomenon. Second, human beings were no more than accidental episodes in the unfolding of physical laws. Grahame wrote of an "ultimate mystery" impenetrable by human reason. He quotes the mathematician and philosopher A. N. Whitehead: "The present type of order in the world has arisen from an unimaginable past and it will find its grave in an unimaginable future."[36]

The last of Clark's published books stressed the uniqueness of humanity in its ability to perceive the dimensions of space and time, as well as by its deliberate expansion of spatial horizons, while also documenting the passage of time in the past and into the future. It received no academic reviews of importance.

"You Have Enriched the Science of Prehistory Immeasurably"

In 1990, Grahame received an extraordinary honor. The Netherlands Foundation had honored classical archaeology with the highly prestigious Erasmus Prize in 1984. In 1990, they decided to "crown the field of Prehistory" and awarded the prize to "Grahame Clark because he recognized the interdisciplinary character of Prehistory quite early, and has linked together, both in theory and practice, the historical, biological and anthropological sciences; because he can be regarded as a pioneer in the study of economic aspects of prehistoric communities; studies which have led to fundamental new insights that have meaningful implications for modern society." The citation also recognized his contributions to world prehistory and to public understanding of the prehistoric past and his "incisive and inspiring working methods . . . [which established] a scholarly institute whose influence is felt throughout the entire world."[37]

The prize was presented at a formal ceremony at the Royal Palace in Amsterdam, attended by His Royal Highness Prince Bernhard and Princess Margret of the Netherlands. Prince Bernhard himself read the "laudation," a formal tribute to Grahame's work. He summarized Clark's concern with the long sweep of the prehistoric past and with the identity of human beings, resulting from their societies with shared values. The prince acclaimed Grahame's concern with human diversity, his recognition of our ability to discriminate, his apprehension over the inexorable homogenization of human culture. He praised his optimism about the future of humanity. "You have enriched the science of prehistory immeasurably. And, in addition, you have illuminated for a large public the meaning of prehistorical insights for modern society. But what stands out

Figure 12.5   **Grahame Clark, left, receives the Erasmus Prize from Prince Bernhard of the Netherlands, November 1990. Courtesy Praemium Erasmianum Foundation and Benelux Press, Voorburg.**

above all your other activities and accomplishments is your great love for and interest in Man." Being human meant being an individual, a particular type of person. "And you, Professor Clark, are indeed a very particular kind of man" (Figure 12.5).[38]

In his acceptance speech, Grahame recalled how Erasmus had taught at Queens College, Cambridge, between 1511 and 1514, "only a couple of hundred meters or so" from Peterhouse, long before prehistory was a conscious academic discipline. He paid tribute to the famous Dutchman who had played an "important part in freeing Christendom from superstition and making possible the growth of modern consciousness." He expressed his delight that the foundation had recognized the importance of prehistory as a way of studying how humans chose alternatives. "The brave sound of the Danish lures [replicas of prehistoric trumpets played earlier in the ceremony] is a tuneful reminder that prehistoric people were not living by bread alone." They also reminded him how much he owed to Danish colleagues, who set high standards for him in the early days. He was touched by the showing of a film on the archaeology of the Somerset Levels chosen by John Coles, "one of the most brilliant of my former pupils." He ended by announcing that he intended to divide the £100,000 prize money between his beloved Prehistoric Society to establish a Europa Fund "to provide an annual monetary prize" for prehistorians, and the British Academy for an endowment "for a medal to recognize achievements in prehistory comparable to those it already awards in other fields." In this way, he hoped that the Erasmus Prize would "help to further the wider recognition of the subject in our continent as a whole." Earlier in the week, he had written to Charles Higham to say that he would use the prize to "help advance prehistory and the esteem in which it is held. It has to be admitted that the older disciplines tend to close ranks and relegate our field to the side-lines. I hope that you and others will continue to show them how wrong they are."[39]

The Erasmus Prize gave Grahame a deep sense of satisfaction and achievement, not so much because of his own work but because archaeology could enjoy such high visibility in a wider world. He could look back over sixty years of active involvement in an archaeological world that had changed dramatically, in considerable measure because of his work. Prehistoric archaeology was now a commonplace on the academic scene, even if much remained to be done to raise public consciousness. Dozens of younger archaeologists in distant lands were adding new chapters to human prehistory, their careers jump-started in Cambridge. Multidisciplinary research was producing exciting results on every side. He was delighted when the first recipient of the Europa Medal was his lifetime friend Stuart Piggott.

More honors followed. In 1992, Grahame received a knighthood for his services to archaeology—his research and leadership in fostering world prehistory. Two years later, Grahame and Mollie were present at the opening of the Macdonald Institute for Archaeological Research in Cambridge. This new research organization had been generously endowed by the inventor of the automatic changer for long-playing records. The institute occupies a handsome, modern building in the Downing Street quadrangle opposite the entrance of the Haddon Museum and is dedicated to multidisciplinary archaeological research. Grahame was deeply touched by the dedication of the Grahame Clark Laboratory for Archaeology as part of the institute on that important day. His career had come full circle. As a young research student, he had entered an archaeological world in which the stone implement and potsherd reigned supreme, a discipline that sometimes resembled mere stamp collecting. In the fullness of his years, he was present at the opening of an institute that was dedicated to the very kinds of multidisciplinary research in all parts of the world to which he had devoted his career.

Grahame was now well into his eighties and was slowing the pace. He was writing yet another book, which he at first entitled *A Path to Prehistory*, in which he would pursue the theme that had engaged his mind throughout the later stages of his life—the qualities that distinguished humans from other animals. Once he was well into the manuscript, he changed his mind and proposed naming it *Man the Spiritual Primate*, but the new title never made its way onto the manuscript. The surviving six-chapter draft preserved in his archives is partly autobiographical, but much of it covers ground already surveyed in *Archaeology at Cambridge and Beyond*, among other works. The manuscript is of interest in that it chronicles some of his thinking behind the Early History of Agriculture Project and records some details of his Australian and American travels, as well as his ponderings on world prehistory. Grahame's restless mind was still focusing on the spiritual dimensions of humankind. He was well aware that archaeology was turning away from artifacts and economic systems into a more profound concern, "the unfolding of the mind which more than anything else has differentiated man from other primates. At the same [time, it] has enabled us to understand or at least confront our predicament as self-conscious beings."[40]

His mind was still sharp, his curiosity undiminished. He continued to attend meetings of the Prehistoric Society, even if the theoretical debates and specialist researches of the younger generation were often uncongenial. His public austerity had mellowed considerably as his natural kindness showed through. A steady stream of former students passed through Cambridge and called to pay their respects and, certainly, to make sure that Grahame knew of his influence on their early careers. A slight stroke that he suffered while he was master of Peterhouse had slowed him down slightly, but he continued writing as he had always done. Mollie persuaded him that it was acceptable to travel in more luxury in their old age. They took a Swan Hellenic cruise to the eastern Mediterranean in June 1995. He suffered a severe stroke off Cyprus, was taken home, and died peacefully with Mollie holding his hand on September 12, 1995.

At a memorial service in Little St. Mary's Church, Lord Renfrew of Kaimsthorn, the current Disney Professor and then master of Jesus College, described Grahame as "a great Peterhouse man, a great Cambridge man." He paid tribute to his commitment and intellectual integrity, to a man "who preferred his kindnesses to be quiet and unostentious." It was in the Cambridge department that "as he would have wished, that we find his greatest memorial: in the scholars to whom he gave inspiration, and in the series of books and papers which helped archaeology make the transition from an anecdotal study of artifacts to a systematic science in touch with other sciences."[41] A *Times* obituary called him "one of the leading prehistorians of this century." Professor Paul Mellars, writing in the *Independent*, mirrored this sentiment and remarked that his death "marks, in every sense, the end of an era in archaeology."[42] An end of an era it was, for Grahame lived long enough to see others build on his pioneering work. To an earnest student asking for a copy of one of his earlier writings, he is said to have replied. "That? Why that is completely out of date. Fancy anyone wanting to read that now." [43] Clark meant it—and therein lay part of his greatness.

13

✥

Retrospect

It's difficult to realize now that I grew up in a climate in which there was absolutely nothing. We had to improvise everything for ourselves. I was very lucky to live at such a time.

Interview, 1994[1]

Grahame Clark never wanted to be anything but an archaeologist, and so it was fitting that he became one of the greatest prehistorians of the twentieth century. Over a career that spanned well over a half century, he watched archaeology transform itself from a largely amateur pursuit into a sophisticated, multidisciplinary science with deep roots in the humanities. At the same time, he was well aware that his research and writings were among the catalysts that engineered this transformation.

Clark pursued his calling with a dedication and an intensity that did not always endear him to his colleagues. He was not a man for small talk or academic gossip and was consumed by prehistory. It was the ruling passion of his life, tempered only by his love for his family, his religion, and an eclectic interest in Asian and modern art. Clark could be arrogant, was ruthless in his criticism of what he considered shoddy work, and could be self-absorbed in his research and writing to the point of rudeness. His was a remote personality, a legacy from a youth plagued with shyness, but underneath the austere exterior was the kindest of men, capable of deep love and caring. But his obsession was archaeology and the furthering of a discipline that he considered central to the future welfare of humankind. He devoted his entire career to this long-term goal, even if the steps along the way were mingled with personal ambitions and a powerful craving for success. As noted earlier, the citation for his Erasmus Prize stated, "You have enriched the science of prehistory immeasurably. And, in addition, you have illuminated for a large public the meaning of prehistorical insights for modern society. But what stands out above all your other activities and accomplishments is your great love for and interest in Man."[2] Grahame Clark was fascinated by human diversity and human progress. The broad sweep of past human achievement was his life, his preoccupation, and his legacy.

Grahame Clark's thinking about archaeology and humanity stemmed from many intellectual strands and a number of defining discoveries and experiences. Strong intellectual influences came early. Throughout his life he was an unself-conscious elitist, his elitism fostered by his public school education, just like that inculcated into thousands of his contemporaries. His notions of leadership, human progress, and cultural evolution always owed much to his early education, from which he also acquired a lasting and an understated Christian faith.

Clark began his archaeological career in the cozy, largely amateur world of the 1930s, when flint artifact typology was all the rage. His seniors were preoccupied with chronology, simple culture history, and little else. This was the archaeology of museum curators, which Grahame professed to despise. In his early years, he wrote often of the stultifying atmosphere of dull museum display cases, of an archaeology that rarely went into the field or saw the archaeological record in the soil firsthand. Nevertheless, he was careful at first not to stray too far from the dictates of his superiors. His first book, *The Mesolithic Age in Britain,* was a conservative document couched in the archaeological language of the day, cautious in its use of distribution maps, and mirroring contemporary thought in its employment of modest diffusionist theories. Clark was still feeling his way, learning basic skills. The basic analytical approaches to artifacts used in his first book and doctoral dissertation were the foundation for an intellectual career that was to venture in very different directions.

Clark's travels to Scandinavia in 1932–1933 were a defining experience that brought him to appreciate the magnitude of the climatic changes after the Ice Age. His stroll along the ancient shore of the Litorina Sea was an epiphanic moment, as was the accidental discovery of the Leman and Ower harpoon by a North Sea trawler skipper in 1931. Both opened young Clark's eyes to the potential of environmental change to Stone Age archaeology. His mentors included Ellis Minns, a Cambridge scholar with an eclectic mind and wide perspective, and later the European prehistorian Gordon Childe, who was also a scholar with wide interests. He was strongly influenced by the economic historian A. W. Clapham, whose ideas left a lasting impression, and by the writings of the ecologist Sir A. G. Tansley, a pioneer of ecosystems. His own contemporaries and fellow researchers at Cambridge were all-important, like botanists Harry and Margaret Godwin, who taught an ambitious and restless-minded archaeologist the value and potential of pollen analysis. So were archaeologists of his age, Young Turks who became lifelong friends, Stuart Piggott and Charles Phillips among them. The Iron Age culture historian Christopher Hawkes was also a contemporary and often an intellectual adversary. Grahame worked with some, sometimes all, of these archaeologists for decades.

Clark had a mind like a sponge and used it to good effect throughout his career. He developed an unusually broad vision of prehistory in a crucible of debate and shared discoveries unusual for a young graduate student—in coffee shops and cramped lodgings, at small conferences, and in countless day-long field expeditions into the fens. He was in at the rebirth of prehistory after a long period of intellectual stagnation, an exciting experience for any scholar, let alone a young researcher. By the time he published his second book, *The Mesolithic Settlement of Northern Europe* (1936), Clark was steeped in state-of-the-art palynology and the basic systems concepts of ecology. Remarkably, he was still in his late twenties. His nascent ideas on environmental archaeology stemmed from the writing of this book, from a melting pot of fresh ideas in Cambridge, from the stimulation of the Fenland Research Committee, and from the Peacock's Farm excavation. Clark's innate conservatism was now tempered with a passion for new ideas and fresh approaches.

The Mesolithic Settlement was a brilliant synthesis for its day, consulted and admired in Scandinavia as much as it was in Britain.[3] Clark's environmental approach was still developing in its pages and did not appear in full force until three years later in *Archaeology and Society*, with its simple diagram of human societies and ecological systems that was to appear in increasingly elaborate forms over the years, in Grahame's Reckitt Lecture on environmental archaeology in 1953 and beyond (see Figure 9.3). The ideas in *Society*, arguably one of his most important books, focused on human adaptation, ecological systems, and the importance of technology to human progress. They lay at the very core of Clark's thinking for more than half a century.

Archaeology and Society also defined Grahame's opinions on the role of prehistory in contemporary life. Archaeology provided "sentiments needful to the stability and, indeed, to the very existence of society," strengthening the links which bound present generations to the past."[4] In the final analysis, he wrote, the standing of archaeology within a society was an index of "its degree of civilization." Clark's views on archaeology were always influenced by ideas and values inculcated from youth—a subtle but pervasive elitism, a deep political conservatism born of his family background and education, and a conviction of the importance of human progress and charismatic leadership, which considered the egalitarian societies of the late twentieth century unfamiliar and a retrograde step. More than one observer commented that Grahame regretted the passing of France's ancien régime of the eighteenth century with its wealthy nobility and supreme monarch. There is much truth in the observation, for Grahame's writings on human progress have an elemental simplicity about them that cannot be attributed to anything but an innate elitism, a conviction of superiority, that was the product of a British public school upbringing, not racism. But the final chapter of *Archaeology and Society*, with its powerful remarks about the misuses of archaeology by Nazis, Communists, and others, were quoted widely for more than a generation. This short but important textbook shaped the archaeological thinking of undergraduates for a quarter century.

The Prehistoric Society loomed large in Grahame's intellectual growth for more than three decades. He was passionately devoted to the society after its birth from the Prehistoric Society of East Anglia at the beginning of his career and edited the *Proceedings of the Prehistoric Society* for thirty-five years. The council made an inspired editorial choice in 1935, for Clark brought a fresh perspective to a once provincial journal. As editor, he had a unique opportunity to widen his own intellectual perspectives and breathe new air into the musty annals of British prehistory. From the beginning, he commissioned papers from archaeologists working far from Britain, thereby forming a much wider community of prehistorians. His own eclectic view of prehistory came from his undergraduate days. He had been an undergraduate at Cambridge when Garrod and Leakey were making their momentous discoveries in Palestine and Kenya, and he had learned from his Scandinavian travels the potential of folk culture for interpretation of ancient subsistence.

The *Proceedings* introduced him to scholars from far afield, whose ideas were a strong thread in his intellectual growth. By 1939, Clark was excited by the possibilities of what today is called "living archaeology," especially by anthropologist David Thompson's research on seasonality among the Wik Monkan Aborigines of northern Australia. Thompson was resident in Cambridge for a while. His paper came from his conversations with Clark and brought home to him just how important ethnography and what today we would call ethnoarchaeology were for the scientific interpretation of ancient subsistence and lifeways. Much of Clark's inspired work on prehistoric European economies was colored by Thompson's work. Had not World War II broken out, he would have tested the Australian's seasonality theories against archaeological data in the fens the following summer.

Clark's influence on prehistory through the *Proceedings* was sustained. Quite apart from being a convenient vehicle for publishing his own work and ideas, he fostered a standard of professional research and writing about human prehistory that was among the finest in the world. His editorial legacy endures in the pages of the journal to this day. At the same time, he learned about and published archaeological discoveries and syntheses from many parts of the world. His later preoccupation with world prehistory began in the pages of *PPS*.

Clark was a devoted member of many other learned societies, notably the British Academy, where he lobbied hard in his later years for a close marriage in research between archaeology and the natural sciences. He was the first chair of the Science-based Archaeology Committee of the academy, which involved close, sustained collaboration with the Royal Society. Clark knew that learned societies were the lifeblood of fund-starved disciplines such as archaeology and provided venues for serious intellectual dialogue.

In retrospect, the World War II years with their enforced idleness were probably beneficial to a young archaeologist driven to pursue the past. Grahame worked long shifts at RAF Medmenham, edited a much attenuated *Proceedings*, and had ample time to think about environmental archaeology. He consolidated and honed his approaches to ancient economy and environment. These musings bore rich archaeological fruit in a stream of papers about prehistoric economic activities that began with bees and bee-keeping in 1942 and culminated in the essays in *Prehistoric Europe: The Economic Basis* a decade later. These synthetic researches were masterpieces of multidisciplinary writing—meldings of archaeological evidence, historical sources, natural history, and folk culture—culled from traveling, days spent in museum collections, and omnivorous, often esoteric reading. This was Grahame Clark's environmental archaeology in full flow—based on a simple systems approach and data from many sources, as well as the premise that prehistoric archaeology was the study of ancient cultures and communities adapting to ever changing ancient environments.

The war years also provided opportunities for thinking about the future of archaeology. At the Future of Archaeology conference in 1943, Clark saw clearly that prehistory's destiny lay in an ardently international perspective, in what he was already calling a world prehistory. As Christopher Evans has pointed out, world prehistory itself came into being as a result of many global developments, among them improved communications and an explosion in scientific research.[5] But its fostering as a serious intellectual conception was in Clark's able hands.

After the Hitler war, Clark's career entered its most productive phase. Before 1954, he was much concerned with progress through time. By that time, he was adding an ecological perspective to his general writings. He continued to write papers on various aspects of economic life in prehistoric Europe, bringing together a final collection of them into *Prehistoric Europe: The Economic Basis* in 1952, which is often hailed as a seminal book. In fact, it was a set of stand-alone Munro lectures given at Edinburgh University assembled in book form. *Prehistoric Europe* is a collection of essays, with but the sketchiest of integrating synthesis. However, this synthesis proposed that economic and cultural stability were the normal state of affairs—disrupted "disequilibrium" resulting from environmental change—which could enlarge and contract opportunities for human societies, changes in the needs and requirements of human societies, and changes in the external environment brought about by human activities. This was a systems approach with an adaptational perspective (although Clark himself never used the word) used on a day-by-day basis long before systems became a buzzword in prehistoric archaeology. *The Economic Basis* profoundly influenced archaeologists in many countries and remains a standard work to this day. The book was a culminating moment in Clark's career, but it was not a defining event, unlike the Star Carr excavations, which were under way as he completed it.

Clark had realized as early as 1932 that the future of Mesolithic studies lay in the investigation of wet sites, where both environmental data and organic artifacts were found. The Leman and Ower harpoon and the Peacock's Farm excavation had fuelled his ambition to find such a site, realized with the discovery of Star Carr by John Moore in 1948. Star Carr, with its organic finds and rich environmental data, was a remarkable excavation by any standard that boosted Clark onto the international radar screen. The first truly multidisciplinary excavation on any scale in Britain, conducted on a shoestring and published thoroughly and promptly, Star Carr was a tour de force of environmental archaeology in which Grahame proved that he did more than talk the talk or synthesize other people's data. Thanks to his prompt, clear reporting, the site became an icon and the epitome of wet site archaeology for a generation. Not until half a century later was Clark's portrait of the settlement modified substantially. This is a tribute to both the archaeologist and the approach behind the research, which, in its basics, still underlies much Mesolithic (and later) prehistoric archaeology in Europe.

Prehistoric Europe and the Star Carr excavations won Grahame Clark the Disney Chair. For all his imperfections as a teacher and an administrator, he was the ideal man for the post at the time. He could now train students in his own mold. The 1953 Reckitt lecture, delivered after the Star Carr excavations and completion of the still unpublished report, was Grahame's ultimate statement on multidisciplinary archaeology, a sophisticated plea for collaboration with natural scientists and environmental archaeology. The message was nothing new, even if many archaeologists were still tied to flints and potsherds, but the tide was changing as the number of professional archaeologists trained in Clark's approach grew. He repeated the same message, albeit with refinements, for the rest of his career. Even before he became Disney, one can sense his perspective shifting, from a relatively narrow focus to the much broader issues of world prehistory. The shift coincided with his growing interest in the origins of European farming and with Clark's last excavation, the abortive search for Neolithic houses at Hurst Fen in 1957–1958. Thereafter, he devoted his time to broad intellectual issues such as European farming, to travel, and to world prehistory.

The intellectual threads of Clark's world archaeology go back to his student days when Dorothy Garrod worked at Mount Carmel, to the early issues of the *Proceedings*, to the broad perspective of *Archaeology and Society*, and to his musings on the future of archaeology after World War II. As Disney, Dorothy Garrod had introduced a world prehistory course at Cambridge directly after the war that had the effect of somewhat widening departmental perspectives. Most of the faculty had worked overseas during the war, which made the transition a logical one. The 1950s saw a growing demand for young archaeologists to work overseas and for formal training in anthropology for future Colonial Service officers. By the time Clark was elected to the chair in 1952, a rapid global expansion of archaeology was under way, in which the Cambridge department played an active part. The Disney Chair himself actively encouraged many now well-known archaeologists to carve out archaeological careers overseas. Clark was proud of his many former students working in distant lands. Their researches and the development of radiocarbon dating provided a catalyst for one of Clark's best known works, *World Prehistory*, the first global account of human prehistory based on radiocarbon chronology.

The development of radiocarbon dating in 1949 was one of the turning points of Grahame Clark's career and coincided with his growing interest in world prehistory. Like many successful scholars, Grahame was a skilled opportunist when it came to new methodologies or working with scientists from other disciplines. Much of Clark's greatness also lay in his ability to recognize the potential of new approaches and scientific methods and then apply them to broad archaeological problems. He heard of radiocarbon dating from his botanical colleagues, notably Harry Godwin, and from archaeologist O. G. S. Crawford, editor of *Antiquity*. He attended conferences on the new method and lobbied hard for archaeological dating with Libby and others. His assiduous courting resulted in a radiocarbon date for Star Carr, the first Mesolithic sample ever processed. But he also realized the potential of radiocarbon dates for developing a truly global prehistory.

By 1949, Clark was already puzzling over the concept of world prehistory and such problems as the independent invention of agriculture in southwest Asia and the Americas. Such exercises were effectively meaningless until a universal dating method came along. Radiocarbon dating was the solution, and it was Clark's genius that applied the new method, perhaps even prematurely, to the global prehistory of humankind. The result was *World Prehistory's* first iteration in 1961.

Clark himself was the first to admit that his synthesis had imperfections. He had no patience, however, with the more myopic of his colleagues, who considered such a summary both impossible and irresponsible. Clark always took the long view and saw his role as propagating both environmental archaeology and world prehistory by any academic means possible. He had openly called *Prehistoric Europe* a work of propaganda. *World Prehistory* had the same objective: to break archaeology out of its provincialism and foster new approaches to the past. For all its mixed reviews, the book was a considerable success and achieved Clark's goal. Like so much of his work, *World Prehistory* was a catalyst, not for more theorizing but for the acquisition of new data. He considered the collection of fine-grained, multidisciplinary data the most fundamental tasks of archaeology. As a result, *World Prehistory* was a descriptive work with no theoretical sophistication—a cardinal sin in some American archaeologists' view, but a book that opened even his critics' eyes to the potential of a truly global prehistory.

Grahame Clark was not a theoretician. He did most of his major work before archaeological theory assumed center stage in the mid-1960s and had little patience for purely theoretical formulations, especially if they could not be backed up in the field. The spirited debates and oratory of the so-called New Archaeology of the 1960s in the United States passed him by. There is little evidence that he read much of Binford and his disciples' writings, with their extravagant claims of scientific breakthroughs based on systems theory. Clark, after all, had been aware of what the Americans called "cultural ecology" in its early, simple forms since the mid-1930s and had used it, albeit superficially, in his writings. He appears to have ignored the New Archaeology, as he ignored discoveries he disagreed with or theoretical posturings that were of no interest to him. He was aware of the debates over processual archaeology and over postprocessualism that exploded in the Cambridge department after his retirement. He refused to be drawn into them, for he was comfortable in his data-driven world and with his multidisciplinary perspectives, even if he was well aware of the dangers of focusing on subsistence and environment at the expense of everything else. Increasingly, and especially after his retirement, he became deeply interested in the unique spiritual qualities possessed by humankind alone.

At the same time, Clark ardently encouraged the young with their new ideas and occasional theoretical excesses. He was very proud of his graduates, who left comfortable Cambridge and went to work in remote, often inhospitable places and applied the environmental archaeology inculcated in them during their undergraduate days. Stories abound of his efforts to steer undergraduates into promising posts overseas, of dinners at Peterhouse where he would work hard to persuade a discouraged Ph.D. student to stay with the game, of unusual research opportunities placed before young men and women whom Grahame perceived to be *serious* about archaeology. He would forgive almost any idea or any transgression in someone who was serious and tried to do good work, even if the ideas were far from what was to him the mainstream.

The brilliant young theoretician David Clarke, a Peterhouse undergraduate who completed a doctorate under Grahame on Beaker pottery, was a case in point. David Clarke had a remarkable mind and a brilliant gift for abstract argument and multidisciplinary argument. He soon became a serious theoretician who, like Lewis Binford in North America, challenged the status quo in archaeology, but with far greater sophistication. He argued for much more sophisticated theoretical models and explicit scientific approaches than the simplistic ways of his elders and contemporaries. In 1968, David Clarke published his ideas in his magnum opus, *Analytical Archaeology*, in which he inveighed against "the murky exhalation which passes for 'interpretative thinking' in archaeology."[6] Grahame disagreed violently with most of what David Clarke said, but he worked hard to foster his career and obtained for him a tutorship at Peterhouse. He probably remembered his own youth, when he was a Young Turk upsetting established ideas. Tragically, David Clarke died prematurely before reaching full intellectual maturity, depriving archaeology of a theoretical voice that promised to be far more influential and longer-lived than many of his contemporaries. Grahame deeply grieved the premature death of the brilliant palaeoanthropologist Glynn Isaac, who had trained at Cambridge and went on to work with Louis Leakey and then at the University of California–Berkeley and Harvard. He had a gift for seeing potential in young and old alike, not only in David Clarke but, for example, in the older Eric Higgs, a former sheep farmer who became the force behind the Early History of Agriculture Project of the 1970s.

World Prehistory was certainly a defining landmark in Clark's long career. The synthesis had a far greater impact on the then small world of archaeology than such a volume would today, partly because his former students were scattered all over the world and used it in their courses, and also because there were far fewer archaeological books than there are today. His intellectual perspective broadened almost overnight. He received invitations to travel—to the United States, Canada, Australia, and New Zealand, as well as to China and, toward the end of his career, India. He never visited China nor tropical Africa, the latter being a serious lacuna in his coverage of human prehistory as a result. His visits to Australia and New Zealand in the mid-1960s enabled him to witness Australian Aboriginal culture first-hand and study Maori traditional culture, reinforcing in him the potential present in controlled analogies for interpreting the remote past. The three editions of the book between 1961 and 1977 show an expert scholar reaching the limits of his potential and exceeding them.

During the last ten years of his formal career Grahame was preoccupied with world prehistory and the origins of agriculture. As far as early farming was concerned, he was more of a facilitator, despite his pioneering articles on the radiocarbon dating of agricultural origins in Europe. He was the force behind the scenes that persuaded the British Academy and Royal Society to support a major research project, The Early History of Agriculture, directed by Eric Higgs. The project's conclusions were not necessarily widely accepted, but they highlighted the value of multidisciplinary research at a far more sophisticated level than that of Clark's Fenland days. Grahame had written papers about the first farming settlement of Europe before the project began. When it was finished, his simple migration model was significantly modified, which pleased him because he knew that science was cumulative. At this stage in his career, it was his task to encourage, foster, and synthesize, with an intellectual authority that few of his contemporaries shared.

World Prehistory: A Revised Outline appeared in 1977, during Grahame's successful mastership of Peterhouse. Sixteen years had passed and a flood of new discoveries, to say nothing of fresh theoretical formulations, had transformed our knowledge of human prehistory. The third edition was a major revision but was lacking. The approach was still largely descriptive, and there was little, if any, discussion of issues such as the origins of food production that went further than the previous editions. Important discoveries were missing from its pages, since Clark seems to have stopped reading new literature. This phenomenon is marked in his *Earlier Stone Age Settlement of Scandinavia*, which appeared two years before the *Revised Outline*. Reviewers of that new work pointed to the numerous recent discoveries that did not appear in its pages. Grahame himself implicitly realized he was getting out of touch and abandoned plans for a companion volume on the later prehistory of the same region.

His powers of synthesis were undiminished, but his knowledge of the literature and new advances now lagged behind his writing. In his later years, Grahame became an even more compulsive writer than before. As soon as he completed one book, he started another, all of them long essays rather than more substantial contributions. He had always pined for a better understanding of the intangible aspects of ancient societies and sought in his last books to identify what was unique about humanity and humanness. In particular, he focused on the human advances made possible by technology and the more hierarchical societies that resulted from such innovations. The *Identity of Man* and *Symbols of Excellence* made much of human progress and of the importance of technology in fostering cultural diversity and change. Clark's innate elitism came through clearly, as if he lamented that human progress created egalitarian, global, industrial culture, not hierarchical societies. He went so far as to deem it a privilege to "explore the values of the civilizations coming within his purview and not least the symbols which have served to define status and acknowledge outstanding achievement."[7]

Clark's later books cannot be called distinguished, for his simple ideas about humanity and technology, about cultural evolution, were based on the values of an earlier time and reflected his profound conservatism. As the anthropologist Edmund Leach rather pointedly remarked in a review of *Identity*, Clark's political views were conservative, "to the right of Margaret Thatcher," and reflected a perspective on the past based on progress and institutionalized social stratification.[8]

A harsh assessment of Clark's last books would call them self-indulgent. Certainly, they were not widely read, nor were they broadly reviewed. He continued to write obsessively until a few weeks before his death. Inevitably, the flow of original thinking was drying up. Fortunately, his reputation was secure, and it was honored in a manner that befalls few scholars: with an Erasmus Prize that commemorated a lifetime spent telling people that prehistory was of the utmost importance to humanity. And in this he was right.

Grahame Clark was a good and gentle man of considerable kindness, who rarely let the outside world see this side of his personality. He could be magisterial in person, even Olympian in print, but it was always in the cause of scholarship. It reflected a writing style that was formal rather than conversational—formality was something that Clark took seriously. He was at his best when writing, in highly technical one-on-one conversation, or in talking about a new idea or fresh archaeological discovery that interested him. Grahame Clark was unique. Few archaeologists have revolutionized a discipline, developed a global archaeology, and trained an entire generation of men and women to follow them. Today such an achievement would probably be impossible. Grahame Clark achieved all that and more because he believed passionately that "anyone programmed for the twenty-first century might well profit by approaching history from the wider background offered by archaeology and anthropology."⁹ Today's prehistoric archaeology is his legacy.

Notes

Preface and Acknowledgments

1. Grahame Clark, ed., *Economic Prehistory* (Cambridge: Cambridge University Press, 1989), p. vii.

2. Bruce Trigger, *A History of Archaeological Thought* (Cambridge: Cambridge University Press, 1989).

3. Grahame Clark, *Archaeology at Cambridge and Beyond* (Cambridge: Cambridge University Press, 1989).

4. John Coles, "John Grahame Douglas Clark, 1907–1995," *Proceedings of the British Academy* 94 (1997): 357–387.

Chapter 1

1. First quote from Clark's unpublished manuscript, "A Path to Prehistory" (1993), preface, p. 1. (Clark subsequently told his wife that he was going to call the book *Man the Spiritual Primate*, but for clarity I have retained the title in the archive copy here.) Second quote, "Path," p. 150.

2. Attributed to Jacquetta Hawkes and quoted to me (among others) by Professor Paul Ashbee, interview by author, May 12, 2000.

3. Throughout this book, I use the word "prehistorian" (likewise prehistory) to refer to archaeologists who study preliterate human societies. "Archaeologist" is a generic term covering amateurs and professionals who study all periods of the human past. Sometimes I use it to refer to prehistoric archaeologists, but I think the meaning is then self-evident.

4. Background biographical information comes from John Coles, "John Grahame Douglas Clark, 1907–1995," *Proceedings of the British Academy* 94 (1997): 357. The same

memoir also appears in John Coles, Robert Bewley, and Paul Mellars, eds., *World Prehistory: Studies in Memory of Grahame Clark* (London: Oxford University Press and the British Academy, 1999), pp. 207–230. This volume of essays updates the prehistoric archaeology of different regions of the world that interested Clark.

5. *Report of the Marlborough College Natural History Society,* 1926, p. 17. In Britain, the term "public school" refers to private high schools, of which Eton and Harrow are the most famous. Grahame Clark received the finest education money could buy at the time. The 1920s and 1930s were exciting times in Neolithic archaeology in Britain, especially with the discovery of causewayed camps, ill-defined enclosures with interrupted earthworks, the ditches of which sometimes contained caches of cattle bones and human remains. Their significance is still debated. Windmill Hill is still the most famous causewayed camp in Britain.

6. Coles, "John Grahame Douglas Clark," p. 358.

7. *Report*, p. 18.

8. This impression is based in part on the author's assessment of Clark's character and also on his own educational experience at Rugby School, another public school, which was, and still is, one of Marlborough's major rivals.

9. Clark, *Report*, pp. 85–89.

10. Clark, *Report,* pp. 73–75. Sarsen is a form of sandstone.

11. A summary of these developments is found in Glyn Daniel, *A Short History of Archaeology* (London: Thames and Hudson, 1981).

12. The eolith controversy is described by Donald Grayson, "'Eoliths,' Archaeological Ambiguity, and the Generation of 'Middle Range' Research," in David Meltzer et al., eds., *American Archaeology Past and Future* (Washington, D.C.: Smithsonian Institution Press, 1986), pp. 77–134.

13. See Daniel, *Short History*; and O. G. S. Crawford, *Archaeology in the Field* (New York: Praeger, 1953). We lack a biography of O. G. S. Crawford, who was a seminal figure in British archaeology from the 1920s to 1950s.

14. A. Lane Fox Pitt-Rivers, *Excavations at Cranborne Chase* (privately printed, 1887), is the primary source. Mortimer Wheeler, *Archaeology from the Earth* (Oxford: Clarendon, 1954), is an archaeological excavation manual based on his modification of Pitt-Rivers's methods. For a biography of Wheeler, see Jacquetta Hawkes, *Mortimer Wheeler* (London: Weidenfeld and Nicholson, 1983). For Avebury excavations, see Caroline Malone, *Avebury* (London: English Heritage, 1989).

15. Clark, "Path," p. 2.

16. Vere Gordon Childe is the subject of a huge and growing literature. Bruce Trigger, *Gordon Childe: Revolutions in Archaeology* (London: Thames and Hudson, 1980), is a good starting point.

17. This passage is based on Grahame Clark, "Prehistory Since Childe," *Bulletin of the London Institute of Archaeology* 13 (1976): 1–21. This, the first Childe Memorial Lecture, is one of Clark's best theoretical papers.

18. Clark, "Prehistory Since Childe," p. 4.

19. For a summary, see Grahame Clark, *Prehistory at Cambridge and Beyond* (Cambridge University Press, 1989), chap. 2.

20. William Ridgeway, "The Relationship of Archaeology to Classical Studies," a lecture in the Classics Library, Cambridge University. Pamphlet OL, Box C9.

21. "Tripos," from the Greek word for a three-footed stool, refers to the two parts of the Cambridge undergraduate honors degree. The word originates from a humorous eighteenth-century custom by which a bachelor of arts would dispute with pending graduates at commencement, seated on a three-legged stool. The term remains in use to this day. A tripos has two parts, Part I being more general, Part II more specialized. Part I can last for one or two years, depending on the subject. A one-part tripos, such as the first archaeology and anthropology curriculum of the 1920s, was combined with a Part I from some other specialty to make up an undergraduate degree. The undergraduate degree typically takes three years, not the four that is typical in the United States and some other countries.

22. Clark, *Prehistory at Cambridge*, pp. 32–33.

23. Clark, *Prehistory at Cambridge*, p. 33.

24. Burkitt's infectious enthusiasm brought dozens of young people into archaeology, including the writer. This paragraph is based on the author's personal experience, also Clark, *Prehistory at Cambridge*, chaps. 3–4.

25. Cambridge undergraduate honors degrees are grouped into Firsts (or first class), Upper and Lower Seconds (2 [1] and 2[2]), Thirds, and Pass, the latter not being an honors degree. Clark, *Prehistory at Cambridge*, p. 3.

26. J. G. D. Clark, "Some Hollow-Scrapers from Seaford, Sussex," *Sussex Archaeological Collections* 68 (1927): 273–276. Also Clark, "Discoidal Polished Flint Knives: Their Typology and Distribution," *Proceedings of the Prehistoric Society of East Anglia* 6 (1928): 40–54.

27. In writing this section, I drew on Clark, *Prehistory at Cambridge*, chaps. 2–3. Also Coles, "John Grahame Douglas Clark," pp. 358–360.

28. Clark, "Path," p. 11.

29. Clark, "Path," p. 12.

30. This passage is based on Clark, *Prehistory at Cambridge* and "Path," p. 13.

31. Clark, "Path," p. 12.

32. Clark, *Prehistory after Childe*, p. 7.

33. Clark, *Prehistory after Childe*, p. 7. The New Archaeology of the 1960s, developed in North America by Lewis Binford and others, was heavily based on systems theory, scientific method, and the principles of cultural ecology.

34. Supervisions are the backbone of the Cambridge system. Undergraduates meet weekly in small groups, or even individually, with an academic supervisor, for whom they write essays. Good supervisions can be intellectual magic and, at their best, create close interaction with teachers.

35. Clark wrote of his debt to Cyril Fox on many occasions, notably in *Cambridge and Beyond*, chap. 3.

36. This passage relies on Clark's recollections, "Path," pp. 12ff., and on Charles Phillips, *My Life in Archaeology* (Stroud, Glos, U.K.: Alan Sutton, 1987), pp. 30–32. Also Coles, "John Grahame Douglas Clark," pp. 359–360.

37. Phillips, *My Life*, p. 36. The paragraphs that follow also make use of Phillips's reminiscences.

38. Clark, "Path," p. 12.

Chapter 2

1. Miles Burkitt, *The Old Stone Age* (New York: Athenaeum, 1964), p. 250.

2. Miles Burkitt, *Prehistory*, 2d ed. (Cambridge: Cambridge University Press, 1925), p. 152. I assume throughout this book that the reader is familiar with the basic cultural terms of the Upper Palaeolithic and Mesolithic. Definitions or further descriptions are only given for terms that are obscure, outdated, or little used.

3. Burkitt in J. G. D. Clark, *The Mesolithic Age in Britain* (Cambridge: Cambridge University Press, 1932), p. xiii.

4. D. A. E. Garrod, *The Upper Palaeolithic Age in Britain* (Oxford: Clarendon, 1926).

5. Acknowledged in the preface to *The Mesolithic Settlement of Northern Europe* (Cambridge: Cambridge University Press, 1936), p. ix.

6. I am grateful to Dr. Michael Reynier of Leicester University for sharing his research on Francis Buckley with me.

7. Clark, *Mesolithic Age*, p. 1

8. Clark, *Mesolithic Age*, pp. 4–5.

9. Quotes in this paragraph are from Clark, *Mesolithic Age*, pp. 6–7.

10. For more extended discussion, see Pamela Jane Smith, "'A Passionate Connoisseur of Flints': An Intellectual Biography of the Young Grahame Clark Based on His Pre-War Publications," *Archaeologia Polonia* 35–36 (1999): 385–408. I am very grateful to Smith for giving me access to this paper before publication.

11. Clark, *Mesolithic Age*, pp. 7–8. The Capsian of North Africa is a widely distributed culture with a highly refined microlithic technology, which is broadly contemporary with the European Mesolithic but now thought to be an independent development.

12. Clark, *Mesolithic Age*, p. 8.

13. The Kunda and Pernau Mesolithic industries of the eastern Baltic region are local variations on the Maglemose and Ertebølle cultures of further west, which are described in Chapter 4.

14. Quotes in this paragraph are from Clark, *Mesolithic Age*, p. 13.

15. Clark, *Mesolithic Age*, p. 19.

16. Clark, *Mesolithic Age*, p. 27.

17. Discussion with references in Clark, *Mesolithic Age*, pp. 59–62.

18. Clark, *Mesolithic Age*, p. 87.

19. Clark, *Mesolithic Age*, p. 88.

20. Clark, *Mesolithic Age*, p. 115.

21. Described by M. C. Burkitt, "A Maglemose Harpoon Dredged Up from the North Sea," *Man* 238 (1932): 99. See also H. Godwin and M. E. Godwin, "British Maglemose Harpoon Sites," *Antiquity* 7 (1933): 36–48. The Leman and Ower harpoon has recently been AMS radiocarbon dated to 11,740 ± 150 B.C., considerably earlier than the Mesolithic date that made it so important to Clark. See R. A. Housley, "AMS Dates from the Late Glacial and Early Postglacial in North-West Europe: A Review," in N. Barton, A. J. Roberts, and D. A. Roe, eds., *The Late Glacial in North-West Europe*, Research Report 77 (London: Council for British Archaeology, 1991), pp. 73–85. ". . . which was being typed." Interview with Grahame Clark by Dr. Peter Rowley-Conwy, September 1994. I am grateful to Rowley-Conwy for access to the text of this interview.

22. Clark, *Mesolithic Age,* appendix 7.

23. Grahame Clark himself once told me, when I was an undergraduate, that the Leman and Ower find was an intellectual turning point for him.

24. V. Gordon Childe, "Review: *The Mesolithic Age in Britain*," *Antiquaries Journal* 13 (1933): 182. Oswald Menghin, "Review: *The Mesolithic Age in Britain*," *Antiquity* 7 (1933): 243.

25. Clark, *Mesolithic Age*, p. 6.

26. Coles, "John Grahame Douglas Clark," p. 360.

27. Phillips, *My Life*, pp. 53–54.

28. Coles, "John Grahame Douglas Clark," p. 360.

29. Coles, "John Grahame Douglas Clark," pp. 360–361.

30. On file in Cambridge University Library.

Chapter 3

1. Grahame Clark, editorial comment in *Proceedings of the Prehistoric Society* 2 (1939): 260.

2. Clark, *Mesolithic Age*, p. 6.

3. A. G. Tansley, "The Use and Abuse of Vegetational Concepts and Terms," *Ecology* 16 (1935): 284–307.

4. Fens are lowlands partially or completely surrounded by water. They form marshy and swampy terrain, also peat bogs, and are often waterlogged. The term is classically applied to the lowlands north and east of Cambridge, which are referred to as the Fenlands. In the 1930s, they were still a remote part of England, with a much

higher water table than today. See also Harry Godwin, *Fenland: Its Ancient Past and Uncertain Future* (Cambridge: Cambridge University Press, 1978).

5. The description of the Fenland Research Committee is based on Clark, "Path," p. 22. Pamela Jane Smith, "Grahame Clark's New Archaeology," *Antiquity* 71 (1977): 11–30, was my source for much of this part of the chapter. She researched the archival materials quoted here. Clark called Harry Godwin "a great ally. He was a Clare man and about three years my senior." Rowley-Conwy, interview by author, September 1994.

6. Burkitt, "Investigations of the Fens," *Antiquaries Journal* 12 (1932): 453. Smith, "Grahame Clark," p. 14.

7. The Fenland Research Committee convened only sixteen meetings during its existence, its activities being interrupted by World War II. The last meeting was held on December 5, 1948, in the Sedgewick Museum of Geology, by which time the focus of its work was moving toward the Roman period. By then, both Clark and Godwin were engaged in research away from the fens. At the final gathering, members voted to dissolve the committee, having learned with satisfaction of the establishment of the new Subdepartment of Quaternary Research under Dr. Harry Goodwin, now a university reader. The university had also agreed in principle to set up a curatorship in aerial photography, which was eventually held by Kenneth St. Joseph. In a nice gesture, the university awarded an honorary M.A. to Major Gordon Fowler, who had done so much for the committee's work.

8. Clark, *Prehistory at Cambridge,* p. 55.

9. On Plantation Farm, see Grahame Clark, "Report on an Early Bronze Age Site in the South-Eastern Fens," *Antiquaries Journal* 13 (1933): 264–296. Quote is from p. 264.

10. Smith, "Grahame Clark," p. 19.

11. For Peacock's Farm, see J. G. D. Clark, H. Godwin and M. E. Godwin, and M. H. Clifford, "Report on Recent Excavations at Peacock's Farm, Shippea Hill, Cambridgeshire," *Antiquaries Journal* 15 (1935): 284–319.

12. J. G. D. Clark, "Report on a Late Bronze Age Site in Mildenhall Fen, West Suffolk," *Antiquaries Journal* 16 (1936): 29–50. Quote is from p. 29.

13. J. G. D. Clark and H. Godwin, "A Late Bronze Age Find near Stuntney, Isle of Ely," *Antiquaries Journal* 20 (1940): 52–71. Quotes are from pp. 59, 71.

14. My account of the Prehistoric Society of East Anglia is based on Pamela Smith, "Grahame Clark," p. 25; and Smith, "The Coup: How did the Prehistoric Society of East Anglia Become the Prehistoric Society?" *Proceedings of the Prehistoric Society* 65 (2000): 465–470. See also Clark's own account, J. G. D. Clark, "The Prehistoric Society: From East Anglia to the World," *Proceedings of the Prehistoric Society* 51 (1985): 1–13.

15. This account draws on Smith, "Grahame Clark," pp. 24–25; Smith, "The Coup."

16. Smith, "The Coup," p. 467. Her paper is based in part on S. J. Plunkett, "Prehistory at Ipswich—An Idea and Its Consequences" (manuscript, Ipswich Museum, 1998).

17. Smith, "The Coup," p. 467.

18. Smith, "Grahame Clark," p. 8 n.

19. Smith, "Grahame Clark," pp. 9–10.

20. Glyn Daniel and C. Chippindale, eds., *The Pastmasters: Eleven Modern Pioneers of Archaeology* (London: Thames and Hudson, 1989). Stuart Piggott's reminiscences are on p. 26.

21. Smith, "The Coup," p. 465.

22. J. G. D. Clark, Hazzledine Warren, Stuart Piggott, M. C. Burkitt, and H. Godwin and M. E. Godwin, "Archaeology of the Submerged Land Surface of the Essex Coast," *Proceedings of the Prehistoric Society* 2 (1936): 178–210.

23. J. G. D. Clark, "The Timber Monument at Arminghall and Its Affinities," *Proceedings of the Prehistoric Society* 2 (1936): 1–51. Quote from p. 39.

24. J. G. D. Clark and W. F. Rankine, "Excavations at Farnham, Surrey (1937–1938): The Horsham Culture and the Question of Mesolithic Dwellings," *Proceedings of the Prehistoric Society* 5 (1939): 61–118.

25. Cambridge University has university-wide academic departments, but students attend individual colleges, of which Peterhouse is one. In simple terms, a fellow of a college supervises students in that college and has rooms there, as well as the right to dine at the fellow's table, often called "high table." Research fellows have no teaching responsibilities.

26. Clark, "Path," p. 23.

27. Smith, "Grahame Clark," p. 26.

28. Smith, "Grahame Clark," p. 27.

29. Smith, "Grahame Clark," p. 27.

30. Forward by Charles McBurney, in G. de G. Sieveking, Ian H. Longworth, and K. E. Wilson, eds., *Problems in Economic and Social Archaeology* (London: Duckworth, 1976), p. xii. An account of Clark's early students, or "pupils," as he always called them, can be found in his *Prehistory at Cambridge*, chap. 3.

31. J. Desmond Clark, "Archaeological Retrospect 10," *Antiquity* 60 (1986): 80.

32. Thurstan Shaw, *Igbo-Ukwu* (London: Faber and Faber, 1970).

33. Stuart Piggott, "Archaeology and Prehistory: Presidential Address," *Proceedings of the Prehistoric Society* 29 (1963): 1–16.

Chapter 4

1. Clark, "Path," p. 24.

2. J. G. D. Clark, *The Mesolithic Settlement of Northern Europe* (Cambridge: Cambridge University Press, 1936), p. 26.

3. Clark, *Mesolithic Settlement*, p. xiii.

4. The varve dating method involves counting annual sequences of glacial meltwater deposits in Postglacial lakes and can be compared, loosely, to tree-ring dating, which is of much broader application.

5. Clark, *Mesolithic Settlement*, p. 23.

6. Clark, *Mesolithic Settlement*, p. 29.

7. Clark, *Mesolithic Settlement*, p. 42.

8. Clark, *Mesolithic Settlement*, p. 74. Font Robert points are a distinctive shouldered point associated with the Upper Palaeolithic Gravettian culture of central and western Europe, dating to c. 24,000 years ago.

9. Quotes in this paragraph from Clark, *Mesolithic Settlement*, pp. 76–78. The Hamburgian culture is a widespread Late Glacial reindeer hunting culture in Late Glacial Central Europe, first identified at Stellmoor and other sites excavated by Rust, and now known in much greater detail from excavations and especially settlement surveys.

10. The Lyngby culture is still a valid local variant of Late Glacial culture in Denmark. Quote from Clark, *Mesolithic Settlement*, p. 84.

11. Clark, *Mesolithic Settlement*, p. 86. In many respects, Clark's account is still the best, partly because no one else has attempted a similar task.

12. Clark, *Mesolithic Settlement*, p. 89.

13. Clark, *Mesolithic Settlement*, p. 90.

14. Clark, *Mesolithic Settlement*, p. 92.

15. These paragraphs are based on Clark, *Mesolithic Settlement*. Quote from p. 115.

16. Clark, *Mesolithic Settlement*, p. 131.

17. The term "kitchen-midden" culture came into use during the nineteenth century, referring to the shell middens from which so many Ertebølle artifacts came. Ertebølle is now the commonly used label. Quote from Clark, *Mesolithic Settlement*, p. 156.

18. Clark, *Mesolithic Settlement*, p. 167.

19. Clark, *Mesolithic Settlement*, p. ix.

20. Clark, *Mesolithic Settlement*, p. 200.

21. W. F. Grimes, "Review: The Mesolithic Settlement of Northern Europe," *Proceedings of the Prehistoric Society* 3 (1937): 255.

22. Clark, *Mesolithic Settlement*, p. 215. Theories of Tardenoisian migration are no longer widely espoused today.

23. A. J. Armstrong, "Review: *The Mesolithic Settlement of Northern Europe*," *Man* 37 (1937): 68–69.

Chapter 5

1. The Clarks had two sons and a daughter. The elder son and daughter predeceased Grahame. Quotes from Clark, *Archaeology and Society*, p. 29. For the rock engraving paper, see J. G. D. Clark, "Scandinavian Rock Engravings," *Antiquity* 11 (1937): 56–69.

2. Travels described in Phillips, *My Life*, pp. 58ff. Quotes are from pp. 58–59.

3. Phillips, *My Life*, pp. 59–60.

4. Quotes in this paragraph from Clark, "Path," p. 30.

5. Clark, "Path," p. 30. Christian Jurgensen Thomsen was a Danish museum curator and archaeologist who grappled with the chaos of a jumble of prehistoric artifacts in the National Museum of Denmark in Copenhagen by arranging them in separate rooms devoted to the Stone, Bronze (Copper), and Iron Ages in 1817–1818. Thus was born the famous Three Age System, which was proved stratigraphically and chronologically valid in excavations by Thomsen's successor, J. J. A. Worsaae.

6. This paragraph based on Clark, "Path," pp. 30–32.

7. Clark, "Path," p. 31.

8. J. G. D. Clark and W. F. Rankine, "Excavations at Farnham, Surrey 1937–38: The Horsham Culture and the Question of Mesolithic Dwellings," *Proceedings of the Prehistoric Society* 5 (1939): 61–118.

9. J. G. D. Clark, *Archaeology and Society* (London: Methuen, 1939), p. 214.

10. Quotes in this paragraph from Clark, *Society*, pp. 2–3.

11. Quotes in this paragraph from Clark, *Society*, pp. 11–12.

12. Clark, *Society*, p. 30.

13. Quotes in this paragraph from Clark, *Society*, pp. 43–44.

14. Quotes in this paragraph from Clark, *Society,* pp. 55–60. Sir Aurel Stein (1862–1943) was a famed Asian explorer who collected artifacts and manuscripts over many remote parts of Central Asia. He was one of the first scientific observers to visit this region, although modern scholars often criticize him for his brutal methods.

15. Quotes in this paragraph from Clark, *Society*, pp. 78–79.

16. Clark, *Society*, p. 85.

17. Clark, *Society*, p. 86.

18. Clark, *Society*, p. 101.

19. Clark, *Society*, p. 111.

20. Quotes in this paragraph from Clark, *Society*, pp. 113–114.

21. Milankovitch used variations in solar radiation in an attempt to date the climatic fluctuations of the Ice Age. Frederick Zeuner was a strong advocate of his chronology, which he described at length in his *Dating the Past* (London: Methuen, 1958).

22. Clark, *Society*, p. 147.

23. Quotations in this paragraph from Clark, *Society*, pp. 152–153, except for the last one, which comes from the 1994 interview with Rowley-Conwy.

24. Clark, *Society*, p. 160.

25. Clark, *Society*, p. 167.

26. Both quotes Clark, *Society*, p. 170.

27. Clark, *Society*, p. 178.

28. Quotes in this paragraph from Clark, *Society*, pp. 187–188.

29. Quotes in this paragraph from Clark, *Society*, pp. 189–191, 197.

30. Quotes in this paragraph from Clark, *Society*, p. 203.

31. Clark, *Society*, p. 207.

32. Clark, *Society*, p. 209.

33. Clark, *Society*, pp. 213–214.

Chapter 6

1. J. G. D. Clark, "Education and the Study of Man," *Antiquity* 17 (1943): 113–121.

2. V. Gordon Childe, "Review of *Archaeology and Society*," *Proceedings of the Prehistoric Society* 13 (1939): 468. Jacquetta Hawkes's review is in *Archaeological Journal* 96 (1939) 182–185. See also Stuart Piggott's review in *Antiquaries Journal* 20 (1940): 399–400. Also see J. G. D. Clark, *Prehistoric Britain* (London: Batsford, 1940).

3. The Sutton Hoo ship burial was a spectacular discovery, made on the eve of World War II. Charles Phillips discovered the outline of the ship's timbers as ghost marks in the sandy soil, as well as rich grave furniture, now in the British Museum. The burial is that of a seventh-century Anglo-Saxon chieftain. The excavations are described by Phillips in his autobiography, *My Life.*

4. David Thomson, "The Seasonal Factor in Human Culture," *Proceedings of the Prehistoric Society* 5 (1939): 209–221.

5. Thomson, "Seasonal Factor," p. 221.

6. Mrs. Claire Wilson, personal communication to author. By one of those bizarre coincidences that make the life of a biographer so fascinating, I met Claire Wilson at a retirement home in Santa Barbara. We agreed to meet again, but, alas, she died before I was able to interview her further.

7. Described in Glyn Daniel, *Some Small Harvest: The Memoirs of Glyn Daniel* (London: Thames and Hudson, 1986). Daniel's lively and, it must be confessed, sometimes slightly inaccurate autobiography is a mine of information on Cambridge personalities of his and Clark's day.

8. Stuart Piggott, *Prehistoric India* (London: Penguin, 1950).

9. Charles McBurney, *The Haua Fteah, Cyrenaica, and the Stone Age of the South-east Mediterranean* (Cambridge: Cambridge University Press, 1967). McBurney also exercised a profound influence on several generations of Cambridge undergraduates, this writer among them.

10. Information received from Mollie Clark, June 11, 2000.

11. Gertrude Caton Thompson was a formidable personality and an archaeologist of great ability. She trained under the Egyptologist Flinders Petrie but elected to study Stone Age, not ancient Egyptian, sites. Caton Thompson discovered early farmers in the Fayum Depression and investigated Stone Age sites in the Kharga Oasis, west of the

Nile. In 1929, she was commissioned by the British Association for the Advancement of Science to study the enigma of Great Zimbabwe in southern Africa. Her brilliant excavations established beyond all doubt that this most famous of African sites was built by black Africans, not immigrant Europeans. Caton Thompson had private means and never held a professional position in archaeology, but she was an extremely influential voice on many committees and in learned societies.

12. This account is drawn from Christopher Evans, "Archaeology Against the State," in Peter J. Ucko, ed., *Theory in Archaeology: A World Perspective* (London: Routledge, 1995), pp. 312–326. I also consulted the primary source: *Conference on the Future of Archaeology, 1943* (London: Institute of Archaeology, 1943). References in this paragraph are from *Conference*, pp. 62, 64.

13. *Conference*, p. 70.

14. J. G. D. Clark, "Education and the Study of Man," *Antiquity* 17 (1943):113–121. Reprinted in Grahame Clark, *Economic Prehistory: Papers on Archaeology by Grahame Clark* (Cambridge: Cambridge University Press, 1989). The pagination from this anthology is used here for the reader's convenience, as many of Clark's papers are assembled under one cover in this volume. *Economic Prehistory* was Clark's only effort to collect his works into a single edited volume. He was more interested in working on his next piece of research than in promoting one just published. He remarked to Peter Rowley-Conwy: "I enclose a copy of a volume dreamed up by the CUP which nobody in their right mind would want to fork up £50 for." Peter Rowley-Conwy, "Sir Grahame Clark," in Tim Murray, *Encyclopedia of Archaeology: The Great Archaeologists* (Santa Barbara, Calif.: ABC-Clio, 1999), 2:508.

15. Clark, *Economic Prehistory*, p. 411.

16. Quotes in this paragraph from Clark, *Economic Prehistory*, p. 413.

17. Quotes in this paragraph from Clark, *Economic Prehistory*, pp. 414–416.

18. Quotes in these two paragraphs from Clark, *Economic Prehistory*, pp. 416–418.

19. Quotes in this paragraph from Clark, *Economic Prehistory*, pp. 419–420.

20. Evans, "Archaeology Against the State," pp. 319ff.

21. Johannes Iversen, "Land Occupation in Denmark's Stone Age," *Danmarks Geologiske Undersøgelse* II Raekke 66 (1941): 70–76.

22. J. G. D. Clark, "Man and Nature in Prehistory, with Special Reference to Neolithic Settlement in Northern Europe," *Conference on the Problems and Prospects of European Archaeology Held at the University of London Institute of Archaeology, September 16–17, 1944* (London: London Institute of Archaeology, 1945), pp. 20–28.

23. J. G. D. Clark, "Bees in Antiquity," *Antiquity* 16 (1942): 208–215.

24. Quotes in this paragraph from Clark, "Bees," pagination from Clark, *Economic Prehistory*, p. 3.

25. Clark, "Bees," pagination from Clark, *Economic Prehistory*, p. 8; J. G. D. Clark, "Water in Antiquity," *Antiquity* 18 (1944): 1–15.

Chapter 7

1. J. G. D. Clark, *Prehistoric Europe: The Economic Basis* (London: Methuen, 1952), p. 171. For an autobiographical account of the thinking behind the book, see J. G. D. Clark, "Prehistoric Europe: The Economic Basis," in G. R. Willey, ed., *Archaeological Researches in Retrospect* (Cambridge, Mass.: Winthrop, 1974), pp. 31–57.

2. Her theory of the origins of modern humans in Europe, laid out in her classic paper "The Upper Palaeolithic in the Light of Recent Discoveries," published in the *Proceedings* for 1938, envisaged a migration from southwestern Asia, a hypothesis that was a simple version of today's theories. For Garrod, see Pamela Jane Smith, Jane Callendar, Paul G. Bahn, and Geneviève Pinçon, "Dorothy Garrod in Words and Pictures," *Antiquity* 71 (1997): 265–270. For the history of the Cambridge department during these years, see Grahame Clark, *Archaeology at Cambridge and Beyond,* chaps. 4–5.

3. J. G. D. Clark, "Report on Excavations on the Cambridgeshire Car Dyke, 1947," *Antiquaries Journal* 19 (1949): 145–163.

4. Gertrude Caton Thompson, "The Levalloisian Industries of Egypt," *Proceedings of the Prehistoric Society* 12 (1946): 57–120.

5. This account of his travels comes from "Path," pp. 46 ff., and from Clark's manuscript travel notes. The quotes in this paragraph are from pp. 47–48 or his travel notes.

6. Clark, "Path," p. 48. Finno-Ougrian (or Ugrian) refers to languages spoken in Finland, Estonia, and Lapland, as well as other locations. They are Uralic languages. The term was sometimes applied to the native culture as well, as Clark did in "Path."

7. J. G. D. Clark, "Seal-Hunting in the Stone Age of North-Western Europe: A Study in Economic Prehistory," *Proceedings of the Prehistoric Society* 12 (1946): 12–48. Page references from *Economic Prehistory*.

8. A. W. Brøgger, "From the Stone Age to the Motor Age," *Antiquity* 14 (1940): 163–181.

9. Clark, "Seal-Hunting," p. 69.

10. Clark, "Seal-Hunting," p. 75.

11. Le Roy Ladurie, *The Mind and Method of the Historian,* trans. Sîan Reynolds and Ben Reynolds (Chicago: University of Chicago Press, 1981).

12. J. G. D. Clark, "Whales as an Economic Factor in Prehistoric Europe," *Antiquity* 21 (1947): 122–136.

13. Michael Postan, *The Medieval Economy and Society* (London: Weidenfeld and Nicholson, 1972). J. G. D. Clark, "Man and Nature in Prehistory, with Special Reference to Neolithic Settlement in Northern Europe," *Conference on the Problems and Prospects of European Archaeology, September 16–17, 1944.* (London: London Institute of Archaeology, 1945), pp. 20–28.

14. J. G. D. Clark, "Folk-Culture and the Study of European Prehistory," in W. F. Grimes, ed., *Aspects of Archaeology in Britain and Beyond: Essays Presented to O. G. S.*

Crawford (London: M. W. Edwards, 1951), pp. 49–65. Quote from Clark, *Economic Prehistory*, p. 136.

15. Quotes in this paragraph are from Clark, *Economic Prehistory*, p. 138–141.

16. Clark, *Economic Prehistory*, p. 144.

17. Quotes in this paragraph are from Clark, *Economic Prehistory*, pp. 145–146.

18. Clark, *Economic Prehistory*, p. 147.

19. Quotes from Clark, *Archaeology at Cambridge*, pp. 90–91.

20. J. G. D. Clark, *Prehistoric Europe,* p. vii.

21. Clark, *Prehistoric Europe*, p. 8.

22. Clark, *Prehistoric Europe*, p. 21.

23. Clark, *Prehistoric Europe*, p. 171.

24. E. Vogt, "Review: *Prehistoric Europe: The Economic Basis,*" *Antiquity* 27 (1953): 105–108.

25. Quotes in these two paragraphs are taken from V. Gordon Childe, "Review: *Prehistoric Europe:The Economic Basis,*" *Antiquaries Journal* 32 (1952): 209; Grahame Clark, "Prehistoric Europe: The Economic Basis," in Willey, *Archaeological Researches*, p. 54; Christopher Hawkes, "Archaeological Theory and Method: Some Suggestions from the Old World," *American Anthropologist* 56 (1954): 161, 163. For a detailed assessment of Hawkes's work, see Christopher Evans, "Christopher Hawkes," in Murray, ed., *Encyclopedia of Archaeology*, pp. 461–479.

Chapter 8

1. J. G. D. Clark, *Excavations at Star Carr: An Early Mesolithic Site at Seamer, near Scarborough,Yorkshire* (Cambridge: Cambridge University Press, 1954), p. 191.

2. Clark and Rankine, "Excavations at Farnham."The Somerset Levels have recently been the subject of intensive research by John Coles and Bryony Coles. For a summary, see their *Sweet Track to Glastonbury* (London: Thames and Hudson, 1986); and *People of theWetlands* (NewYork: Guild, 1989).

3. Recounted in Clark, "Path," pp. 50ff. The general account of the excavations that follows is taken from this work.

4. Clark ultimately published Moore's account of these finds in the *Proceedings*. John Moore, "Mesolithic Sites in the Neighborhood of Flixton, North-East Yorkshire," *Proceedings of the Prehistoric Society* 16 (1950): 101–108. Also Clark, interview by Peter Rowley-Conwy, September 1994.

5. Clark, *Star Carr*, p. 1.

6. Clark's excavation methods, the author (Hurst Fen), and opinions of observers who wish to remain anonymous. For Ulkestrup comparison, see Peter Rowley-Conwy, "Sir Grahame Clark," in Murray, ed., *Encyclopedia of Archaeology*, pp. 515–516. On Ulkestrup, see K. Andersen, S. Jorgensen, and J. Richter, *Maglemose Hytterne ved Ulkestrup Lyng* (Copenhagen: Det Kongelige Nordiske Oldekriftselskab, 1982).

7. Appendix in J. G. D. Clark, "A Preliminary Report on Excavations at Star Carr, Seamer, Scarborough, Yorkshire, 1949," *Proceedings of the Prehistoric Society* 15 (1949): 52–65.

8. Clark, "Preliminary Report, 1949."

9. Clark, "Preliminary Report, 1949," p. 55.

10. Clark, "Preliminary Report, 1949," p. 64.

11. Clark, *Star Carr*, p. 2

12. J. G. D. Clark, "Preliminary Report on Excavations at Star Carr, Seamer, Scarborough, Yorkshire, 1950," *Proceedings of the Prehistoric Society* 16 (1950): 52–65. The quote in this paragraph is from p. 117.

13. J. G. D. Clark, "The Earliest Settlement of the West Baltic Area in the Light of Recent Research," *Proceedings of the Prehistoric Society* 16 (1950): 87–100. Quotes in this paragraph are from p. 93.

14. Clark, *Star Carr,* p. 4.

15. Clark, *Star Carr*, p. 1. The full citation for the monograph is at note 1.

16. Clark, *Star Carr*, p. 9.

17. Clark, *Star Carr*, pp. 10–11.

18. Clark, *Star Carr*, p. 13.

19. J. G. D. Clark and M. W. Thompson, "The Groove and Splinter Technique of Working Reindeer and Red Deer Antler in Upper Palaeolithic and Mesolithic Europe," *Proceedings of the Prehistoric Society* 19 (1953): 148–160. See also J. G. D. Clark, "The Groove and Splinter Technique of Working Reindeer and Red Deer Antler in Upper Palaeolithic and Mesolithic Europe," *Archivo de Prehistoria Levantina* 4 (1953): 57–65.

20. Clark and Thompson "Groove and Splinter," p. 157.

21. Quotes in this paragraph from Clark, *Star Carr*, p. 191.

22. Hallam L. Movius, "Review: *Star Carr*," *Antiquaries Journal* 36 (1956): 86–88.

23. Gordon R. Willey, *Prehistoric Settlement Patterns in the Virú Valley, Peru* (Washington, D.C.: Smithsonian Institution, Bureau of American Ethnology). The achievements of both these scholars are summarized in Daniel and Chippindale, *Pastmasters.*

24. Ozette is summarized in Ruth Kirk, *Hunters of the Whale* (New York: William Morrow, 1975).

25. For a summary, see Lewis Binford, *In Pursuit of the Past* (London: Thames and Hudson, 1983). See also Brian Fagan, "Grahame Clark and American Archaeology," in Coles, Bewley, and Mellars, *World Prehistory*, pp. 67–74.

26. Richard Lee and Irven DeVore, eds., *Man the Hunter* (Chicago: Aldine, 1968).

27. J. G. D. Clark, *Star Carr: A Case Study in Bioarchaeology* (Reading, Mass.: Addison-Wesley Modules in Anthropology, 1972). Reprinted in Clark, "*Economic Prehistory*," pp. 481–538, which is now the most accessible source for this paper.

28. For example, A. J. Legge and Peter Rowley-Conwy, *Star Carr Revisited* (London: Birkbeck College).

29. Paul Mellars and Petra Dark, *Star Carr in Context* (Cambridge, U.K.: McDonald Institute for Archaeological Research/Vale of Pickering Research Trust, 1998).

30. Accelerator mass spectrometry (AMS) has revolutionized radiocarbon dating, allowing the dating of tiny samples, even individual seeds, as opposed to the required handful of charcoal needed in Clark's day. For a description of the methodology, see Colin Renfrew and Paul Bahn, *Archaeology*, 3d ed. (London: Thames and Hudson, 2000).

31. Legge and Rowley-Conwy, *Star Carr Revisited.*

Chapter 9

1. J. G. D. Clark, *The Study of Prehistory: An Inaugural Lecture* (Cambridge: Cambridge University Press, 1954), p. 23.

2. For details of Garrod's career, see Smith, Callendar, and Bahn, "Dorothy Garrod."

3. Clark, "Path," p. 114. The Litt.D. and Sc.D. are the highest degrees offered at Cambridge and can best be described as senior doctorates. They are awarded on the basis of meritorious published work. Few scholars take them, except major professors.

4. Daniel, *Some Small Harvest*, p. 212.

5. J. G. D. Clark, "The Economic Approach to Prehistory: Albert Reckitt Archaeological Lecture, 1953," *Proceedings of the British Academy* 39 (1953): 215–238. Reprinted in Clark, *Economic Prehistory*, pp. 149–168, whose pagination is used here. Quotations in this paragraph from pp. 150–151.

6. Quotes in this paragraph from Clark, *Economic Prehistory*, pp. 152, 156–157.

7. Clark, *Economic Prehistory*, p. 161.

8. Quotes in this paragraph from Clark, *Economic Prehistory*, p. 166.

9. Clark, *Study of Prehistory*, p. 7. By prehistory, Clark meant what happened in the past. Prehistoric archaeology is the study of prehistory.

10. Clark, *Study of Prehistory*, p. 33.

11. Clark, *Study of Prehistory*, p. 35.

12. Letter from Childe dated July 26, 1957. Second letter is undated but is later than the first. Clark Archives, Cambridge University Library, Box 11.1. The article referred to is V. Gordon Childe, "Retrospect," *Antiquity* 32 (1958): 69–74.

13. J. G. D. Clark, "A Microlithic Industry from the Cambridgeshire Fenland and Other Industries of Sauveterrian Affinities from Britain," *Proceedings of the Prehistoric Society* 21 (1955): 3–20.

14. J. G. D. Clark and H. Godwin, "A Maglemosian Site at Brandesburton, Holderness, Yorkshire," *Proceedings of the Prehistoric Society* 22 (1955): 6–22.

15. J. G. D. Clark, "Blade and Trapeze Industries of the European Stone Age," *Proceedings of the Prehistoric Society* 24 (1958): 24–42.

16. Grahame Clark, "Neolithic Bows from Somerset, England, and the Prehistory of Archery in North-Western Europe," *Proceedings of the Prehistoric Society* 29 (1963): 50–98.

17. Gerhard Bersu, "Excavations at Little Woodbury, Wiltshire," *Proceedings of the Prehistoric Society* 6 (1940): 42–111. For Bersu during World War II, see Christopher Evans, "Constructing Houses and Building Context: Bersu's Manx Round-house Campaign," *Proceedings of the Prehistoric Society* 64 (1998): 183–201.

18. J. G. D. Clark and C. I. Fell, "The Early Iron Age Site at Micklemoor Hill, West Harling, Norfolk and Its Pottery," *Proceedings of the Prehistoric Society* 29 (1953): 1–40.

19. Lady Grace Briscoe, "Neolithic Pottery from Hurst Fen, Suffolk," *Proceedings of the Cambridge Antiquarian Society* 47 (1954): 13–24.

20. Potboilers are lumps of stone, in this case flint, heated in a fire, then dropped into water to heat it.

21. J. G. D. Clark, E. S. Higgs, and I. W. Longworth, "Excavations at the Neolithic site at Hurst Fen, Mildenhall, Suffolk (1954, 1957 and 1958)," *Proceedings of the Prehistoric Society* 26 (1960): 202–245.

22. Longworth, in Clark, Higgs, and Longworth, "Hurst Fen," pp. 228–240. Specialist references to contemporary Mesolithic publications, including Isobel Smith's work, will be found there.

23. Clark, Higgs, and Longworth, "Hurst Fen," p. 242.

24. J. G. D. Clark and Harry Godwin, "The Neolithic in the Cambridgeshire Fens," *Antiquity* 36 (1962): 10–23. Stuart Piggott had advocated a later, traditional chronology in his *Neolithic Cultures of the British Isles* (Cambridge: Cambridge University Press, 1954)

25. Clark, "Path," pp. 57ff.

26. Professor John Coles, personal communication to author, 1999.

27. Clark describes his Wenner-Gren experience in "Path," pp. 56ff. See also John Dodds, *The Several Lives of Paul Fejos* (New York: Wenner-Gren Foundation for Anthropological Research, 1973).

28. J. G. D. Clark, "Perspectives in Prehistory: Presidential Address," *Proceedings of the Prehistoric Society* 25 (1959): 1–14. Quote from p. 5.

29. Quotations in this paragraph are taken from Clark, "Perspectives," pp. 10–14.

Chapter 10

1. Clark, *Prehistory at Cambridge*, p. 153.

2. John Coles, "John Grahame Douglas Clark," p. 370.

3. J. G. D. Clark, *From Savagery to Civilization* (London: Cobbett, 1946). Quotes are from pp. v–vi.

4. Clark, *From Savagery*, p. 68.

5. This section draws on Clark, *Prehistory at Cambridge*, the author's own Cambridge experience, and interviews with contemporaries too numerous to list here. Their assistance is gratefully acknowledged. The map appears in *Prehistory at Cambridge*, p. 100. Another map, of Cambridge prehistorians in Britain, is on p. 149.

6. Eric S. Higgs, "The Excavation of a Late Mesolithic Site at Downton, near Salisbury, Wilts," *Proceedings of the Prehistoric Society* 25 (1959): 209–232.

7. Charles Higham, "Recent Advances in the Prehistory of South-east Asia," in Coles, Bewley, and Mellars, *World Prehistory*, p. 75.

8. The book is Brian M. Fagan, *Iron Age Cultures in Zambia,* vol. 1, *Kalomo and Kangila* (London: Chatto and Windus, 1967). Clark, letter dated November 17, 1967.

9. Clark, "Path," p. 63.

10. Harry Godwin, "The Croonian Lecture: Radiocarbon Dating and Quaternary History in Britain," *Proceedings of the Royal Society of London*, B153 (1960).

11. Account in Glyn Daniel, *Some Small Harvest;* and Daniel, personal communication with author, June 1984.

12. Grahame Clark, *World Prehistory: An Outline* (Cambridge: Cambridge University Press, 1961). Quotes in this paragraph are from pp. xii, 1.

13. Stuart Streuver, ed., *Prehistoric Agriculture* (Englewood Cliffs, N.J.: Natural History Press, 1961) offers an excellent anthology of key papers on the origins of food production of the day.

14. Clark, *World Prehistory,* p. 4.

15. Loess is a windblown glacial dust that provides a good relative chronology for late Ice Age sites in Central Europe. The simple framework of glacials and interglacials that had been in use for over three quarters of a century by 1961 was about to evaporate in the face of startling new advances in paleoclimatology, including ice cores, deep sea borings, coral growth rings, new palynological methods, and AMS dating.

16. *Australopithecus africanus*, the "southern ape-human," was first identified by Professor Raymond Dart in South Africa in 1924. He was ridiculed for suggesting that this tiny hominid lay on the direct line of ancestry to humans. Dart was finally vindicated in the 1950s, when Australopithecines were widely accepted as being close to the human line, if not on it. At the time Clark wrote *World Prehistory*, the Leakeys were revolutionizing human evolution with their Olduvai Gorge discoveries, notably with a robust Australopithecine, *Australopithecus boisei*, named after one of their benefactors, and *Homo habilis*, "handy person," a more gracile, more humanlike hominid found at a slightly higher level in the gorge. Great controversy surrounded the Leakeys' claim that *H. habilis* was the first human toolmaker. The passage of over forty years has shown that they were probably right, even if the earliest representatives of *Homo* were much more diverse than suspected in 1960.

17. Clark, *World Prehistory,* p. 23. The Mount Carmel discoveries were described by Dorothy Garrod, *The Stone Age of Mount Carmel*, 2 vols. (Oxford: Clarendon, 1937–1939).

18. Clark, *World Prehistory,* p. 25.

19. Clark, *World Prehistory,* p. 26.

20. The Leakeys' claims of living floors at Olduvai were widely publicized at the time, thanks to articles in *National Geographic Magazine* as well as specialized journals.

It is surprising that Clark did not mention them. For today's meat cache and scavenging theories, see Robert Blumenschine and John Cavallo, "Scavenging and Human Evolution," *Scientific American* 257 (1992): 90–96.

21. Clark, *World Prehistory,* p. 45.

22. Clark, *World Prehistory,* p. 50.

23. Clark, *World Prehistory,* p. 56.

24. Clark, *World Prehistory,* p. 62. Ma'lta is a well known Upper Palaeolithic site near Lake Baikal, Siberia, dating to c. 21,000 B.C., which is famous for its ivory figurines.

25. Quotes in this paragraph from Clark, *World Prehistory,* p. 71.

26. Clark, *World Prehistory,* p. 80. Mugharet el-Wad, excavated by Dorothy Garrod before World War II, contained a long sequence of Middle and Upper Palaeolithic cultures, as well as important Postglacial Natufian culture remains.

27. Summarized for a popular audience by Kathleen Kenyon, *Digging Up Jericho* (London: Michael Joseph, 1957).

28. Clark, *World Prehistory,* p. 85.

29. Quotes in this paragraph are from Clark, *World Prehistory,* p. 90.

30. The Narmer palette, found at Hierakonopolis (ancient Nekhen) in the 1880s, is adorned with a symbolic depiction of the unification of Lower and Upper Egypt by the first pharaoh, the shadowy King Narmer. A discussion of this remarkable artifact is found in Barry Kemp, *Ancient Egypt: The Anatomy of a Civilization* (London: Routledge, 1988), pp. 44ff.

31. Both quotes, Clark, *World Prehistory,* p. 113.

32. The expansion of Bantu-speaking peoples from somewhere in West Africa through most of sub-Saharan Africa about 2,000 years ago is one of the defining moments of recent African history and a matter of great controversy among African archaeologists and historians. See David Phillipson, *African Archaeology*, 2d ed. (Cambridge: Cambridge University Press, 1994); and Roland Oliver, *The African Experience*, 2d ed. (Boulder: Westview, 2000).

33. Both quotes are from Clark, *World Prehistory,* p. 117. Meroe was a major iron-working center on the Nile in the first few centuries A.D., Aksum an important highland Ethiopian state that traded as far as India. The East African coastal towns were connected to the monsoon trade of the Indian Ocean as early as A.D. 1000. Great Zimbabwe is the most famous of all African sites and was at its apogee in the fourteenth century A.D., just before European contact. For Axum (Aksum), Meroe, and the East African coast, see Graham Connah, *African Civilizations* (Cambridge: Cambridge University Press, 1987).

34. Both quotes are from Clark, *World Prehistory,* p. 118.

35. Described by Colin Renfrew, *Before Civilization* (New York: Alfred Knopf, 1971).

36. The Indus civilization is now commonly called the Harappan civilization. Mortimer Wheeler, *The Indus Civilization,* 3d ed. (Cambridge: Cambridge University Press, 1968), is the latest version of his discoveries. For a modern account, see Gregory Possehl, *Harappan Civilization,* 2d ed. (New Delhi: Oxford University Press/IBH, 1993). Also Jane McIntosh, *A Peaceful Realm: The Rise and Fall of the Indus Civilization* (Boulder: Westview, 2001).

37. Clark, *World Prehistory,* p. 212. For an up-to-date, continent-wide account, see Brian Fagan, *People of the Earth: An Introduction to World Prehistory,* 10th ed. (Upper Saddle River, N.J.: Prentice-Hall, 2001).

38. Quotes in this paragraph are from Clark, *World Prehistory,* pp. 215, 217.

39. Quotes in this paragraph are from Clark, *World Prehistory,* pp. 224–229.

40. Clark, *World Prehistory,* p. 238.

41. Clark, *World Prehistory,* p. 242. For an up-to-date account, see Derek Mulvaney and John Kamminga, *The Prehistory of Australia* (Washington, D.C.: Smithsonian Institution Press, 1999).

42. Quotes in this paragraph are from Clark, *World Prehistory,* pp. 252, 260–261.

43. J. Desmond Clark, "Review: *World Prehistory,*" *Proceedings of the Prehistoric Society* 28 (1962) 392–393.

44. Quotes are from Robert J. Braidwood, "Review: *World Prehistory,*" *Antiquity* 35 (1962): 321–322.

Chapter 11

1. Grahame Clark, *Aspects of Prehistory* (Berkeley: University of California Press, 1970), p. 51.

2. My account of the Harvard semester is based on many sources, among them "Path," p. 107, recollections from Professor Dena Dincauze (letter dated September 30, 2000), to whom I am grateful for the seminar reading list, and my own recollection of comments by Clark about Movius and Abri Pataud back in Cambridge.

3. A manuscript catalogue in Clark's hand summarizes his travels over the last thirty years of his career. I am grateful to Professor John Coles for providing me with a copy.

4. Clark, "Path," p. 69.

5. Clark, "Path," p. 70. Robert J. Rodden, "Excavations at the Early Neolithic Site at Nea Nikomedia, Greek Macedonia (1961 season)," *Proceedings of the Prehistoric Society* 27 (1962): 267–288. Hutchinson and the German general quote are from Professor Higham's journal, July 8, 1961. He refers to the celebrated incident of the capture of the general commanding German troops in Crete by a group of British officers and Cretan partisans in 1941. I am grateful to Professor Higham for this extract from his unpublished diaries and that quoted below (see note 7).

6. Nea Nikomedia story in a personal communication from Charles Higham to Mollie Clark, November 6, 1995. James Mellaart's excavations at Çatalhöyük revealed a remarkable early farming village of huddled dwellings having unique shrines adorned with fine wall paintings, which caused a considerable stir at the time of its discovery. The site is now being reinvestigated by Cambridge archaeologist Ian Hodder and an international team of researchers. See James Mellaart, *Çatal Höyük* (London: Thames and Hudson, 1967); and Ian Hodder, "Symbolism at Catalhöyuk," in Coles, Bewley, and Mellars, *World Prehistory*, pp. 177–192. I have used the modern spelling for the site here.

7. Account in Clark, "Path," pp. 70ff. The results of this work are summarized in three important papers by Higgs and other authors: "The Climate, Environment, and Industries of Stone Age Greece," published in three parts in the *Proceedings* for 1964, 1966, and 1967. Quote about plums is taken from the Higham diary, July 31, 1962.

8. J. G. D. Clark, "Radiocarbon Dating and the Expansion of Farming Culture from the Near East over Europe," *Proceedings of the Prehistoric Society* 31 (1965): 58–73. Quotes are from pp. 58, 64. Also J. G. D. Clark, "Radiocarbon Dating and the Spread of Farming Economy," *Antiquity* 154 (1965): 45–48.

9. This brief account of the setting up of the Early History of Agriculture project draws on John Coles, "John Grahame Douglas Clark," pp. 379–380.

10. Grahame Clark, foreword to E. S. Higgs, ed., *Papers in Economic Prehistory* (Cambridge: Cambridge University Press, 1972), pp. vii–x.

11. E. S. Higgs and M. R. Jarman, "The Origins of Animal and Plant Husbandry," in E. S. Higgs, ed., *Papers in Economic Prehistory* (Cambridge: Cambridge University Press, 1972), pp. 3–13. Quote from p. 12.

12. E. S. Higgs, ed., *Palaeoeconomy* (Cambridge: Cambridge University Press, 1975).

13. Claudio Vita-Finzi and E. S. Higgs, "Prehistoric Economy in the Mount Carmel Area of Palestine: Site Catchment Analysis," *Proceedings of the Prehistoric Society* 36 (1970): 1–37. The primary publication on this method.

14. E. S. Higgs and M. R. Jarman, "Palaeoeconomy," in Higgs, *Palaeoeconomy*, pp. 1–8. Quote is from p. 7.

15. E. S. Higgs, introduction, in Higgs, *Palaeoeconomy*, p. vii.

16. M. R. Jarman, G. N. Bailey, and H. N. Jarman, *Early European Agriculture: Its Foundations and Development* (Cambridge: Cambridge University Press, 1982). Quote is from p. 257.

17. The flotation method of recovering seeds from archaeological deposits originated in the Midwest region of the United States and in southwest Asia during the 1960s, when it consisted of little more than passing seed samples and their matrix through water and screens. Froth flotation involves a more elaborate setup with multiple screens, capable of processing much larger quantities of seed materials. This

enables the recovery of large statistical samples of plant materials and was used with great success at the early farming village at Abu Hureyra, Syria, in the 1970s.

18. Grahame Clark, "The Economic Context of Dolmens and Passage-Graves in Sweden," in V. Markotic, ed., *Ancient Europe and the Mediterranean* (Warminster, U.K.: Aris and Phillips, 1977), pp. 35–49; and Grahame Clark, "Coastal Settlement in European Prehistory with Special Reference to Fennoscandia," in Evon Vogt and R. M. Leventhal, eds., *Prehistoric Settlement Patterns: Essays in Honour of Gordon R. Willey* (Albuquerque: University of New Mexico Press, 1983), pp. 295–317. The cow remark is quoted in "Contribution to Discussion," in G. Burenhult, *The Archaeology of Carrowmore*, Theses and Papers in North-European Archaeology, no. 14 (Stockholm: Institute of Archaeology, University of Stockholm, 1984), p. 112. See discussion in Rowley-Conwy, "Sir Grahame Clark," p. 522.

19. Clark's New Zealand visit is recounted in Peter Gathercole, "Otago 1958–1968 (Part 1)," *Archaeology in New Zealand*, 2000, p. 43(3) 206–219; and "Otago 1958–1968 (Part 2)," *Archaeology in New Zealand*, 43(4) 283–296;. I am grateful to the author for making these articles available to me in advance of publication. The New Zealand travels are also described in Clark, "Path," pp. 98–99. Helen Leach's quote comes from a letter to Peter Gathercole dated October 18, 1995, which he quotes in the second paper cited above. *Moas* were flightless birds that were hunted into extinction by the first human settlers within a few centuries.

20. Account in "Path," pp. 99–106. Also see Coles, "John Grahame Douglas Clark," p. 377. I have also drawn on Clark's manuscript travel notes, which offer a cursory summary of the trip.

21. D. J. Mulvaney, "D. J. Mulvaney," in Glyn Daniel and Christopher Chippindale, eds., *Pastmasters*, pp. 158ff. The Keilor skull is evidence for human settlement in Australia at least 30,000 years ago.

22. Quotes in this paragraph from Clark, "Path," pp. 104–105. A *tjuringa* is an axe.

23. J. G. D. Clark, "Traffic in Stone Axe and Adze Blades," *Economic History Review,* 2d series, 18 (1965): 1–28.

24. This account is drawn from Coles, "John Grahame Douglas Clark, pp. 376–377.

25. MacNeish's Tehuacán excavations of the early 1960s documented the shift from hunting and gathering to maize and bean cultivation in a dry Mexican valley, where preservation conditions allowed the preservation of early maize cobs, still the earliest in the world, dating to before 3,000 B.C.

26. Grahame Clark, *World Prehistory: A New Outline* (Cambridge: Cambridge University Press, 1977). Quotes from p. 46.

27. Thurstan Shaw, "Africa in Prehistory: Leader or Laggard," *Journal of African History* 12, no. 1 (1978): 143–153.

28. Grahame Clark, *Aspects of Prehistory* (Berkeley: University of California Press, 1970). Quotes in this paragraph are from pp. 48–49.

29. Clark, *Aspects*, p. 51.

30. Hugh Hencken, "Review of *Aspects of Prehistory,*" *Antiquity* 55 (1971): 306.

31. Grahame Clark, *World Prehistory in New Perspective* (Cambridge: Cambridge University Press, 1977). Quotes in this paragraph are from pp. xvi–xvii.

32. Honors listed by Coles, "John Grahame Douglas Clark," p. 378. The Society of Antiquaries citation appears in *Antiquaries Journal* 58 (1978): 8. Grahame was greatly amused by the misspelling of his name, Grahme, on the Wharton Medal by an Italian goldsmith (Peter Rowley-Conwy, personal communication to author).

33. John Coles, ed., "Contributions to Prehistory Offered to Grahame Clark," *Proceedings of the Prehistoric Society* 37, no. 2 (1971).

34. Gale Sieveking, Ian Longworth, and K. E. Wilson, eds., *Problems in Economic and Social Archaeology* (London: Duckworth, 1976).

35. D. L. Clarke, "Prehistoric Europe: The Economic Basis," in Sieveking, Longworth, and Wilson, eds., *Problems*, pp. 449–482.

36. Clark Archive, Box 15.3. Kent Flannery, "The Cultural Evolution of Civilizations," *Annual Review of Ecology and Systematics* 4 (1972): 399–426.

Chapter 12

1. Clark, in "Path," p. 111.

2. Mollie Clark, personal communication to author, 1999.

3. This account of the mastership, the events of which are largely irrelevant to this intellectual biography, is drawn from Coles, "John Grahame Douglas Clark," p. 383, and also from conversations with Mollie Clark.

4. Grahame Clark, *The Earlier Stone Age Settlement of Scandinavia* (Cambridge: Cambridge University Press, 1975). The term "Gudenaa culture" was first used by the German prehistorian Gustav Schwantes in 1928 to describe material from the interior of Jutland, which he thought was similar to what he called the Oldesloe culture in Holstein. Gudenaa came into widespread use in 1937 when Therkel Mathiassen published an article on the subject in *Aarbøger for Nordisk Oldkyndighedog Historie* in 1937. In recent years, the Gudenaa culture has been discredited, as the sites where it occurred have been shown to contain artifacts from both Mesolithic and Neolithic cultures. See S. H. Andersen and N. Sterum, "Gudenåkulturen," *Holstebro Museums Årsskrift*, 1970–1971, pp. 14–32. This paper in a regional journal was published before Clark completed *Earlier Settlement*. (Information kindly supplied by Dr. Peter Rowley-Conwy.)

5. See Chapter 11, note 13.

6. Carl Axel Mobery, "Review of *The Earlier Stone Age Settlement of Scandinavia*," *Antiquity* 59 (1976): 310–311.

7. Clark, *Earlier Stone Age Settlement*, p. xxiv.

8. Clark, *Earlier Stone Age Settlement*, p. xxv.

9. Coles, "John Grahame Douglas Clark," p. 384.

10. Coles, "John Grahame Douglas Clark," p. 382.

11. Grahame Clark, "World Prehistory and Natural Science," J. C. Jacobsen Memorial Lecture, *Historisk-filosofiske Meddelelser* 50 (1980): 1–40.

12. Mollie Clark, personal communication to author, 1999.

13. Grahame Clark, *Sir Mortimer and Indian Archaeology*, Wheeler Memorial Lectures, 1st series, 1978 (New Delhi: Archaeological Survey of India, 1978).

14. Clark, "Path," p. 97.

15. Grahame Clark, *Mesolithic Prelude* (Edinburgh: Edinburgh University Press, 1980). Quotes in this paragraph are from pp. 6–7.

16. By this time, dendrochronologies were providing accurate ways of calibrating radiocarbon dates from radiocarbon years into calendar year. This calibration became necessary when it was discovered that the amount of C14 in the atmosphere varied over time.

17. Quotes in this paragraph are from Clark, *Mesolithic Prelude*, p. 107.

18. Grahame Clark, *The Identity of Man as Seen by an Archaeologist* (London: Methuen, 1983). Quotes in this paragraph are from pp. 8–9. The Clark article referred to is "Archaeology and Human Diversity," *Annual Review of Anthropology* 8 (1979): 1–20.

19. Grahame Clark, "Prehistory Since Childe," *Bulletin of the Institute of Archaeology* 13 (1976): 1–21.

20. Quotes in this paragraph are from Clark, *Identity*, pp. 66, 69.

21. Clark, *Identity*, p. 148.

22. Quotes from Clark, *Identity*, pp. 161, 164.

23. Quote from Clark, *Identity*, p. 166. Rolf Dahrendorf, *Essays in the Theory of Society* (Stanford: Stanford University Press, 1968), p. 42.

24. Edmund Leach, "Human Strata: Review of *The Identity of Man as Seen by an Archaeologist*," *Nature* 305 (1983): 341–342. Quotes in the paragraphs that follow are from both pages.

25. Grahame Clark, *Symbols of Excellence: Precious Materials as Expressions of Status* (Cambridge: Cambridge University Press, 1986). Quote from p. 26.

26. Quotes in this paragraph are from Clark, *Symbols*, pp. 2, 6.

27. Thorstein Veblen, *The Theory of the Leisure Class: An Economic Study in the Evolution of Institutions* (New York: Macmillan, 1899). Veblen's persuasive books, of which *The Leisure Class* is the most enduring, were immensely popular in the early twentieth century.

28. Clark, *Symbols*, p. 65.

29. Quotes in this paragraph are from Clark, *Symbols*, p. 106.

30. Quotes are from Clark, *Symbols*, p. 106.

31. Colin Renfrew, "Review of *Symbols of Excellence*," *Antiquity* 60 (1986): 238–239.

32. Grahame Clark, *Space, Time, and Man: A Prehistorian's View* (Cambridge: Cambridge University Press, 1992). The quote occurs in a letter from Clark to Higham, April 24, 1989. I am grateful to Professor Higham for sharing this letter with me.

33. Clark, *Space, Time*, p. 55.

34. Quotes are from Clark, *Space, Time*, pp. 124, 129.

35. Clark, *Space, Time*, p. 131.

36. A. N. Whitehead, *Religion in the Making* (Cambridge: Cambridge University Press, 1928).

37. *Praemium Erasmianum MCMXC*. "Erasmus Prize Programme," November 21, 1990. Quotes in this paragraph are from p. 13 of the program.

38. *Praemium Erasmianum*, pp. 23–24.

39. Relevant quotes from *Praemium Erasmianum*, pp. 26–28. The letter to Charles Higham dates to November 18, 1990, and is used courtesy of Professor Higham.

40. Clark, "Path," p. 150.

41. Lord Renfrew, "The Death of Professor Sir Grahame Clark, KBE, ScD, FBA" (address delivered at a memorial service on November 4, 1995). I am grateful to Peterhouse for a copy of the address. Quotes are from pp. 40, 42. Colin Renfrew also wrote about Clark in a volume of essays on Cambridge scholars: "Three Cambridge Prehistorians," in Richard Mason, ed., *Cambridge Minds* (Cambridge: Cambridge University Press, 1994), pp. 58–71.

42. Obituaries appeared in *Times*, September 14, 1995; *Independent,* September 19, 1995.

43. Peter Rowley-Conwy informs me in a personal communication dated December 18, 2000, that Grahame signed his secondhand copy of *The Mesolithic Settlement* in 1984 with the following inscription: "That old thing. Can't think why you want it."

Chapter 13

1. Grahame Clark, interview by Peter Rowley-Conwy, 1994.

2. *Praemium Erasmianum,* p. 23.

3. See C. J. Becker, "C. J. Becker," in Daniel and Chippindale, *Pastmasters*, p. 118.

4. Clark, *Archaeology and Society*, p. 187.

5. Christopher Evans, "Archaeology Against the State," in Peter J. Ucko, ed., *Theory in Archaeology: A World Perspective* (London: Routledge, 1995), pp. 312–332.

6. D. L. Clarke, *Analytical Archaeology* (London: Methuen, 1968), p. 27.

7. Clark, *Symbols of Excellence*, p. 106.

8. Edmund Leach, "Human Strata," p. 342.

9. Clark, *Archaeology at Cambridge and Beyond*, p. 153.

Credits

Frontispiece

Photo of Sir Grahame Clark: From the Grahame Clark Estate. Printed by permission of Lady Clark.

Chapter 1

Photo of Grahame Clark, age fifteen: From the Grahame Clark Estate. Printed by permission of Lady Clark.

Photo of excavators at the Trundle, 1930: From the Grahame Clark Estate. Printed by permission of Lady Clark.

Chapter 2

Map of Mesolithic sites in Britain: Map created by Jack Scott. From the Grahame Clark Estate. Printed by permission of Lady Clark.

Photo of Francis Buckley: From the Grahame Clark Estate. Printed by permission of Lady Clark.

Microliths from Lakenheath: *The Mesolithic Age in Britain* by Grahame Clark (Cambridge University Press, 1932). Fig. 15. Permission granted by Cambridge University Press.

The microburin technique: *The Mesolithic Age in Britain* by Grahame Clark (Cambridge University Press, 1932). Fig. E (App. 1). Permission granted by Cambridge University Press.

Mesolithic tranchet axe from Horsham: *The Mesolithic Age in Britain* by Grahame Clark (Cambridge University Press, 1932). Fig. 47. Permission granted by Cambridge University Press.

Drawing of the Leman and Ower harpoon: 9A Maglemosian site at Brandesburton, Holderness,Yorkshire, 9 by J. G. D. Clark and Harry Godwin, *Proceedings of the Prehistoric Society* 22 (1955): 6–22. Permission granted by the Prehistoric Society (Salisbury, England).

Drawing by Grahame Clark of microliths from West Heath, West Hastings: From the Grahame Clark Estate. Printed by permission of Lady Clark.

Chapter 3

Photo of the Peacock's Farm excavation: From the Grahame Clark Estate. Printed by permission of Lady Clark.

Photo of the sequence from the Peaccock's Farm excavations: From the Grahame Clark Estate. Printed by permission of Lady Clark.

Chapter 4

Map showing European Late Glacial, Mesolithic, and Neolithic sites: Map by Jack Scott. From the Grahame Clark Estate. Printed by permission of Lady Clark.

Chronological Table: *The Mesolithic Settlement of Northern Europe* by Grahame Clark, (Cambridge University Press, 1936). Fig. 13. Permission granted by Cambridge University Press.

Distribution map of bone points: *The Mesolithic Settlement of Northern Europe* by Grahame Clark, (Cambridge University Press, 1936). Fig. 47. Permission granted by Cambridge University Press.

Ertøbolle artifacts: *The Mesolithic Settlement of Northern Europe* by Grahame Clark, (Cambridge University Press, 1936). Fig. 53. Permission granted by Cambridge University Press.

Maglemose art motifs: *The Mesolithic Settlement of Northern Europe* by Grahame Clark, (Cambridge University Press, 1936). Fig. 61. Permission granted by Cambridge University Press.

Chapter 5

Photo of Rock engravings from Rødoy, Norland, Norway: From the Grahame Clark Estate. Printed by permission of Lady Clark.

Photo of a Mesolithic living surface at the Farnham Mesolitihic site:From the Grahame Clark Estate. Printed by permission of Lady Clark.

Chapter 6

Figure of honey catchers: 9Bees in Antiquity,9 by J. G. D. Clark, *Antiquity* 16 (1942). Reprinted by permission of Antiquity Publications Ltd.

Chapter 7

Olaus Magnus (1539): Seal hunting at the head of the Gulf of Bothnia. This drawing appeared in Clark's 9Seal-hunting in the Stone Age (Fig. 10): From the Grahame Clark Estate. Printed by permission of Lady Clark.

Distribution map of whale bones at prehistoric sites: 9Whales as an economic factor in prehistoric Europe,9 by J. G. D. Clark, *Antiquity* 21, (1947): p. 94. Reprinted by permission of Antiquity Publications Ltd.

Oil on Canvas painting by Finnish artist Eero Järnefelt: 9Under the Yoke (Burning the Brushwood)9 owned by Ateneum Art Museum, Helsinki. Permission granted by The Finnish National Gallery, Helsinki.

Chapter 8

Photo of the Star Carr Excavations: From the Grahame Clark Estate. Printed by permission of Lady Clark.

Photo of the birch wood platform at Star Carr: From the Grahame Clark Estate. Printed by permission of Lady Clark.

Photo of Grahame Clark showing a stag antler headdress to John Evans: From the Grahame Clark Estate. Printed by permission of Lady Clark.

Photo of Star Carr artifacts: From the Grahame Clark Estate. Printed by permission of Lady Clark.

Photo of a stag antler frontlet from Star Carr: From the Grahame Clark Estate. Printed by permission of Lady Clark.

Selected raw materials and their uses, Star Carr: *Excavations at Star Carr* by Grahame Clark, (Cambridge University Press, 1954) p. 154. Permission granted by Cambridge University Press.

Chapter 9

Elk antler mattocks: *Excavations at Star Carr* by Grahame Clark, (Cambridge University Press, 1954) Oil painting by Ruskin Spear. p. 159. Permission granted by Cambridge University Press.

Photo of Stuart Piggott and Grahame Clark at Stonehenge. Permission granted by professor John Mulvaney (Australia).

Diagram of the refined systems, as used in the Reckitt Lecture, 1953: From the Grahame Clark Estate. Printed by permission of Lady Clark.

A sectioned pit at Hurst Fen, 1957: From the Grahame Clark Estate. Printed by permission of Lady Clark.

Drawing of Mildenhall ware: 9Excavations at the Neolithic site at Hurst Fen, Mildenhall, Suffok (1954, 1957, and 1958),9 by J. G. D. Clark E. S. Higgs, and I. W. Longworth, *Proceedings of the Prehistoric Society* 26 (1960): 202–245. Permission granted by the Prehistoric Society (Salisbury, England).

Chapter 11

Photo of excavations at Nea Nikomedia: From the Grahame Clark Estate. Printed by permission of Lady Clark.

Photo of Grahame Clark examining the stratification at Fromm's Landing, Australia: Photograph by W. S. Tindale. Printed by permission of South Australian Museum

Chapter 12

Photo of sailing at Aldeborough: From the Grahame Clark Estate. Printed by permission of Lady Clark.

Photo of Mollie and Grahame with the Taj Mahal in the background: From the Grahame Clark Estate. Printed by permission of Lady Clark.

Photo of Grahame Clark's painting of Henry Moore's sculpture: From the Grahame Clark Estate. Printed by permission of Lady Clark.

Photo of Grahame Clark's painting of Barbara Hepworth's *Family of Man* sculpture: From the Grahame Clark Estate. Printed by permission of Lady Clark.

Photo of Professor Clark receiving the Erasmus Prize from Prince Bernhard of the Netherlands: Permission granted by Praemium Erasmianum Foundation; Photo by Benelux Press, Voorburg.

Microliths: *Excavations at Star Carr* by Grahame Clark, (Cambridge University Press, 1954) p. 101. Permission granted by Cambridge University Press.

Non-geometric microliths from Lominot: *The Mesolithic Age in Britain* by Grahame Clark (Cambridge University Press, 1932). Fig. 6. Permission granted by Cambridge University Press.

Tardenoisian artifacts from Belgium: *The Mesolithic Age in Britain* by Grahame Clark (Cambridge University Press, 1932). Fig. 12. Permission granted by Cambridge University Press.

Index